NO SENSE OF DECENCY

NO SENSE OF DECENCY

The Army-McCarthy Hearings:
A Demagogue Falls and
Television Takes Charge of
American Politics

ROBERT SHOGAN

Ivan R. Dee
CHICAGO 2009

www.ivanrdee.com

Library of Congress Cataloging-in-Publication Data:
Shogan, Robert.
    No sense of decency : the Army McCarthy hearings / Robert Shogan.
        p. cm.
    Includes bibliographical references and index.
    ISBN-13: 978-1-56663-770-1 (cloth : alk. paper)
    ISBN-10: 1-56663-770-8 (cloth : alk. paper)
    1. Army-McCarthy Controversy, 1954. 2. McCarthy, Joseph, 1908–1957—Trials, litigation, etc. 3. Legislative hearings—United States—History—20th century. 4. United States—Politics and government—1945–1953. 5. United States—Politics and government—1953–1961. 6. Television and politics—United States—History—20th century. 7. Political culture—United States—History—20th century. I. Title.
UB23.S53 2009
973.921092—dc22

                                        2008030760

For Ellen Shrewsbury Shogan
in loving memory
and for our daughters
Cynthia and Amelia

Contents

Preface

WHEN THE Army-McCarthy hearings opened in the caucus room of the U.S. Senate in the spring of 1954, many in
Washington anticipated that history was in the making. This
despite the fact that the proximate cause of the controversy
between the Wisconsin senator and the Army that boiled over
and forced the hearings was pretty small potatoes by historical
measurements. At the center of the dispute was a former aide to
McCarthy's investigating committee, G. David Schine. He had
been inducted into the service as McCarthy was in the midst
of a probe of alleged spying at one of the Army's most sensitive
installations, the Signal Corps center at Fort Monmouth.

In what amounted to an indictment made public a month
before the start of the hearings, the Army charged that McCarthy and his staff had relentlessly pressured the military to gain
favorable treatment for Private Schine. But McCarthy and his
cohorts immediately fired back. They charged that the Army
was trying to use Schine as a "hostage" of sorts, to get McCarthy to ease up on his investigation, if not drop it altogether.

Juicy gossip, but nothing more. But what transcended
the petty details of this argument was the stature of the two
chief protagonists. McCarthy was at that point arguably the

most powerful and certainly the most feared politician in the country. He had more than seven years of Senate seniority and headed one of its most potent agencies, the Permanent Subcommittee on Investigations. By ruthlessly—and many said recklessly—exploiting the tensions of the cold war between the United States and the Soviet Union, and public anxiety about Communist subversion at home, he had come to dominate the political scene. Hardly anyone, either among the opposition Democrats or his own GOP, had the gumption to challenge him.

McCarthy's nominal opponent was the Army. But what everyone understood in Washington was that the senator's principal adversary was actually the Army's commander-in-chief and the head of the administration that McCarthy regularly harassed and intruded on, Dwight David Eisenhower. Ike, as he liked to be called, was probably the most widely admired American politician of the twentieth century. Yet for reasons that mystified even his closest aides, he seemed unwilling and unable to meet McCarthy's challenge to his governance. Now many believed that the general who had conquered the Axis could afford no further retreats. Eisenhower's supporters feared that unless their man held the line, the upstart senator from Wisconsin would make a mockery of his presidency.

As others saw it, from a historical perspective, the stakes in the confrontation in the Senate caucus room transcended even the future of the Eisenhower presidency. In his four years of crusading against Communist subversion, McCarthy had helped generate a national wave of paranoia the likes of which the nation had not seen since the great post–World War I Red Scare. Reputations had been ruined, constitutional rights had been trampled, and dissent had come to be viewed as disloyalty. Everyone conceded that the nation faced real peril from abroad and that in the nuclear age national survival was at risk every day. But this threat seemed likely to persist for years to come.

The crucial questions that faced Americans, on which some thought the hearings would cast light, was how in this harrowing era America could balance freedom against security? How would the nation protect its citizens and their freedom too?

As it turned out, history would show that the decisive factor in the hearings was none of these ingredients but rather a wild card, a very recent entrant in the American political wars: television. The decision to televise the hearings had been made almost as an afterthought by senators preoccupied with parliamentary esoterica. Little did they realize that television, just by its presence, would take over the hearings, transforming the literal record into a far more compelling event, heightening the impact not only for the millions who watched the live telecast but also for the millions more who eagerly read the printed accounts of the drama that television had created. In this fashion were the fates of McCarthy and the Eisenhower presidency decided. More than that, this demonstration of potency would pave the way for a new political world in which television would be the dominant force, making history again and again as it had during that fateful spring in the Senate caucus room.

For better or for worse? The answer of course is both. "I believe television is going to be the test of the modern world," E. B. White wrote in 1938 when the medium had barely reached its nascent stage. "We shall stand or fall by television, of that I am quite sure." White did not say which outcome he thought likely. And seventy years later, as Chairman Mao famously said about the impact of the French Revolution, it is still too soon to tell.

This book owes a primary debt to the staff of the Milton Eisenhower Library at the Johns Hopkins University, where I am fortunate enough to teach. I particularly wish to thank James Gillispie, head of the government publications section in Baltimore, who supplied the transcripts of the committee hearings without which the book could not have been completed, and in the Washington Center library Zena Mason and Audrey A. MacDonell. I am also very grateful to William Lee, a partner in Wilmer, Cutler, Pickering, Hale and Dorr, the descendant of Joseph Welch's old law firm, who provided valuable material relating to Welch and to the hearings, to which I otherwise would not have had access. Benjamin Stamplis's research at the Library of Congress made an important contribution. An old friend, Anne Wexler, got me a rare copy of Frederick G. Fisher III's memoir of his father and Ann Littlejohn shared the recollections of her late husband Fritz, a TV news pioneer.

Among those who gave encouragement and helpful counsel were Thomas B. Allen, Victor Gold, Alonzo I. Hamby, Tom Hannon, Art Pine, Aric Press, and my daughters, Cynthia D. Shogan and Amelia Ford Shogan. I also thank my publisher, Ivan Dee, for keeping faith.

R. S.

Chevy Chase, Maryland
November 2008

"Have you no sense of decency, sir, at long last? Have you left no sense of decency?"

—Attorney Joseph Welch, responding to an attack by Senator Joseph McCarthy, June 9, 1954

NO SENSE OF DECENCY

I

The Curtain Rises

With its Corinthian pilasters, marble columns, ornate ceiling, and three-tiered chandeliers, the Senate caucus room, Room 318 in what is now called the Russell Senate Office Building, resembles a mausoleum and is usually just as dreary and barren. But on Thursday morning, April 22, 1954, this cavernous space hummed with tension and overflowed with politicians, lawyers, and journalists. They had been drawn by the prospect of a power struggle that promised to be one of the most memorable of the twentieth century, now just past its halfway mark. In one corner was Republican senator Joseph McCarthy of Wisconsin, the most feared politician in the land and perhaps the most powerful. Against him were arrayed one of the nation's proudest institutions, the Army of the United States, and along with the Army, the reigning administration of the country.

Spectators had begun collecting in the rotunda of the building before dawn. By mid-morning more than eight hundred had gained entrance past the massive oaken doors into the seventy-four-foot-long room designed to hold no more than three hundred persons. Conducting the hearings was a committee of the United States Senate, officially styled as the Special

Subcommittee on Investigations, known more popularly—or just as often unpopularly—as the McCarthy Committee, after its chairman.

But no one, friend or foe, was calling it that today.

Senator McCarthy had been forced to step aside from his chairmanship. After four fractious years of stirring up trouble for others, he had ignited a firestorm that threatened to engulf this prodigious troublemaker himself. Like all the other furors initiated by McCarthy this one had begun by his choosing a target for charges of Communist subversion. But in this case his intended victim, the Department of the Army, after weeks of enduring abuse from McCarthy, had struck back and leveled charges of its own. It claimed that McCarthy had threatened to depict the Army to the country "in the worst light" unless it gave preferential treatment to a recently inducted McCarthy aide, G. David Schine. The Army alone would have made a formidable foe. But in challenging the Army McCarthy also had to reckon with the prestige and power of the Army's commander-in-chief, the thirty-second president of the United States, Dwight D. Eisenhower.

Since for the time being, at least, Eisenhower chose to remain in the background, it was Senator McCarthy who most commanded attention as the hearings prepared to open. During his three-year crusade against what he proclaimed to be the insidious threat of Communist subversion in America, McCarthy had made himself into the great intimidator of American politics. He had won the admiration, indeed the devotion, of millions of Americans. Other millions regarded him with scorn and derision. But even among his enemies, most—if they were honest—would admit they were too fearful of political retribution to speak against him.

Under these conditions, even as the hearings commenced, it was difficult to predict who if anyone would rise to challenge McCarthy in this public arena. But it was clear who besides

McCarthy himself had the most at stake. This was Eisenhower, the most admired American of his time. Despite his plain reluctance to square off against McCarthy, Eisenhower's own advisers wondered whether he could afford *not* to confront the senator. Unless McCarthy was stopped, if he continued unchecked on his reckless course, he would be well positioned to wreck Eisenhower's presidency in midstream. And it was clear to everyone on both sides of this struggle that if McCarthy were ever to be taken down, it had better happen at the Senate hearings on which the curtain was about to rise.

The conflict between the Army and McCarthy was not the only troublesome news about national security that month. Ten days before the hearings opened, the country learned that Dr. J. Robert Oppenheimer, the physicist who had directed development of the atomic bomb, had been denied his security clearance and suspended by the Atomic Energy Commission. The charges against Oppenheimer included associating with Communists and opposing the development of the hydrogen bomb after President Truman had given the project a green light. Oppenheimer admitted his past Communist sympathies but denied resisting development of the H-bomb. Although he later appealed the action against him, his security clearance was never restored.

Even more ominous was the news from halfway around the world, in Indochina. There Communist Vietminh forces had laid siege to the French fortress of Dienbienphu in what many viewed as the climactic battle in the struggle to overthrow French rule of its colony. On the day the hearings opened, the French admitted that Vietminh forces had tightened their band of flesh and steel around the fortress, in preparation for a final assault. Only a week earlier, Vice President Richard Milhous Nixon, in remarks he tried to keep off the record, warned the nation's newspaper editors that if France were forced to surrender Indochina, the United States might have to send its own troops there. Washington could not afford further retreat in Asia, Nixon claimed.

But in the nation's capital, all the news, no matter how portentous, was transcended by the remarkable events that were about to unfold in Room 318. Although officially designated as a legislative hearing, these proceedings would in reality be more like a trial. And when they concluded, the judgment of the participating lawmakers would be far outweighed by the opinions of millions of ordinary Americans who would function as an informal but potent jury.

Not that there was space in the hearing room for average folk. The great demand for seats from the capital's officialdom and the need to accommodate the national press corps left little room for any but officials and celebrities. Even the senators on the committee found themselves surrounded by relatives of the witnesses who would be called. The witnesses themselves were crammed in by the spectators. Aides to committee members wandered among the chairs and tables, seeking a place to work.

But there was no danger the public would be left in the dark. A glance around the room made clear why. A three-tiered platform had been constructed along the back wall of the hearing room to accommodate a battery of television cameras, which glared out at the senators as they sat at their table. Other cameras behind the committee table faced the witness table and the spectators. Still more cameras were positioned at one side of the room, able to pivot at various angles. And along the outside wall, in front of the room's three windows that would have offered its occupants a glimpse of the changing spring sky, four high-powered floodlights had been positioned to provide television the illumination it needed.

As the presence of the cameras testified, the senators, without much debate and without fully realizing the consequences, had agreed to allow television coverage of these hearings. It was a decision that would assure an audience of millions, define the nature of the proceedings and their outcome, and have a profound impact on the nation's politics for generations.

Americans would be drawn to this spectacle in part by the uneasy realization that the federal government was seriously out of joint. Eisenhower, the crusader who had brought down Hitler, now had as his command post the Oval Office, seat of ultimate political power. But much of Ike's authority had been undercut by Senator McCarthy. A relative upstart in national life, Joseph Raymond McCarthy was a man of modest intellect and limited experience. He was nevertheless possessed of boundless ambition, exceptional cunning, and unsurpassed gall. McCarthy obstructed Eisenhower's nominations for high office, upstaged his State Department, abused his generals, and waged a vendetta against the institution that had propelled Ike to greatness, the U.S. Army. For many in the capital, including Eisenhower's own supporters, the president's timidity in the face of McCarthy's excesses was epitomized in a drawing by the *Washington Post*'s Herbert Block, who depicted McCarthy wielding a bloody meat cleaver as he confronted a pathetic-looking Eisenhower. "Have a care, sir," the president says, as he pulls from his scabbard a feather.

As the second year of Eisenhower's presidency began in 1954, it was McCarthy, not the man in the White House, who in many respects ruled American politics. He had already established his primacy during his meteoric rise to national prominence that had begun only four years earlier. Democrats cowered before his vindictive anger, having witnessed the political demise of colleagues who dared to challenge him. "You may get a lot of moral support for fighting Joe," one Democrat more candid than most explained, "but if you lose your seat in the Senate, that's no good."

In private conversation with a trusted journalist, Lyndon Baines Johnson of Texas, then the leader of the Senate

Democrats, put the matter with characteristic succinctness, laced with hyperbole: "I will not commit my party to some high school debate on the subject 'Resolved that communism is good for the United States' with my party taking the affirmative."

"Let the Republicans take him on," was the almost unanimous response of Democrats when called upon to confront McCarthy as a matter of conscience. But the Republicans, with a bare handful of exceptions, clearly had no intention of doing any such thing.

For all the tongue-clucking that some of them did, many believed they benefited from McCarthy's swinging the bludgeon of anti-communism against the Democrats, leaving them to remain sanctimoniously aloof from such crude tactics. Besides, some of them feared that if they questioned McCarthy's methods, they themselves might be scarred with the same axe. Whatever their motives, when it came to any criticism of McCarthy, the silence of the Republicans was thunderous.

Eisenhower the war hero, the man whose patriotism was presumably immune from attack even by McCarthy, intentionally or not had established in his 1952 presidential campaign the pattern that his party now followed. When Ike made plans to defend the reputation of his old comrade in arms, George C. Marshall, his advisers warned that if he went ahead with his intended statement on Marshall's behalf, he would lose votes in McCarthy's home state of Wisconsin. Where upon Eisenhower backed down.

The consequence of Eisenhower's passivity became apparent barely three months into his presidency when McCarthy secretly negotiated an agreement with Greek shipowners to halt their flourishing trade with Red China, whose troops were then battling American soldiers in Korea. The agreement was in blatant violation of diplomatic protocol and federal statutes. But no less an eminence than Secretary of State John Foster

Dulles excused this outrage. While foreign relations were the responsibility of the executive branch, Dulles said, in shutting down the Greek trade to China McCarthy had acted in the national interest.

A striking indication of McCarthy's status in the capital was provided in September 1953 at his wedding to Jeannie Kerr, a longtime member of his Senate staff. Some 2,500 well-wishers crowded the curbside after the ceremony in St. Matthews Cathedral. More than 1,000 attended the reception. Eisenhower begged off, pleading the need to entertain the visiting president of Panama. But Vice President Nixon, White House chief of staff Sherman Adams, and Attorney General Herbert Brownell were on hand. So were prominent Democrats, notably ex–New Dealer, ex-ambassador, and current staunch McCarthy admirer Joseph P. Kennedy, and three of his children, John, the junior senator from Massachusetts, his younger brother Robert, a staff member of the McCarthy Committee, and their sister Pat. As if this bipartisan demonstration of admiration were not enough, from the Vatican came a cable offering Pope Pius XII's "paternal apostolic blessing."

The newlyweds flew off for a three-week honeymoon in the British West Indies. But even his own nuptials could not keep McCarthy from pursuing the danger he perceived to the Republic. After only a week in the islands, McCarthy was alerted by his chief aide, Roy Cohn, that the committee's investigators had turned up evidence of one of the most serious security threats they had yet encountered, in of all places the United States Army. So McCarthy left the pleasures of the Caribbean and the comforts of the conjugal bed to return to the United States. Immediately he launched a probe of one of the nation's most vital military installations, Fort Monmouth, New Jersey, the main research center for the Signal Corps, which liked to bill itself as the eyes and ears of the Army.

At first it seemed that McCarthy was off on another wild ride that would bring him new headlines and new influence while the rest of the government quailed. But this investigation would have ramifications that no one, not even the senator from Wisconsin, could have anticipated. The wild card was the major role to be played in the proceedings by an imponderable force—television. Over time this new medium would transform American politics in many ways, and in the Army-McCarthy hearings it would find its impetus toward political influence. As these chapters will show, the clash of ambitions, personalities, and beliefs in politics and in journalism during the decade following the end of World War II set the stage for television's decisive role in the climactic episode of the saga of Joe McCarthy.

In the spring of 1954, television was scarcely a brand-new feature of American politics. As far back as 1950 Democratic senator Estes Kefauver of Tennessee had exploited the still nascent power of the medium by leading hearings into organized crime. Despite the minuscule size of the television audience at the time, Kefauver's investigations transfixed the nation. A flock of Damon Runyonesqe characters paraded before the Kefauver Committee and its klieg lights, attracting enough attention to elevate Kefauver from the obscurity of the Senate backbenches to the pantheon of national political celebrity. But once the hearings ended, memories faded quickly. Nothing much came of this crime inquiry, in part because there was no urgent imperative for it to happen in the first place, except as a promotion for Kefauver's career. Nevertheless, to anyone watching closely, the hearings demonstrated the political potency of such a televised event.

Among those impressed was a veteran North Carolina lawman named Frank N. Littlejohn, the police chief of Charlotte, his state's largest city. Littlejohn had won national recognition in 1933 for his role in capturing Basil "The Owl" Banghart and other henchmen of Chicago mobster Roger

"The Terrible" Touhy after they robbed a mail truck in Charlotte of $120,000. The money supposedly was intended to help pay lawyers for Touhy, who was in a Chicago jail facing kidnapping charges. The exploits earned Littlejohn praise from FBI chief J. Edgar Hoover, not known for applauding the work of local cops, as the finest detective in the country. In the midst of his other duties, Littlejohn had trouble keeping his eye off the TV screen and the Kefauver hearings. He raved about them to his son, Fritz, an editor with NBC radio in New York City. And Fritz Littlejohn mentally filed away his father's enthusiastic reaction until the spring of 1954, by which time he had become news director of ABC television. He was now well positioned to exploit the potential demonstrated by the Kefauver hearings by broadcasting what came to be known as the Army-McCarthy hearings.

As a test of television's power, what made the Army-McCarthy hearings all the more stringent was that the medium would take on these proceedings with one, or more precisely, two hands tied behind its back. Initially all four networks had been expected to carry the full hearings live; but NBC, after trying it for a day, and CBS, which never even tried, balked at the loss of revenues from commercial programming. That left only ABC, the weakest of the Big Three, which had little in the way of other programming to lose. What ABC did have was Fritz Littlejohn as its news editor. Bolstered by his father's judgment, Littlejohn persuaded ABC president Robert Kintner to cover the hearings gavel to gavel. The DuMont network, the financially strapped stepsister of the industry, which would go out of business in a couple of years, also decided to provide coverage. And even the two holdouts, NBC and CBS, would broadcast nightly roundups edited from kinescope recordings of the daytime ABC telecasts.

Despite limited coverage, the telecasts would have dramatic impact. The audience for television had expanded by several orders of magnitude since Kefauver grilled the leaders of the underworld and their highly placed benefactors before the cameras. An estimated 45 million would view at least part of the 188 live-telecast hours of the hearings—and 120 million would watch the nighttime summaries or read newspaper accounts. Unlike the Kefauver hearings, the Army-McCarthy sessions were more than a contrivance. They grew out of a profound and genuine conflict which forced the antagonists, the Army and the Eisenhower administration on one side, and McCarthy and his allies on the other, to air their grievances in public.

The proximate cause of the hearings was the treatment or alleged mistreatment of an Army private, twenty-five-year-old G. David Schine, the scion of a hotel and movie-theater empire founded by his father, and an unpaid consultant to McCarthy's investigating committee. By a pregnant coincidence, Schine had been drafted into the Army just as McCarthy's committee was in the midst of probing allegations of communism within the Army's ranks. The Army publicly accused McCarthy and his high-strung and supremely arrogant chief aide, Roy M. Cohn, of threatening to cause more trouble than their probe had already brought to the Army unless Schine were granted privileges accorded no other private soldier in the history of the American military. For their part, McCarthy and Cohn claimed that the Army was holding Schine as a sort of "hostage," to forestall further embarrassment from McCarthy's investigations.

Adding a prurient note to the brouhaha was the suspicion that Cohn's devotion to improving the lot of Schine was inspired by a sexual relationship between the two young men, and that McCarthy himself was in on the game. The liberal playwright Lillian Hellman even referred to the three men as "Bonnie, Bonnie, and Clyde."

Whatever the truth of this innuendo, serious politicians in Washington realized from the start that Schine was only a pawn in a far greater struggle. The stakes were much higher than this young soldier's chances for a weekend pass and promotion. At issue was whether the leadership of the two political parties could find a way to control McCarthy's excesses before he caused permanent damage to the political system. Not since Huey P. Long burst on the national scene out of the bayous of Louisiana to steal Franklin Roosevelt's New Deal thunder with his promise to "make every man a king" had any political figure posed such a threat to the existing power structure. Long had planned a third-party candidacy in 1936 that would drain enough votes from FDR to elect a Republican that year, ultimately paving the way for Long's own presidency in 1940. But an assassin's bullet ended the Kingfish's schemes and his life. Now McCarthy's foes, Republican and Democrat alike, had to hope that the televised confrontation with the Army would dispose of McCarthy's threat—if not as violently, just as decisively.

But everyone understood this would be a formidable task. For McCarthy's demagoguery was a product not only of his own ingenuity and skills but of a deep-rooted national phobia of communism. This had led to an orgy of cold war witch-hunting, the second such binge in little more than a generation. The first great Red Scare had its roots in World War I, when Woodrow Wilson sounded the alarm against any protest that might impede his crusade to make the world safe for democracy. In leading the nation into war, Wilson had confided to the journalist Frank Cobb that he was reluctant to awaken "the spirit of ruthless brutality" that would infect "the very fiber of our national life." But then the scholarly, moralistic Wilson did much to make his premonition come true. Obsessed with the threat to the war effort from sabotage and criticism—which he seemed to equate—the president prodded Congress into passing a series of repressive measures.

The most notorious of these, the Espionage Act, prohibited not only spying and sabotage but also public utterances that could be considered harmful to the military. Its most celebrated victim was Eugene V. Debs, the perennial Socialist party presidential candidate and longtime leader of the railroad workers. Debs was convicted after a particularly scathing attack on the war and on the government's prosecution of fellow Socialists. "This year we are going to sweep into power and destroy capitalist institutions," he predicted, taking an optimistic view of Socialist prospects in the full congressional elections.

It was sheer rhetoric. But it was enough for a federal judge to sentence Debs to ten years in prison, an occasion that prompted him to deliver what would become his most memorable public utterance. "While there is a lower class I am in it," Debs told the court. "While there is a criminal element I am of it. And while there is a soul in prison I am not free." But Debs's eloquence did not halt the crackdown on dissent.

In March 1918, a year after America entered the war, Russia's new Bolshevik rulers, having made a separate peace with Germany, called upon workers everywhere to rise up and end the war of the capitalist oppressors. Nothing of the sort happened. But the threat, real or imagined, gave new impetus to the onslaught against subversion that persisted even after the carnage in Europe ground to a halt on November 11, 1918.

Americans had emerged from the war militant in their patriotism and confirmed in their allegiance to what was often called "the American way." Although no one knew exactly what this credo meant, businessmen assumed that it included their right to bar union organizers from their premises. War stories of spies and international intrigue had fed the public's imagination and stretched its credulity. In 1919, Russia's much feared Bolshevik regime was being wracked by civil war; in the supposedly Red-ridden United States, the *Atlantic Monthly* estimated the total members of the Socialist, Communist, and Communist Labor parties at a not-so-grand total of 130,000, barely more than two-tenths of 1 percent of the country's adult population. But such statistics were overshadowed in the spring and summer of 1919 by a series of genuinely alarming incidents of violence and near misses.

Alerted by the explosion of a bomb sent through the mail to the home of a U.S. senator, a conscientious postal clerk turned up more than thirty similar, neatly wrapped infernal devices, which had been set aside for insufficient postage. Their addressees made up a pantheon of American business and government, including John D. Rockefeller, J. P. Morgan, and Supreme Court Justice Oliver Wendell Holmes. Also on the target list was Attorney General A. Mitchell Palmer, who was already leading a nationwide crackdown on anything or anyone suspected of radical beliefs.

A few weeks after escaping that threat, whose perpetrators were never discovered, Palmer was going to bed for the night when he heard a bang, as if something had hit his front door. Then came a blast. Rushing outside, he found some human limbs, all that remained of his uninvited caller who had been blown to pieces by his own contraption. Nearby was found a telltale clue, a copy of the radical publication *Plain Words*.

In the fall of 1919, with the president weakened by illness and distracted by events abroad, the nation shaken by domestic turmoil, and with no apparent heir to Wilson as the 1920 Democratic standard-bearer, Palmer saw opportunity and seized it with both hands. Earlier that turbulent year, shortly after his own house was bombed, he had gotten a special $500,000 appropriation from Congress to bolster efforts to ferret out subversives. Palmer used the funds to establish a new agency, the General Intelligence Division, and installed at its head an eager young agent named J. Edgar Hoover, who soon compiled a list of 60,000 purportedly dangerous radicals. The nation's new top Red hunter also sent to every newspaper and periodical of note in the country letters over Palmer's signature warning of "the real menace of the Red Movement."

To root out this danger, in January 1920 Palmer's agents raided alleged nests of subversion around the country, arresting more than four thousand individuals and deporting hundreds of them. Often arrests were made without the formality of warrants. Suspects were routinely held incommunicado and denied the right to legal counsel. Describing the prisoners caught in his net, Palmer declared, "Out of the sly and crafty eyes of many of them leap cupidity, cruelty, insanity and crime; from their lopsided faces, sloping brows and misshapen features may be recognized the unmistakable criminal type."

Within a year the great Red Scare petered out as the public gradually began to realize that the perils proclaimed by Palmer and his cohorts were greatly exaggerated. But if the virus of national hysteria subsided, it did not perish. It would be revived by another threat from abroad that emerged soon after World War II.

At first Americans were in a mellow mood after V-J Day marked the end of the war—"The Good War," in Studs Terkel's phrase. Unlike World War I, World War II left no legacy of disillusionment. *The Best Years* was the title the journalist Joseph Goulden chose for his chronicle of the immediate postwar era. Goulden found the nation caught up in a "general euphoria," possessed of a broad national confidence in individual futures and in the country's ability to solve postwar problems.

Yet in the midst of the prosperity and peace, anxiety began to mount. The cold war was a term coined to describe the bitter conflict between the United States and America's wartime ally, the Communist-ruled Soviet Union, a struggle that had begun even when the war still raged. At the Yalta Conference in February 1945, three months before Hitler's final defeat, the United States and Britain, eager to gain Soviet help in finishing off Japan, made important "spheres of influence" concessions to the Soviets in Eastern Europe. No sooner had Germany surrendered than Joseph Stalin took advantage of hazy agreements with his former allies to establish Soviet control in Poland, Czechoslovakia, and the Balkans. Stalin kept his promise to join in the assault on Japan. But after V-J Day antagonism between East and West mounted, fed by the collision of U.S. and Soviet interests at trouble spots around the world.

When Great Britain, its economy crippled by war, was forced to abandon its traditional role as guardian of Western interests in the Balkans, the United States stepped in. With congressional backing, President Harry Truman proclaimed the Truman Doctrine, pledging support to Greece and Turkey against the threat of a Communist takeover and in the process formalizing the cold war.

The "long twilight struggle," as John F. Kennedy later called it, would dominate the second half of what *Time* publisher Henry Luce had dubbed the American Century. It was true enough that in the decade of the fifties the dreaded nuclear collision between the two superpowers did not materialize. But there was still plenty of reason for Americans to brood. Over three years of fighting in Korea cost more than 130,000 casualties, the fourth bloodiest war in U.S. history until Vietnam.

Fully as important as the threat of Communist aggression abroad in darkening the public mood were revelations of espionage at home, lending momentum to a crusade against domestic subversion that presaged McCarthy's rise. The two most sensational episodes involved personalities who could hardly have been more different. In one instance the chief protagonist was Alger Hiss, a pillar of the Eastern establishment who had served in the highest councils of government. In the other major case the principals were Julius Rosenberg and his wife Ethel, two Jews with working-class backgrounds raised on New York's lower East Side. The Hiss controversy first made headlines during the summer of 1948 before the Committee on Un-American Affairs of the House of Representatives, known as HUAC. The committee had been formed before the war to root out fascist as well as Communist subversion. But from its origins, under Congressman Martin Dies of Texas, it had concentrated on Red hunting, particularly among labor leaders and their New Deal supporters.

The onset of the cold war only added to the committee's enthusiasm for this course. Its main function seemed to be as a public confessional booth for contrite ex-Communists who were eager to own up to their sins—and not incidentally expose the activities of some of their former comrades. So there was little reason to expect that the testimony of Whittaker Chambers, another ex-Communist who also had been an editor at *Time* magazine, would be anything but routine. Chambers, regarded by other journalists as an intellectual, was also a gifted translator. What no one knew outside his family and a circle of intimate friends was that during the 1920s he had been active in the American Communist party, not just as a member but as an agent for Soviet intelligence. Late in the 1930s he broke with the party, revolted by the brutal excesses of Stalinism.

Chambers's tale of ideological commitment and remorse was too familiar to attract much attention. What could not be dismissed, however implausible it seemed on its face, was his shocking claim that the ranks of Soviet agents in the 1930s included a number of New Deal officials. Most prominent of these was Alger Hiss, with whom Chambers contended he had enjoyed a warm relationship.

Hiss's was a name for journalists and Red hunters to conjure with. A native of Baltimore, he had trained at Harvard Law, where he was a protégé of FDR confidant and future Supreme Court Justice Felix Frankfurter. With Roosevelt in the White House, Hiss became one of the celebrated "little hot dogs" whom Frankfurter dispatched to Washington to staff the New Deal. Posted to the State Department in 1936, he moved steadily up the career ladder for more than a decade. Roosevelt took Hiss with him to the Big Three conference at Yalta, where the seeds of the cold war were sowed. And later that year Hiss was dispatched to San Francisco for the charter conference of the United Nations. In 1948 he left government and took a post that seemed appropriate to the credentials he had earned in government: the presidency of the Carnegie Endowment for International Peace.

While many others who had been accused of perfidy by witnesses before HUAC took the Fifth Amendment, Hiss did not duck the charges against him. In response to Chambers's accusations, which received large attention in the media, Hiss sent a telegram to HUAC's chairman, J. Parnell Thomas, categorically denying Chambers's testimony, claiming he had never even met Chambers, and demanding the chance to testify before Thomas's committee.

That wish was easily granted. Only two days after Chambers's appearance Hiss took the stand, where he repeated his denials before a packed hearing room. His performance was impressive enough to convince most members of the committee that the investigation should be dropped. President Truman called the Capitol Hill spy inquiry "a red herring." HUAC was under fire.

Certainly by comparison with the suave Hiss, Chambers seemed like last week's wash. He was rumpled and portly with double chins and bad teeth. His character was no asset, either. A dropout from Columbia and from various occupations, he was suspected of alcoholism and homosexuality. At best he was an admitted double turncoat, who by his own account had betrayed his country for communism, then deserted its false god.

Hiss, on the other hand, was elegant in appearance and patrician in manner. A Harvard Law School classmate, Lee Pressman, himself named by Chambers as a comrade along with Hiss in the New Deal spy ring, once said of Hiss: "If he were standing at the bar with the British Ambassador and you were told to give a package to the Ambassador's valet, you would give it to the Ambassador before you gave it to Alger."

Perhaps Hiss's air of distinction was why Richard Nixon, then a freshman congressman from California, was one of the few members of the committee who openly questioned Hiss's story. Nixon had seen FBI files that raised doubts about Hiss's denial. In addition, Nixon realized that Hiss was just the sort of figure who, because of his manner and breeding, aroused instinctive resentment and mistrust from middle-class voters. Nixon shared those instincts and was in the process of forging a political identity as a champion of the middle class, whom he would later call the "Silent Majority." He decided he could bolster that image by taking on Hiss.

Nixon persuaded Thomas to appoint him to head a special subcommittee to look into the case against Hiss. Under prodding by Nixon, and by another dedicated Red hunter, South Dakota congressman Karl Mundt, the initial favorable impressions of Hiss faded into suspicion and eventual disbelief. Testifying before Nixon's subcommittee in executive session, Chambers buttressed his version of events with detailed recollections of his friendship with Hiss and his wife, Priscilla—such an odd assortment of minutiae it did not seem anyone could have invented it.

By the time Hiss was recalled for further questioning, the affair had achieved such a degree of notoriety that television cameras were deployed to capture the event. It became one of the earliest hearings to be beamed into American living rooms. After Hiss's grilling, HUAC published a report calling his testimony "vague and evasive." By contrast, Chambers was described as "forthright and emphatic."

Determined to restore his tarnished reputation, Hiss sued Chambers for slander, demanding that Chambers produce "any correspondence, either typewritten or in handwriting, from any member of the Hiss family." In response, Chambers visited the Baltimore home of his nephew's mother, reached into a dumbwaiter shaft in the bathroom, and pulled out a large, weathered envelope. Its contents were sufficient to incriminate Hiss. Fortunately for him the statute of limitations for espionage had long since passed. But that left the federal government free to charge him with perjury for lying to the grand jury by denying that he had turned over documents to Chambers and by claiming not to have had contact with him after 1937.

Hiss's trial in May 1949 ended in a hung jury, but the government tried again. A second trial in January 1950 found Hiss guilty on both counts. After his attempts at appeal failed, he was sentenced to prison for five years. He continued to maintain his innocence for forty-four years until his death in 1996 at the age of ninety-two. His case became the focus of unending controversy.

No one outside the federal prosecutor's office worked harder to convict Alger Hiss than Richard Nixon, and no one benefited more from his conviction politically. The case helped Nixon win election to the U.S. Senate in 1950, the year of Hiss's conviction, and also put him on the road to the vice presidency in 1952, and ultimately to the White House. Nixon's fire-eating anti-Communist rhetoric on the campaign trail helped condition the environment for Senator McCarthy. Although McCarthy had no direct role in the Hiss case, it gave him a license to launch his war on subversion, which began with a specific charge against the State Department, Alger Hiss's old stamping grounds, as "infested with Communists."

The Hiss case, combined with the announcement of the Soviet atomic bomb; the emergence of China, America's old ally, as a Communist state; and the Korean War were, as the historian Eric Goldman put it, "shocks of catalytic force." But yet another trauma was in store for Americans: the arrest of Julius and Ethel Rosenberg on charges of smuggling atomic secrets to the Soviet Union.

The way for the prosecution of the Rosenbergs was paved by the arrest in 1950 of Klaus Fuchs, a German refugee theoretical physicist. Fuchs had worked for the British as part of the Manhattan Project, the top-secret effort of U.S. and Allied scientists to develop the atomic bomb; it turned out that throughout the war he had given key documents to the Russians. Fuchs's confession led to the arrest of other confederates involved in the development of the U.S. bomb, among them David Greenglass, Ethel Rosenberg's brother. Greenglass, an Army sergeant, had been assigned to the Los Alamos laboratories in New Mexico while the atomic bomb was being assembled there during World War II.

It was Greenglass, and his wife, Ruth, both members of the American Communist party, who claimed that Julius Rosenberg, with the help of his wife, Ethel, recruited him to collect information about the bomb, which Rosenberg then passed on to the Soviets. The son of a Polish garment worker, Julius was a quiet, serious youth whose early success in Hebrew studies led his father to hope that he might become a rabbi. Julius's interests lay in other directions. Soon after entering New York's City College at age sixteen, he joined the Young Communist League. Two years later he met Ethel, whom he married in 1939 when he graduated. Both were members of the Communist party. After graduation Rosenberg took a civilian job with the Army Signal Corps where he worked on radar until he was fired in 1945 because of his pro-Soviet views. He was then not only an avowed member of the Communist party but a leader of a network of secret agents working in defense plants and military bases who stole secrets for the Soviets.

In July 1950, a few weeks after the outbreak of the Korean War, Julius Rosenberg was arrested mainly on the basis of Greenglass's testimony. The next month the FBI arrested his wife too. Although the evidence against Ethel Rosenberg was meager, the FBI hoped to use her as a lever to force her husband to name others involved in the spy ring. The tactic failed.

But the prosecution pushed ahead anyway. The Rosenbergs went on trial in March 1951, a year after Alger Hiss's conviction, for conspiracy to commit espionage, a capital crime. But what they were rhetorically charged with was giving the secrets of the atomic bomb to the Soviet Union, a point made clear by the prosecution as the trial began. U.S. Attorney Irving Saypol, the prosecutor of Hiss, told the jury that the defendants "have committed the most serious crime which can be committed against the people of this country." The Rosenbergs conspired, Saypol said, to deliver to the Soviet Union "the weapons the Soviet Union could use to destroy us."

Saypol's chief aide in the prosecution, and McCarthy's future lead assistant, was a brilliant, high-handed twenty-three-year-old attorney named Roy Cohn, son of a state supreme court justice who was a power in the New York Democratic party. Composed in manner and supple in tactics beyond his years in the courtroom, Cohn laid the cornerstone for the case against the Rosenbergs with his convincing direct examination of Greenglass, the principal witness against them. But Cohn's impact on the trial went beyond his courtroom performance. Mindful that the prosecution of the Rosenbergs had provoked charges of anti-Semitism, Cohn by his own account arranged for the presiding judge at the trial to be Irving Kaufman, who, like Saypol and Cohn himself, were co-religionists of the Rosenbergs.

Kaufman, in imposing the death penalty after the Rosenbergs were convicted, blamed them not only for helping the Soviets get the atomic bomb but for the deaths of American soldiers in Korea. In June 1953 the Rosenbergs became the first persons in American history to be executed for espionage during peacetime. Ethel Rosenberg was the first woman to be executed by the United States government since Mary Surratt was hanged for her role in Lincoln's assassination.

And all of this was grist for Senator Joe McCarthy's mill.

McCarthy was cautious about overtly exploiting the Rosenberg case, out of fear of being accused of anti-Semitism. But his cause inevitably benefited from the furor. Like the downfall of Alger Hiss, the convictions of Julius and Ethel Rosenberg fed the national paranoia about communism that fostered a Manichean outlook toward the conflicts of the cold war, at home and abroad.

In the midst of this turmoil, without anyone anticipating it, McCarthy and his bizarre feud with the Army had brought the country to a moment of decision. By calling into question the high-handed and heavy-handed tactics of McCarthy, the hearings suggested an issue even broader and just as important as the health of the political system: What kind of nation would America become in the second half of the twentieth century? No one doubted that the world was a dangerous place. Some said the danger must be defended against at all costs, even by shrinking some of the freedoms that had long defined the national character. But others claimed that a sacrifice of civil liberties was too great a price to pay for security. This was the choice that hovered over the proceedings in Room 318.

One thing was certain: for better or worse, this would be a very public argument. The presence of the media assured that. A horde of print correspondents were on hand to cover the story, among them some of the big names of the trade such as Walter Winchell, wearing his habitual grey fedora with black headband. Their combined output over the next few weeks would exceed a million words and reach readers throughout the nation and the world.

Yet for all their prestige and prolificacy, these traditional reporters mattered less than in the past. It was Karl Mundt, chairing the hearings, who gave the game away. Early in the proceedings he reprimanded the news photographers who ranged around the room, as they always did, bobbing up and down as they struggled to get the best shot. After a few days of that, Mundt laid down the law, ordering the photographers, who had once been sovereign in such situations, to crouch or kneel rather than get in the way of the cameras. "There are a great many complaints from the television audience and from the television people that all their cameras are getting are the backs of photographers," Mundt declared. He himself had seen television playbacks, "and I want to confirm the legitimacy of these complaints."

In such quotidian fashion was notice given that the old order had passed, supplanted by the still unfathomable horizons of television. The big question was whether television would be able to help a nation define itself. It would take three months of hearings to find out, but a look back at the brief history of television news showed that the hearings now about to begin represented a far greater challenge than any the new medium had yet faced.

2

A Torch in the
Troubled World

If members of the journalistic establishment were caught off guard by the dominant role assumed by television at the Army-McCarthy hearings, it was easy to understand why. In the world of media contenders, television news to that time had been relegated to the featherweight class. Early on it had been heralded as a blessing to humanity. But its growth had been stunted in infancy by calamitous events—war and economic collapse—and now it had to contend with the vagaries of an angst-ridden age. And while it seemed to be steadily growing in importance, television news continued to struggle against the skepticism of other branches of journalism and the disadvantage of its secondary status in a medium designed mainly to entertain the public, not enlighten it.

These growing pains obscured the reality that by the time the Army-McCarthy hearings opened, television had been around, at least in nominal existence, for three decades. It was in fact born not much later than radio, in the 1920s. And it got off to a flying start. On April 7, 1927, the American Telephone and Telegraph Company sponsored a public demonstration of television both in the nation's capital and in its largest city, featuring coverage of a speech by then Secretary of Commerce Herbert Hoover. The coming-out party won page-one headlines in the *New York Times*, the *Washington Post*, and the *Washington Evening Star.*

When asked about the commercial potential for this new wonder of technology, AT&T president Walter S. Gifford would say only, "I will have to leave that to your imagination." What Gifford could not imagine was that in a little more than two years a great economic disaster would engulf the nation. The Great Depression devastated enterprises already flourishing and made the idea of ambitious new innovations like television seem like sad illusions.

But when after a grim decade the economic gloom finally lifted, television pioneers pressed forward. When the New York World's Fair, with its theme of the "world of tomorrow," opened in the spring of 1939, RCA showed off its new commercial TV receivers. RCA president David Sarnoff hailed television as nothing less than "an art which shines like a torch in the troubled world, a creative force which we must learn to utilize for the benefit of all mankind." His view would be echoed later by Paul Raibourn, an executive at Paramount Pictures and DuMont, who declared that "television alone holds the promise of becoming the ambassador of goodwill that will bring about an enduring peace."

But just as television's early hopes had been smashed by the depression, the dreams of this new wave of promoters were sidetracked by World War II, when all the nation's technological resources and manpower were concentrated on defeating the Axis powers. Even after V-J Day, TV's rise seemed slow. "Instead of standing up and walking like its big brother, radio, it has crawled along without getting very far," *Time* chided in early 1946.

By April in that first postwar year, when the initial experimental station in the nation's capital, W3XWT, began transmitting for an hour a day, the city counted fewer than 150 sets. TV sets in the whole country totaled only about 8,000. Television's development was slowed not only by early technological kinks but by bureaucratic decision-making. The Federal Communications Commission took the obvious and easy way out, approving a television system modeled on radio. Although the FCC paid lip service to the idea of local control, its regulations allowed the radio networks to buy individual local stations and provide programming to others who chose to affiliate with them. While local concerns may have suffered, the harnessing of the networks' economic power and know-how, developed through radio, helped TV gain a footing in the media world.

But TV's development continued to be spastic and slapdash. It was all very well for General Sarnoff to describe the medium he dominated early on as "a torch in the troubled world." But with few exceptions the managers of Sarnoff's NBC and of the other networks spent little time pursuing such lofty goals. Instead they devoted themselves mainly to enlarging their share of the advertising dollar. And TV news, with no claim as a revenue producer, was swept along on the mercenary tide while it struggled to make the best of penny-ante budgets. Thus TV news moved into the future by fits and starts, by guess and by gosh, reacting to events rather than planning for them.

By 1948 television antennas were mushrooming from U.S. rooftops and set manufacturers were selling a thousand a day. By one reckoning only one American in ten had yet seen a television broadcast, but everyone was talking about the new medium. TV boosters predicted that children would go to school in their own living rooms. Presidential candidates would win elections from a television studio while housewives would pick out on the screen the dresses and groceries they wanted, and shop by phone.

But hardly anyone pointed out that the government-ordained system, which assured that TV would be controlled by powerful corporations—either local enterprises or the national networks—also guaranteed that this newest media form would share the same biases and limitations of its older brethren, radio and print. Americans gloried in their freedom of the press as one of the cherished guarantees of the Bill of Rights. But few seemed to realize that all the First Amendment provides is protection against direct government intervention. It does not shield the press from the indirect pressures of government and private institutions alike. As the 1940s radio satirist Henry Morgan pointed out, "Sure we have freedom of the press; anyone with ambition, integrity—and $10 million can start a newspaper."

Nor does the First Amendment ensure that the media will have the backbone to resist the informal pressures that combine to form what Noam Chomsky, and Edward Herman, leading intellectual analysts of the media, termed "a propaganda system." As Chomsky argues, this apparatus is camouflaged by the surface aspects of the media environment. Newspapers and broadcasters do compete against one another for information, access, and audiences, occasionally expose wrongdoing both by corporate interests and the government, and strive to portray themselves as tribunes for the public.

But such episodes are relatively few and far between. Meanwhile the media output reflects the great inequities of wealth and power between the public interest and the special interests. These include the corporations that own and run the media and provide them with revenue, and the agencies of government, national and local, that have an inherent interest in defending and promoting themselves. Both are well positioned to influence the media—the private interests by providing advertising revenue, the public agencies by granting or withholding access and approval. So while on the face of things diversity and freedom are protected by the great numbers of newspapers, magazines, and radio and television stations, the numbers are misleading. As the media critic Ben Bagdikian and others have pointed out, in reality only a handful of media corporations account for most of the output of newspapers and most of the sales and audiences in magazines, broadcasting, books, and movies.

The net result is that the media system—of which television would become the most conspicuous part—is marked by a conformity that mocks the promise of diversity implicit in the guarantee of free speech. This circumstance was epitomized during World War II when the mass media demonstrated a notable sensitivity to the demands and needs of the federal government, even when they were not directly expressed. Indeed, the media morphed into what the University of Wisconsin's James Baughman has called "voluntary propagandists" for the war effort.

Support for America's involvement in the war was only to be expected; the country had been attacked and its very existence threatened. But the media not only backed America's effort to defeat the Axis, they almost never challenged the way the government was conducting that battle. Thus the media relentlessly reported progress on the battlefronts, even when there was little, and minimized casualties and setbacks. Black newspaper publishers resentful of the federal government's failure, in a war to preserve democracy, to disturb established patterns of racial segregation felt the hot breath of the FBI on their necks. And the federal government's internment of more than 110,000 Japanese Americans, many of them U.S. citizens, in what amounted to concentration camps stirred scarcely a whisper of protest from the established press.

The war was a wonderful boon for the media. Coverage of the global struggle boosted newspaper and magazine circulation among readers hungry for information, however much it was sanitized. It also provided radio with millions of additional listeners. But in a broader sense, despite the tremendous social and political upheaval that World War II created, the coverage of this great tumult did little to alter the zeitgeist on America's home front. Instead it served mainly to intensify the conformity and complacency that pervaded the national mood, and colored the media's own view of its role.

This attitude was underlined soon after the war in 1947 by the reception given to the report of the Commission on Freedom of the Press, chaired by the iconoclastic chancellor of the University of Chicago, Robert M. Hutchins, and made up of other prominent educators and civic leaders. The commission, whose creation was suggested and backed by Henry Luce, warned that freedom of the press was in grave peril largely because of the press's own failure to meet its obligation to provide the understanding and information the public needed to meet its responsibilities as citizens. As remedies the report urged "vigorous" mutual criticism by the press and stricter enforcement of anti-trust laws by the government. But the chance for any positive response to this challenge was undercut by the media's reaction. Luce turned his back on the commission he had inspired. And Wilbur Forrest, president of the American Society of Newspaper Editors, reflected the resentment of his profession at being called to account by complaining—without explaining how that the commission's criticism had damaged freedom of the press around the world.

Although ignored by the Hutchins commission as not important enough to warrant mention, television was making great strides thanks to postwar breakthroughs in technology. AT&T's development of the coaxial cable linked local stations to the fountainheads of programming, the networks. The result was the birth of four TV networks—NBC, CBS, and ABC, which had been doing business in radio for years, and a newcomer, DuMont, whose primary business had been as a maker of television sets.

Only nine cities were on the coaxial cable, which stretched from Boston in the north to Richmond in the south. But the linking of two of these cities, New York and Washington, in 1947 enabled CBS to broadcast live from the Capitol in January the opening of the Eightieth Congress, a historic moment because it was the first Congress with a Republican majority since the onset of the Great Depression. To show evenhandedness, CBS that same month also broadcast the State of the Union Address of Democratic president Harry Truman.

Even with TV's boost from technology, print journalists did not regard television as a serious competitor for news in those days. "Television is going the way of radio, as fast as it can, toward entertainment," the editor of the *Louisville Courier-Journal* remarked. TV broadcasters could justify their priorities on the basis of viewer demand. If they had their druthers, said 65 percent of New York City's TV set owners polled in 1948, they would like to see more variety shows; only 7 percent asked for more news, a result borne out in other surveys.

Given these preferences, the wonder is that television bothered to cover as much news as it did. But at a time when broadcasters were scrambling for programming, news events provided cheap and readily available material. Thus the early sessions of the United Nations, meeting in its first home in Lake Success, New York, became a staple of early television. Broadcasters did not have to pay a fee for covering news events. Just as important, the networks and the local stations saw news coverage as a way to meet their vague obligation to serve the public interest as mandated by the FCC.

There were intangible reasons too behind television's early approach to news. Coverage of important events brought to the infant medium a measure of prestige roughly equivalent to the significance of the event itself. And the personages being covered, particularly politicians, saw in the camera's eye an opportunity to promote their own stature. That dynamic helps explain the marriage of television news and both political parties, which made possible the coverage of the 1948 nominating conventions, a first for television.

It was somehow appropriate that television make its national political debut at a nominating convention. After all, radio had broken into national politics at a convention too—the Democratic conclave of 1924, the like of which has never been seen or heard since. The site was New York's Madison Square Garden, then in its second incarnation, which during three decades of prizefights, six-day bicycle races, and circuses had never housed the sheer raucousness produced by the national nominating convention of the world's oldest and largest political party in this sweltering summer of 1924. The conclave dragged on for 103 ballots and 14 days, and saw 60 persons receiving votes for the party's presidential nomination.

In 1924, despite an economic slump, sales of radios more than doubled over the preceding year, reaching $360 million, the largest increase in the entire booming decade of the twenties. And the Democratic convention had a lot to do with it. Americans discovered that "a seat by the radio was as good as a ticket to the Garden," wrote Frederick Lewis Allen in his celebrated chronicle of the decade, *Only Yesterday.* "Better in fact, for at any moment you could turn a knob and get 'Barney Google,' or 'It Ain't Gonna Rain No More,' by way of respite."

News would remain for radio—as it would become for television—a sideline to its primary reason for existence, entertainment. But it was a sideline that brought prestige and helped justify the claim of both media to the public airways. Meanwhile radio's entry into political coverage at strife-torn Madison Square Garden established a legacy that would benefit television: the sense for listeners and later for viewers of immediacy, of sharing in the making of history.

Eventually that legacy led to television's role at the Army-McCarthy hearings, thirty years after the Democratic tumult at Madison Square Garden. TV's first important step in that direction was coverage of the 1948 presidential nominating conventions, which proved a tough place to begin. Interest in the campaign that summer was at a low ebb since most journalists—and most Americans, to the extent they thought about it—were convinced that the Republicans would oust Truman from the White House. Nevertheless the idea of getting involved in the making of the president was a potent lure for television. As for the parties, they were drawn to the opportunity to be immortalized in living black and white. It was true there were fewer than a million sets in the country, only eighteen cities with television stations, and only half of those on the cable and able to transmit live coverage. But the TV networks pledged gavel-to-gavel live coverage—in contrast with radio, which covered only major events—plus kinescopes, made by filming broadcasts off the TV screen, shown to the rest of the country.

In return, both parties agreed to nominate their standard-bearers in Philadelphia, the second-largest city on the cable. For the networks, at first glance this seemed like a terrific bargain. Besides helping them fill airtime, which they would have had difficulty doing otherwise, they could save a big piece of their operating budgets on the salaries they did not have to pay to performers and writers. In advance of the convention the networks worried most about adjusting to the newfangled technology of television, but their lack of journalistic experience turned out to be just as big a headache. The savviest journalists available to them, the stars of their radio newscasts, regarded television as a step down. They dragged their feet when called upon for convention coverage on camera. CBS found that the best it could get from its star, Edward R. Murrow, the nation's best-known newscaster, was a promise to help out—an attitude that Murrow would ultimately change. The network had to settle for a backup announcer, Douglas Edwards, to anchor its coverage of the conventions. Similarly NBC had to resort to a second-echelon announcer, the little-known John Cameron Swayze, as anchor.

The Republicans came first to Philadelphia and provided little in the way of suspense, thanks to the ruthless efficiency of New York governor Thomas E. Dewey, front-runner for the GOP nomination. Dewey had his problems, particularly in the emerging new age of television. He was, in the modern idiom, vertically challenged, short enough so that he sometimes stood on an unabridged dictionary or a stack of phone books while delivering a speech. But such defects were overlooked because of the manner in which Dewey lived up to advance billing, swiftly recruiting the additional delegates he needed to nail down the nomination and—or so nearly everyone thought at the time—the White House.

All four TV networks were on hand to record Dewey's expected victory, on the third ballot. He embellished his convention triumph by persuading Earl Warren, then governor of California and later chief justice of the United States, to be his running mate.

The coast-to-coast reach of a ticket anchored in the nation's two most populous states darkened the already bleak outlook for the Democrats when they assembled in the same city three weeks later. Few even in their own party gave them any chance to regain the White House because of President Truman's unpopularity. But once the convention was under way, and under the gaze of the television cameras and what the networks would claim to be ten million viewers, the Democrats came to life. One of their first speakers, India Edwards, head of the Democrat's women's division, proved a quick study when it came to television. Warning that a Republican takeover would unleash the devastation of inflation, she set helium balloons floating to the ceiling to demonstrate the heights prices would reach. Then, reaching into a shopping bag, she produced a carton of milk and a steak, items she warned were sure to cost families more than they could afford if the Republicans had their way. No sooner had Edwards finished her remarks than Don Hewitt of CBS, later producer of the fabled *60 Minutes*, raced to the podium, snatched the steak and milk that had been left behind, and brought them to the CBS control room so that Ed Murrow could use these visual aids as props for his commentary.

Not all the Democratic special effects went off as smoothly. Someone had the idea of releasing a flock of pigeons, heralded as "doves of peace," which fluttered over the platform and did what pigeons usually do. The dignitaries seated below could do nothing but brush off their clothes.

The real drama of the Democratic convention was un-orchestrated. It centered on the battle between Southern states determined to preserve the party's long allegiance to segregation in Dixie, and Northern liberals committed to change. The liberals won this battle when the party adopted a strong civil rights plank. In response, Southern delegates stormed out of the convention and eventually backed their own Dixiecrat candidate for president, Strom Thurmond, then governor of South Carolina. Seeking to make the most of the Southern walkout, NBC herded some of the insurgent delegates into its studio where, on cue, the rebels threw down their Democratic credentials on a cigarette-burned desk.

That incident touched off a row later that night, after Harry Truman was nominated, at a party hosted by NBC to celebrate its coverage. CBS's Murrow showed up and angrily confronted Andrew Heiskell, the publisher of *Life*, which sponsored the NBC broadcast and gave Heiskell the opportunity to oversee NBC's coverage. Murrow roundly denounced him for undermining the integrity of television's convention debut by staging the Southern discarding of credentials. It was one of the first disputes over TV's tendency to orchestrate the news to make it fit better into its entertainment script—but it would not be the last.

Nothing happened at either major party convention to alter the prevailing view among politicians and pundits that Dewey's victory was inevitable. But while TV and most of the rest of the media were looking the other way, with rapt admiration for Republican Dewey, Truman transformed himself into a feisty and persuasive candidate. Amid chants of "Give 'em hell, Harry," he whistle-stopped his way to the greatest upset in the history of the modern presidency. TV's reporters, for all the prestige their medium had gained from its convention coverage, were caught looking just as foolish as all the other pundits. The lesson, oft to be repeated, was that the glamour and drama of network television was no substitute for nuts-and-bolts reporting.

With the election over, TV news returned to its status as poor cousin, not only in the eyes of print media but even in its own broadcasting industry. In the summer of 1950, by which time both CBS and NBC had begun daily newscasts as outgrowths of their convention coverage, *Newark News* reporter Reuven Frank signed on as an NBC "newswriter" for $110 a week. This was $10 more than he was making at the *News*, he told NBC—actually $20 more than he was really getting. When Frank, who later became president of NBC news, asked why the network did not tap one of its radio newswriters for the vacancy, he got a brutally candid answer. "Well, to be honest, nobody down there who is worth hiring thinks this is going to last," he was told.

This low regard for television news was easy to understand. CBS modeled its product on radio news, dragooning the lesser lights of its radio staff into TV. For content the network relied on a syndicated service called Telenews, which it occasionally supplemented with material from its own hired crews. Douglas Edwards, building on the exposure and experience he had gained at the conventions, anchored the show. CBS's budget for its daily newscast was less than what it spent on its featured weekly radio documentary starring Edward R. Murrow, a differential that strengthened Murrow's reluctance to sign on as a TV news anchor.

NBC, the only other network that came close to matching CBS's efforts to cover the news in those early days, premiered its nightly newscast in 1948, just after the conventions concluded. It was called the *Camel Newsreel Theater* after its cigarette sponsor, and was narrated off camera by John Cameron Swayze, who like Edwards had made his mark as NBC's chief announcer at the 1948 convention but who worried "that the real money was in radio." In 1949 Camel and NBC changed the name of the show to the *Camel News Caravan*, expanded it to fifteen minutes, and put Swayze's face on the screen.

Whatever the show's name or length, it was clear that Camel was in charge. The money the tobacco company laid out for its news version of *Caravan* supported the entire worldwide operations of NBC news—salaries, equipment, and overhead—with enough left over to pay for other programming. In addition to allowing Camel carte blanche in naming the show, NBC was obliged to indulge the sponsor's other idiosyncrasies having to do with the promotion of cigarette smoking. Swayze, a nonsmoker, was required to place an ashtray prominently on his desk. The network was prohibited from showing any footage in which a "no smoking" sign was visible. And it could not show anyone smoking a cigar, not even Groucho Marx, except for Winston Churchill, and that exemption was won only after a bitter struggle waged by Reuven Frank.

In these early days, TV's working conditions were often primitive. This was particularly true at the ABC news operation, which ran well behind the big two in financial resources.

The inflated rhetoric of Sarnoff and other promoters about the "miracle of TV" contrasted with the reality of everyday programming, as Fritz Littlejohn later recalled. "The miracle was that we got on the air at all," he said. "First the movie camera could run out of film at precisely the wrong moment. Reloading took place while the critical moment sped past. Or the lab, always across town, could foul up."

Despite such early logistical problems, television news gained importance in large part because of the cold war. TV had missed out on the gains in prestige and audiences that World War II brought to radio. But now the cold war was to do much the same for television. "In many ways, the cold war shaped television news," wrote Reuven Frank, "and television news helped shape the cold war."

The first great center of action was Berlin, during the airlift of 1948 when East and West seemed on the verge of a disastrous collision. The juxtaposition of DC-3s landing every thirty seconds, carrying coal and bread to West Berlin's trapped citizens, with the goose-stepping Red Army brigades dominated television news and captured the public imagination.

There were more viewers when the shooting started in Korea two years later, and television rushed to the battlefront. Some of the starkest clips showed frostbitten Marines in desperate retreat after they had been ambushed by troops of the Chinese Red Army in overwhelming force. Years later Frank would recall the images: "the knitted scarves around their faces under their helmets, hollow eyes and bearded cheeks showing through, rags over their combat boots to keep in a little body heat."

Meanwhile the cold war was spilling over into the domestic political arena and creating new opportunities for television to demonstrate its growing clout. In 1948 TV cameras captured Whittaker Chambers's startling testimony before the House

Un-American Activities Committee charging that Alger Hiss had been a Soviet agent. Far less welcome was the internal anguish created by the fear of communism within television itself, including television news. On June 22, 1950, three days before the outbreak of the Korean War, a newsletter called *Counterattack*, printed over a hammer and sickle and dedicated to exposing the "Communist Fifth Column," published a slim volume called *Red Channels*. Produced by three former FBI agents, it purported to be a list of Communists and Communist sympathizers in television and radio. The 150 names, some as famous as Orson Welles and Gypsy Rose Lee and others relatively obscure, had been gleaned from the pages of the *Daily Worker*, the letterheads of suspect organizations, HUAC reports, and a hodgepodge of other sources.

Once listed in *Red Channels*, an individual became "controversial" and therefore undesirable for employment. To pressure television into compliance with this blacklist, anti-Communist groups threatened boycotts of the sponsoring companies' products if a show featured someone who was on one of the lists. Even after blacklisted individuals were cleared, industry officials often hesitated to hire them because their reputations remained sullied or because their careers had lost momentum while they were removed from the public eye.

People who appeared on a blacklist could become eligible for employment if they were "cleared" by the *Red Channels* publishers, either by demonstrating mistaken identity or by publicly repenting their earlier activities. The clearing process sometimes required individuals to hire the organization that had blacklisted them to perform an investigation in order to certify that they were, indeed, "clean." Thus between selling the lists to government agencies and industries and performing security investigations and clearing operations, the resourceful blacklisters were able to earn a living from their exposés. The television and radio blacklist lasted through the

1950s and came to an end only when lawsuits by victims made the blacklisters financially liable for the consequences of their listings.

Meanwhile Congress too was busy in the domestic cold war against the Communist threat within television. In 1951 the House Un-American Activities Committee, which had already spotlighted charges of alleged Communists in Hollywood, decided to investigate the increasingly influential new medium of TV. The Senate Internal Security Subcommittee followed suit. Television presented a more ominous threat than movies or radio, argued Jack O'Brian, television critic for the *New York Journal-American,* part of the Hearst chain, which was glad to encourage any offensive against communism. "In TV the actors come right into our living rooms," O'Brian wrote.

Despite the unjust harm done to innocent blacklist victims by the obsession with domestic communism, the broader struggles of the cold war benefited TV in the long run. Coverage of the global contest between East and West lent television a certain gravitas, helped it establish a prominent place in the news media chorus, and suggested its potential as a political weapon.

Paradoxically, the first politician to maximize this potential, the previously little-known Senator Estes Kefauver of Tennessee, turned the camera eye on an issue that appeared far removed from the international affairs that had been grist for the mill of TV news—organized crime. But it was a subject that, like the threat of communism, fed on a paranoia that gripped the nation in the 1950s. At the same time the United States confronted the power of the Soviet Union abroad, Americans in their own country were caught up in an unprecedented wave of violence. Criminologists attributed rising crime rates to the wartime disruption of families, shortages of goods, and a mounting public demand for illicit gambling. But Kefauver targeted another villain: "the mob," otherwise known as "the syndicate" or the Mafia. By whatever epithet is was labeled, to many ordinary citizens this evil conglomerate seemed particularly menacing in those fearful days because it had one fundamental thing in common with Communist subversion: it was also an "enemy within."

3

Racket Buster

When Senator Estes Kefauver launched his probe of organized crime in 1950, there was no way he could know that his televised investigation would serve as a sort of dress rehearsal for the televised Army-McCarthy hearings nearly four years later. Coincidentally, Kefauver had to compete against Senator McCarthy to get Senate approval for his crime inquiry. Having lost out on one front, crime, McCarthy moved ahead on another where the Republic was also supposedly threatened: Communist subversion. Within a month he would make headlines and begin building a national reputation for himself as a fighter of communism. Meanwhile Kefauver's crime investigation showed the almost hypnotic appeal of television to millions of Americans and its consequent power to dramatize a political issue. This was an experience broadcasters and politicians would bear in mind in April 1954 when McCarthy's long-running crusade against communism went off the tracks, leading to the televised hearings of his dispute with the Army.

But these events were still sleeping in the future when Kefauver set out to take on organized crime. His venture had as much to do with his own political predicament as with the threat against law and order. In January 1950, Kefauver, then beginning his second year in the Senate, was in a quandary: he was a reform politician without a cause. For the forty-seven-year-old senator this was no small matter. Reform of one sort or another had from the start been the lifeblood of his political career. He was a throwback of sorts to the nineteenth-century progressives who had set aside ideology in favor of the faith that nothing was wrong with our democracy that could not be cured by a bit of tinkering with its machinery.

Coming from Tennessee, Kefauver had never before had much trouble finding dragons to slay. When he entered politics he found the political order of battle in his state dominated by Ed Crump, who had built an apparently impregnable political base rooted in his hometown of Memphis. Crump viewed Kefauver with intense suspicion from the time he first trod onto the state's political stage. And with good reason. Kefauver may have been a political outsider, but he was no underdog and would have no need to kowtow to Crump. He could trace his lineage in this country to the Jamestown colony. Both his father and his mother had come from families highly respected in the state and strategically located, one in east Tennessee, the other in the west.

Following graduation from Yale Law School young Estes married well, to the red-haired Nancy Patterson Pigott, daughter of an expatriate American later knighted by Great Britain's George VI, whose own vivid nature refreshingly contrasted with her husband's tepid personality. After establishing himself as a leading corporate lawyer in his native Chattanooga, Kefauver set his cap for the state senate in 1938, running on a platform devoted to upgrading zoning standards and backed by his own small army of idealistic volunteers. Appalled even by this specter of mild change, the local bosses managed to stuff enough ballot boxes to defeat the young reformer. But Kefauver emerged with his reputation as a crusader stronger than ever. When he entered the bidding for a vacant House seat in 1939, the bosses threw up their hands and let Kefauver have his way.

As a junior congressman he first achieved distinction in 1942 when he voted for anti-poll-tax legislation. This was a stand unheard of among Southern Democrats, prompting the notorious Mississippi segregationist John Rankin to point a finger at the Tennessean on the House floor and shout, "Shame on you, Estes Kefauver."

In 1948 he sought to move up, seizing the opportunity created by the weakness of the incumbent Democratic senator to challenge him for renomination. Kefauver's biggest drawback was that he was little known outside his own House district. A solution to this problem came from, of all people, his fiercest enemy, Boss Crump. The sultan of Memphis climaxed a crusade against Kefauver's candidacy with full-page ads in the state's major newspapers calling Kefauver "a darling of the Communists." Most memorably, the ads compared Kefauver's denials of this charge to the sneakiness of a "pet coon."

Kefauver lost no time responding. "Mr. Crump defames me," he declared, "but worse than that he defames the coon, the all-American animal. We coons can take care of ourselves," Kefauver added, following with a thrust that brought his audience to its feet cheering and laughing: "I may be a pet coon, but I ain't Mr. Crump's pet coon." To exploit the point, as Kefauver campaigned he donned a coonskin cap, which became the talisman of his political career. With this uncharacteristic burst of folksy showmanship, Kefauver put an end to Boss Crump's seeming invincibility in Tennessee politics, winning the Democratic nomination handily and then crushing his GOP opponent in the general election.

Once in the Senate, having nailed Crump's coonskin to the wall, Kefauver began to explore the possibilities of even higher office. "I suppose it is just a natural desire on the part of every boy to want to be president," he said with seeming modesty.

With the end of World War II, public concern over crime had mounted, spurred by the grim forecasts of law enforcement experts who warned that a wave of unprecedented lawlessness was about to engulf the land. The cause, most people agreed at first, was the undermining of family discipline and general social dislocation as a consequence of the war. But a series of newspaper and magazine stories brought attention to the idea that the root of the problem was a national network of organized crime.

The central villain, by these accounts, was a New York gambling boss named Frank Costello, with past links to the gang once headed by the late Al Capone. Costello made the journalists' work easy by styling himself the "king of slots." Although no one could describe exactly how he operated, that did not prevent the press from labeling him "Prime Minister of the Underworld," profiling him in a two-part series in *Collier's*, and plastering his face on the covers of *Time* and *Newsweek*. The clamor raised by the media forced the federal government to respond. In 1947 President Truman's Justice Department established a special "racket squad" to visit major cities and lay the groundwork for grand jury probes. Truman himself addressed a nationwide conference on crime, blaming the problem mainly on the social upheaval caused by the war. As a path to a solution, rather than an all-out crackdown by police the president urged an emphasis on the "gentler forces" of church and family to cure the distemper among the young. And he cautioned against violating civil liberties.

But this was not what the crime hawks on Capitol Hill wanted to hear. In the Senate two ambitious freshmen, one in each party, had the same idea and sought to put their own imprimatur on the battle against the underworld. On the Republican side was Joe McCarthy of Wisconsin, desperate for an issue to help his 1952 reelection campaign. First among the Democrats was Kefauver, who had set his sights on the White House in 1952, or at least a spot on the national ticket. But to satisfy the public Kefauver offered a more substantive predicate for his proposed assault on crime—his previous work on a House judiciary subcommittee which had investigated charges of judicial corruption in Pennsylvania and recommended the impeachment of a federal district judge. The probe had brought him useful contacts with prosecutors who were familiar with the machinations of organized crime and journalists who had been ballyhooing the menace of the "syndicate" and who now offered him guidance and support.

In January 1950 Kefauver introduced a resolution calling for the Judiciary Committee on which he served to launch an investigation into gambling and racketeering "and of the manner in which the facilities of interstate commerce are made a vehicle of organized crime." No sooner had Kefauver offered his proposal than McCarthy suggested that the inquiry be turned over to the Senate's Investigations Subcommittee of which he was a member, and would eventually become chairman. But Kefauver had beaten him to the punch. And besides, Kefauver's Democrats controlled the Senate.

But Kefauver also faced opposition within his own party. Its leaders feared the impact a probe into organized crime would have on Democratic machines entrenched in big cities and often entangled with the mob. It took a headline-grabbing event to break down resistance and get Kefauver a green light. On April 6, 1950, a gambling kingpin highly placed in the Kansas City machine of Democratic boss and former Harry Truman patron Tom Pendergast, and one of his henchmen, were murdered in a Democratic clubhouse in the center of the city that liked to call itself "The Heart of America." To add to the damage, the bodies were positioned in such close juxtaposition to a large wall photo of Truman that both the bodies and the presidential portrait were emblazoned on front pages across the nation.

As the *Kansas City Star-Times* called for immediate action against the "national crime syndicate," papers across the country joined in the cry. Almost immediately Truman himself approved a Kefauver investigation, and the full Senate soon provided its backing. As his special counsel Kefauver chose Rudolph Halley, a brilliant New Yorker who had graduated from Columbia Law School at age twenty and gone on to work with the Senate War Investigating Committee headed by then senator Harry Truman. As the hearings progressed Halley would demonstrate not only keen political and legal acumen but also, through television, a sense of showmanship that helped galvanize the public.

By the late spring of 1950, as Senator McCarthy pursued the menace of Communist subversion, Kefauver began holding hearings that would continue around the country through the summer and fall. In that midterm election year Kefauver's probe seemed to bear out the worst fears of Democratic politicos. His committee's revelations of the Illinois Democratic party's ties to organized crime was blamed by many in the party for the defeat that November of Illinois senator and Democratic majority leader Scott Lucas.

But while the Illinois hearings made enemies for Kefauver within his own party, antagonism that would take a toll on his national ambitions, it also helped foster the reputation of his committee for unbiased muckraking. Even more important for Kefauver and the committee, his contacts with journalists helped assure local stories, and in cities such as New Orleans they brought a new and profoundly important factor into the coverage: television. At the start Kefauver had apparently given little thought to television, which was still only a minor player in the worlds of media and politics. He was chiefly interested in getting the hearings reported in the newspapers.

But the telecasts of the hearings, which developed more or less spontaneously, were to give him more attention than he could have dreamed of.

The Kefauver hearings were only the fifth time in political history that congressional hearings had been televised, the most notable being Alger Hiss's testimony before the House Un-American Activities Committee. But television coverage of Kefauver's probe was far more sustained than the earlier proceedings and gained vastly greater public attention than anyone had anticipated. The initial televised hearings, in New Orleans, overshadowed the newspaper accounts, brought overflow crowds to the hearing rooms, and reached tens of thousands in adjoining states. Sure enough, at Kefauver's next stop, Detroit, a reporter got Kefauver's okay for his paper's television station to televise the hearings locally, and created another huge response. The TV arm of another Detroit paper jumped on the bandwagon, canceling its commercial programs.

"Detroiters, through the eyes and ears of TV and radio were able to attend a real life whodunit," breathlessly reported the trade publication *Broadcasting/Telecasting*. "Nearly every other activity paused as televiewers riveted themselves before an estimated 90 percent of the city's screens to watch hoodlums squirm under the relentless questioning of the committee."

Two weeks later Kefauver brought his road show, complete with squirmers, to television screens in St. Louis. There one witness claimed that his right to privacy was being violated. But Kefauver argued that television was simply an extension of the already recognized right of other media to cover the hearing. The witness testified, but the controversy he raised would rage on for years afterward.

In Los Angeles, where the anti-crime caravan stopped next, KECA-TV moved its cameras into the Federal Building for two days of hearings. Headlines were immediately made when a local police official testified about an underworld plot to assassinate the city's police chief William H. Parker, a figure of nationwide renown because of his being regularly mentioned on the weekly *Dragnet* radio crime drama, then one of the most popular shows on the air. The plot, which resembled a *Dragnet* script, apparently was intended to clear the way for racketeers, posing as legitimate businessmen, to take over the city when Los Angeles "opened up."

That went over big. While the hearings continued, KECA's switchboards were jammed with more than three thousand phone calls from enthusiastic viewers. And Mayor Fletcher Borwin offered his thanks to the station "for performing this vital public service." By the time he finished in Los Angeles, after ten months of probing, Kefauver and his committee were big news—big enough so that the senator who had denied being Boss Crump's pet coon made the cover of *Time*. "It Pays to Organize," *Time* said, thus taking the words right out of the committee's mouth. "The evidence demonstrates quite clearly that organized crime today is not limited to any single community of any single state, but occurs all over the country," the committee's report asserted.

This fanfare turned out to be only a buildup to the event that would make the Kefauver Committee a landmark in the nation's politics—its hearings in New York City beginning March 12, 1951. Kefauver was widely accused of transforming the New York hearings into a video "circus" to promote his own career. And it was certainly true that he was greedy for publicity, as his far-flung contacts with journalists demonstrated. But the truth was, given the opposition from the established political leadership, Kefauver desperately needed the publicity for his enterprise to survive. Yet there is little evidence that when the hearings began Kefauver recognized the gargantuan difference that TV would make.

At first the committee reacted rather than initiated requests from television stations. In New York, for example, WPIX, owned by the nation's biggest-circulation newspaper, the *Daily News*, on its own initiative sought permission to televise the hearings in February 1951, a month before they began. But it seems clear that in the wake of the initial TV exposure, Kefauver grasped the potential of television. After the New York federal judiciary, following tradition, turned down the WPIX request to televise the hearings in the federal courthouse in downtown Manhattan, Kefauver asked the judges to reconsider. They finally agreed to admit the cameras, though they relegated the hearings to a small courtroom on the twenty-eighth floor.

Chief Counsel Halley had arranged for the New York hearings to pack plenty of dramatic material. The plot was ready-made. At its center was William O'Dwyer, former mayor and more recently Harry Truman's ambassador to Mexico, who had originally made his reputation as a crusading, racket-busting district attorney along the lines of Thomas E. Dewey. But in later years O'Dwyer became the target of charges that he was far from being the deadly enemy of organized crime. Instead it was alleged that he had built his reputation by sending the satraps of the mob away to prison while letting the higher-ups get away, sometimes literally with murder.

Unlike the earlier televised sessions, the hearings in New York were picked up by three national networks as well as several local stations and broadcast to twenty major cities in the eastern half of the country. TV fare in the mornings was so dull that only 1.5 percent of the homes with television normally had their sets in use. This made the morning hours relatively inexpensive for sponsors, and *Time* shrewdly decided to sponsor the hearings over ABC. Having invested in televising hearings, the magazine saw no reason to underplay the drama of the event in its weekly print coverage. "The dignified law chambers of Foley Square had never seen anything like it," the magazine declared, "even during the dramatic trials of Alger Hiss or the Communist Party hierarchy."

For some citizens the option of watching on television was not enough to keep them away from the actual scene. Many stood in line for hours for seats in the small upstairs room, until finally the New York judges relented and allowed Kefauver to move his show to a large third-floor courtroom where flashbulbs flared amidst a jungle of television and newsreel cameras.

Although Kefauver had originally planned to have O'Dwyer as his leadoff witness, the former mayor came down with a severe case of bronchitis, coupled with pulmonary congestion. His testimony was put off for a week, a delay that turned out to be serendipitous. It resulted in the hearings opening with an even bigger lure than O'Dwyer—Frank Costello, the "Mr. Big" of New York crime. Costello immediately took the offensive. Through his lawyer he objected to the television cameras. "Mr. Costello doesn't care to submit himself as a spectacle," his lawyer declared loftily. Anxious not to lose their star, the committee agreed that Costello's face should not be televised. So the WPIX camera focused alternately on the questioners and on Costello's hands, which provided a telling portrait of the witness at bay as he crumpled a handkerchief, grasped for a glass of water, picked at his fingers, and fumbled with his eyeglasses.

Costello strove to give a positive impression by answering questions instead of taking the Fifth Amendment. But his responses were so evasive and in some cases obviously untrue that they undercut the image of candor and openness he sought to create. Under harsh questioning his early confidence waned and his voice grew hoarse.

After being granted a few days off to recover, he came back to testify in a voice that *Time* described as "midway between the speaking voice of radio comic Eddie Cantor and the death rattle of a seagull." Years later Costello revealed that his condition had been the result of a physician accidentally singeing his vocal chords when removing polyps from his throat. His gravelly voice made an enduring impression, so much so that Marlon Brando reputedly later mimicked it in the title role of *The Godfather.*

Costello's resistance brought him only limited benefits. The committee gleaned enough evidence from other witnesses to support its claim, at least in the minds of its members, that he was the boss of one of the nation's two big crime syndicates. The committee had also, as *Time* picturesquely put it, "charted some tortuous trails that led straight out of Costello's underworld and wound up in ex-Mayor William O'Dwyer's anteroom."

Finally came the moment Halley had been waiting for, the testimony of the erstwhile mayor himself. Halley and O'Dwyer had been raised on opposite sides of the New York political street. Halley was a child of New York City reform, the movement that had helped elect the city's most celebrated mayor, Fiorello LaGuardia. O'Dwyer was born and bred a regular Democrat, which meant that even though he hailed from Brooklyn he could not escape the influence of the Democratic organization in neighboring Manhattan, the infamous Tammany Hall. Much of Halley's interrogation of O'Dwyer seemed aimed at dispelling the former mayor's efforts to present himself as a foe of Tammany, linking him to various unsavory characters in New York who were said to be part of Tammany's web. O'Dwyer acknowledged that there probably had been large-scale gambling in New York when he was mayor, and that it could not have existed "without police protection." Weary and exasperated, he confessed that "the man in City Hall," running a city of eight million, could not pursue every such detail.

Everyone acknowledged that Halley had succeeded in embarrassing O'Dwyer and building a case of corruption. While never proven, it haunted the former mayor for the rest of his life. But some skeptics questioned whether in doing so Halley had served the stated purpose of the committee's investigation. By focusing on O'Dwyer, the committee implied that racketeering and gambling in New York could be blamed on the weaknesses of one man.

Overlooked was that O'Dwyer's predecessor in City Hall, the sainted LaGuardia, despite his many attacks on "tinhorn gamblers," had by his own admission failed to wipe out corruption and gambling during his long tenure as mayor. Beyond being unfair to O'Dwyer, the committee's emphasis on personal misfeasance buried the crucial reality that crime and corruption were rooted in fundamental issues—the blurring of the distinctions between law and morality that had prevailed in America since its Puritan beginnings, and the structural weakness of the governing system, particularly the fragmenting of authority among various law enforcement agencies and jurisdictions.

This distortion of reality could not be blamed on television, but the telecast of the hearings heightened their impact and thus exacerbated the confusion. By its prominence, television had an opportunity to put the case against O'Dwyer, and the committee's entire thrust, in perspective. This it never attempted to do.

Not that the public minded: the response to the New York hearings was overwhelming. Seventeen times as many people viewed the morning telecasts as watched the usual programs, numbers that perhaps reached twenty to thirty million people around the country. It was estimated that on the average more than 85 percent of those viewing television at the time watched the hearings, and that viewership doubled that of a weekday World Series game the preceding fall.

In Chicago, people stood outside in fifteen-degree temperature watching the testimony through the windows of appliance stores. In Minneapolis, people jammed early in the morning into bars and restaurants that had TV sets. When Kefauver reminded viewers that Red Cross blood donors were needed because of demands from the combat zone in Korea, the Brooklyn Red Cross installed a TV set among its cots and saw donations double. To handle the extra drain on electricity from television sets tuned to the hearings, New York's largest utility, Consolidated Edison, brought a giant generator on line.

The reviews were huzzahs. "No event TV has yet covered—the United Nations, political conventions, the presidential inauguration—presented high drama on so continuous a scale," cheered *Billboard*. Local lawmen joined in the chorus of praise, though some critics worried about the fairness of subjecting witnesses to hostile questioning before the cameras. "Unquestionably the knowledge that his actions are being recorded on millions of screens must be disquieting to a witness," observed the *Washington Post*. Even more important were "the broader questions of decorum and whether the fundamental rights of the witness are being invaded."

But the *Post* was in the minority. For the most part the hearings were greeted with approbation. "From the standpoint of public enlightenment, the union of television and the Senate Crime Investigating committee has been uniquely timely and beneficial," wrote Jack Gould, the prestigious television critic of the *New York Times*. "Such conditions as exposed by the hearings could not much longer exist," Gould suggested, "if the blazing lights and cameras of television were kept trained against the rulers of the darkness of this world." In central New Jersey the Greater Paterson Council of Churches urged "citizens interested in honest law enforcement" to watch the hearings.

Kefauver was showered with honors. The Father's Day Council named him Father of the Year for his "high principled leadership" of the committee, "which dramatically aroused public interest and morality." *Look* magazine gave him its annual award for best public affairs TV programming. And the Academy of Television Arts and Sciences awarded him an Emmy for "bringing the workings of our government into the homes of the American people." It seemed not to matter that the hearings lacked continuity or that much of the most dramatic testimony had only a tenuous connection to the supposed main purpose of the committee, which was to explore how organized crime exploited interstate commerce to expand its empire.

The Kefauver Committee's work reached its climax with the dramatic sessions in New York. Hearings dragged on through the summer, but Kefauver himself stepped down from the chairmanship to promote anti-crime legislation that might have provided a tangible result for all the *sturm und drang* the televised hearings had generated. But his major proposal, for a federal crime commission, went nowhere. The opposition Republicans were not eager to add to the prestige Kefauver had gained. Among his fellow Democrats, despite the laurels Kefauver had won from the public, the *New York Times* reported, "he was about as popular as a skunk at a lawn party." His exposure of the connections between crime and big-city officialdom had damaged their party in its strongholds. Moreover, as Democratic leaders correctly anticipated, the committee's findings would help strengthen the battle cries of "crime" and "corruption" that, with the frustrations of the war in Korea, would make up the Republican strategy for the 1952 presidential campaign.

While the committee's work may not have paid off in legislation, it did provide significant rewards for Kefauver personally—to a point. He emerged from the hearings second only to Truman in the polls as the favored Democratic standard-bearer in 1952. He rang up a series of impressive primary victories and came to the convention with the largest single bloc of delegates—but not enough for a majority. Resentful party leaders, including Truman, brought his bandwagon to a halt and persuaded Illinois governor Adlai Stevenson to make the first of what turned out to be two unsuccessful runs for the White House.

Above and beyond Kefauver's political ambitions was the debate that centered on the other major new force on the political stage, television. Not all politicians were prepared to join in the encomiums for the new medium. While one GOP committee member, New Hampshire's Charles Tobey, denounced the wrongdoers who appeared before him with such passion that he moved himself to tears, his committee colleague and fellow Republican Alexander Wiley of Wisconsin was more restrained. Determined to avoid "hamming and phony theatrics or an unjust inquisition of people under klieg lights," Wiley proposed in the wake of the hearings that the Senate Rules Committee establish "common sense standards of good taste and restraint" for televising the work of Congress. Kefauver himself supported the proposal, though it ultimately went nowhere.

Serious-minded cultural critics like Gilbert Seldes were swept off their feet by the hearings. "Television actively entered the public mind by the broadcasts of sports and political conventions, to which nothing creative was contributed," he wrote. "And it has now come to a position of pre-eminence with an event reflecting no skill, no art, no imagination— nothing but the honest report of an event."

But such a blank-check endorsement begged the question that would arise again and again in television's future. Does merely recording an event fulfill the responsibility of television and other media involved in political journalism? What television showed the viewing audience, as the novelist and journalist Ivan Doig wrote in a retrospective on the Kefauver hearings, "was just exactly what the committee wanted it to see: carefully garnered evidence of a great crime conspiracy. The point is that the great audience served by the nation's journalism was presented the story of the Kefauver committee virtually with no questions asked." Doig acknowledged some virtue in the "cold objective eye of the camera," but he added that "a cold hard stare often is less revealing than a good look around."

Twenty years before the Kefauver hearings, a federal commission on crime had pointed out that "the things which are considered as contributing to crime are merely the effects of larger and more fundamental causes"—the social, political, and economic problems facing the nation. But neither in its conduct of the hearings nor in its report did the Kefauver Committee exhibit an awareness of the importance of this context. Instead the committee presented a much dramatized and overly simplified picture.

Yes, organized crime and the mob did exist. But the fault with the hearings, and with television's coverage of them, lay in what was omitted—an omission amounting to a distortion. As one academic critic of the committee pointed out, instead of probing the conditions giving rise to organized crime, the Kefauver panel fostered the impression that this evil "originated outside of American society and was imposed upon the public by a group of immoral men, bound together by a mysterious ethnic conspiracy." Individuals, like the unfortunate Bill O'Dwyer, plunged into the conspiracy not because of the conditions of their environment but because of some weakness in their character. And television, by raising no questions about this interpretation, reinforced the committee's conclusions. It was true that neither did any challenge come from the print press, but television was the medium through which most Americans heard the committee's story. Nor did any of the media point out that the committee never inquired into the social and economic causes of crime nor weigh the idea of legalizing gambling. The committee heard from more than a thousand witnesses—police, politicians, and alleged criminals. But not a single sociologist or criminologist was summoned to testify. That certainly created an opening for an imaginative television producer, but none took advantage. Three years after the Kefauver hearings concluded, the Army-McCarthy hearings would test what lessons if any television news would take from the experience of the organized-crime hearings.

4

The Road to Room 318

Joe McCarthy watched with envy as journalists swarmed around crimebuster Kefauver like moths around a flame. But McCarthy did not need his Tennessee colleague to teach him the value of publicity to a career in national politics. Conniving for media exposure had been part of his stock in trade since he had first come to the Senate. Immediately on arriving in Washington in the winter of 1947 he called a press conference on the coal strike then in progress, proposing the conscription of the miners and their leader John L. Lewis. If that didn't get miners back to the pits, McCarthy suggested, they should be court-martialed.

For all his wild talk, many reporters found McCarthy a gregarious and amiable type who did not usually take himself as seriously as some of his fellow solons. And he went out of his way to cement good relations. He sent wheels of Wisconsin cheese and cases of Wisconsin beer to the National Press Club, gave out phone numbers of bars where he could be reached after hours—and made a point of returning reporters' calls. He also joined them in their poker games, though the senator, who was something of a card shark, was careful not to come out too far ahead.

But press relations was more than fun and games to McCarthy. He made himself into an expert on the trade craft of contemporary American journalism. He knew when deadlines fell and when reporters would have to print what he said. "His IQ was goddam high," said George Reedy, Lyndon Johnson's press secretary. "And, boy, he really had the press figured out."

McCarthy's success with the press, due not only to his own skills but also in part to lack of professional rigor among journalists responsible for covering him, helped him scale the heights of American politics. But it also contributed to an arrogance that encouraged him to take on all comers, including ultimately the U.S. Army and his own party's leaders. And this would lead him into the grave peril he would face before the television cameras in April 1954 in Room 318 of the Senate Office Building.

In his early Senate years it seemed that McCarthy's shrewd instincts with the press would safeguard him from harm. Dan Hanley, who covered the senator from Madison, Wisconsin, for the United Press would call McCarthy with a quote from the *Milwaukee Journal* and dutifully ask: "Is that what you said?"

"Sure," McCarthy would say. "And I'll say that for you too, or do you want something else? Tell me what you want and I'll say it."

McCarthy was particularly astute at providing "overnight leads" to hard-pressed wire-service reporters. In those days when America was still served by many afternoon as well as morning papers, the wire services had to cater to both. Typically most news breaks during the normal nine-to-five workday and is reported for the morning papers, the "a.m. cycle." But the afternoon papers wanted a fresh story, or at least a story that looked fresh because it had a new lead. "That's where Joe came in," recalled the UP's John L. Steele. "He was always on the lookout for a fresh angle for the p.m. cycle. Call him, he'd always have something for a new lead."

But when dealing with journalists whom he regarded as hostile, McCarthy used a heavy hand. After several unfavorable articles by the Associated Press's Marvin Arrowsmith, McCarthy complained to him personally. When Arrowsmith ignored him, McCarthy sent letters to hundreds of papers, denouncing the AP for its supposedly biased coverage. Arrowsmith's next story was positive, recounting the floods of supportive mail McCarthy was getting.

On at least one occasion McCarthy resorted to violence. Furious at Drew Pearson, who had attacked him countless times in his widely read syndicated column, McCarthy cornered him in the cloakroom of Washington's exclusive Sulgrave Club, kneed him twice in the groin, and took a swing at him. It took Senator Richard Nixon to stop the brawl. "Let a Quaker break up this fight," Nixon cried.

The determination, energy, and shrewdness that McCarthy displayed in his dealings with the press, along with his willingness to take risks that would have deterred most other politicians, were shaped by the cards that life had dealt him. Early on he had learned that time for him was no luxury; he could not afford to waste it.

One of seven children born to Timothy Thomas McCarthy, a farmer, and his wife, Bridget, the boy grew up in the country outside Appleton and Manawa, Wisconsin, and was educated in the one-room Underhill country school, completing the eighth grade at age fourteen. He was no idler. Besides working on the family farm, he ran his own chicken-raising enterprise and managed an outlet in a grocery chain. In the fall of 1929, as the Great Depression descended on America, the twenty-year-old McCarthy entered Manawa's Little Wolf High School, where—within nine months—he completed a four-year program with honors.

Enrolling in Marquette University in 1930 as an engineering student, he soon switched to law and graduated with a law degree five years later. Throughout his school years he supported himself with part-time jobs—grocery worker, flypaper salesman, theater usher, construction worker, dishwasher, and manager of a filling station. He also picked up spare change by gambling, playing poker with such reckless abandon that he often drove players with better hands to fold. It was said that during a football weekend in Pittsburgh he made enough from several unwitting Marquette alumni to cover his college bills for the full semester. Brash and indifferent to academic routines and rules, he found time to coach the school's boxing team and to make many friends among his fellow students.

About his political beliefs he left no doubt: young Joe was an ardent New Dealer. Soon after law school graduation, he entered practice in a small town outside Appleton and got himself elected president of the local Democratic club. In 1936 he ran a strong though losing race for district attorney. All the while he made a show of professing his admiration for President Franklin D. Roosevelt, enthusiastically backing New Deal relief programs. By his own account he voted for FDR three times.

Three years after his first election bid, McCarthy tried again, this time for a circuit judgeship. And this time he won, defeating a 24-year incumbent, partly by overstating his opponent's age—claiming he was 73 when in fact he was only 66—but mostly by outhustling him for votes. When McCarthy took his seat on the Wisconsin circuit bench in 1939 he was only 30 years old, the youngest circuit judge in his state's history. As a judge, McCarthy continued to be a young man in a hurry: within months he had cleared a backlog of 250 cases from the docket.

McCarthy was soon criticized for his practice of granting divorces within five or ten minutes, though in most of these cases the couples had already reached agreement on terms. Indeed, some lawyers in the circuit viewed his speedup as a service to the couples involved. In general, local attorneys praised him for his energy and fair-mindedness, and he remained in good standing with his state's highest court.

McCarthy's unpretentious manner and his rough-and-ready humor made him popular with constituents. His main recreations were gambling and drinking in the back rooms of Appleton's fraternal clubs and dating the attractive young women he hired to work in his office. He made plain his disinterest in marriage. "I can't work at politics if I have to call in every half-hour," he liked to say.

In 1942, with America at war, Judge McCarthy, though not subject to the draft, but with his eye on the political future, saw the need for a war record. Taking the advice of a friend who counseled, "Look if you've got to be a hero to be a politician, join the Marines," McCarthy did just that, receiving a commission as a second lieutenant rather than—as he later boasted—a "buck private." Shipped to the Pacific, he talked his way into receiving a Distinguished Flying Cross he had done little to earn. He did perform ably as a briefing officer and occasionally came under enemy fire. But the foot injury he suffered did not result from, as he would claim, Japanese shelling but rather from shipboard shenanigans while crossing the equator. That did not prevent McCarthy from faking a limp and claiming that he carried ten pounds of shrapnel in his leg.

In 1944 political opportunity called again. This time it led him to take a leave from the Marines and return home to run for the Senate, as a Republican of all things. If the philosophy behind his move was never clear, it nonetheless made practical sense. Wisconsin had always been more of a Republican state than a Democratic preserve, and in 1944 the glow from the New Deal that McCarthy had once so much admired was wearing off rapidly. And McCarthy, as he later told reporters, had the advantage of being "a Republican with a Democratic name." Campaigning that year on his war record as "Tail Gunner Joe," he entered the Republican senatorial primary against the incumbent Alexander Wiley, who beat him easily. But McCarthy got what he wanted: name recognition in the state and a following in the GOP, where he gained grudging acceptance.

As always, he had his eye on the future, and the future came up fast. In 1946, two years after he lost to Wiley, McCarthy targeted the Senate seat held by Robert M. La Follette, Jr., son of the legendary "Fighting Bob." La Follette senior had been a Wisconsin hero, but his son was no fighter, nor much of a politician either. He neglected his base in Wisconsin's Progressive party and ultimately decided to disband that liberal group and instead to seek the nomination of the Republican party.

That was a mistake. La Follette's old supporters refused to follow him into the GOP, and McCarthy with his boundless energy narrowly defeated him for the Republican nomination. That fall he trounced his Democratic opponent. Although McCarthy branded his foe, Howard J. McMurray, a political scientist at the University of Wisconsin and a former New Deal congressman, as "communistically inclined," this seemed to be no more than a passing slur. The "Red menace" was not a major issue in the campaign.

Instead in that memorable year which saw the Republicans seize control of Congress for the first time since the Great Depression, McCarthy leveled broad attacks on the Truman administration for its mishandling of conversion to a peacetime economy. "Had enough?" was the damning question campaigning Republicans everywhere asked. And the voters in most places, including Wisconsin, answered resoundingly by voting the GOP ticket, making the Marine Corps veteran and district judge into a United States senator.

McCarthy's youth again distinguished him, this time in Washington. Now thirty-eight, he entered the Eightieth Congress as its youngest member. Although his enemies later claimed that McCarthy suffered from an inferiority complex, the charge was not borne out by his behavior. Described by the *Saturday Evening Post* as "handsome in a dark, square-jawed way," he took full advantage of his appearance and pursued the same pattern of carousing that had diverted him in his courthouse days in Appleton.

Far from being withdrawn, McCarthy was brash in a way that soon marked him as a rebel in the Senate. That body, which puts great weight on tradition and custom, demands patience, restraint, and moderation, particularly from its junior members. These were qualities that ran counter to the restless energy and freewheeling behavior that defined McCarthy's drive for attention and success. For the most part he was a typical Republican of his era. He was conservative on labor policy and opposed most welfare measures. He favored tax reductions and fought controls on prices and rents, notably a bill extending wartime price controls on sugar (Wisconsin beet sugar producers were an important constituency for him). But what was striking about McCarthy's role as a mainstay of the opposition, and foreshadowed his future in the Senate, were his crude attacks on his colleagues and his recklessness with the truth, leading to public denunciations of the freshman senator by some of his Republican colleagues.

His career slumped in 1948 when the Democrats, aided by Truman's stunning upset victory over Dewey, regained control of Congress. With his party in the minority and himself low in seniority and lacking an important committee post, McCarthy was having trouble gaining traction. His reelection in 1952 looked like an uphill struggle.

Desperate for attention, McCarthy took on the unlikely cause of seventy-three German SS troopers who had been convicted by an American war-crimes court of massacring American prisoners of war in the Belgian village of Malmedy during the Battle of the Bulge. The troopers contended that they had been tortured to force confessions and that the court proceedings had violated traditional legal standards. One Wisconsin newsman had suggested to McCarthy that backing the SS men would help him build a political base among Wisconsin's German-American farmers.

Paradoxically, McCarthy, who would later become a major threat to civil liberties, agreed to champion the rights of a group who to most Americans were among the most unpopular imaginable. But in carrying out this role on the committee set up to investigate the controversy, McCarthy displayed the same overbearing style that would later become his hallmark. Allowed to sit in on the hearings, though he was not a member of the investigating panel, McCarthy dominated by bullying the committee members. In the end the committee upheld the trials of the troopers and found they had been treated fairly. McCarthy denounced the committee's report and charged that its chairman, Republican senator Ray Baldwin of Connecticut, was "criminally responsible" for a whitewash. The episode convinced Baldwin to leave politics and resign from the Senate. But for McCarthy, the attention he won from the incident helped set him on a course that would pay little attention to legislation and instead make his priority investigation, backed by intimidation.

But this was a potential yet to be exploited. At the moment McCarthy was still looking for an issue to boost his chances of reelection. No wonder then that as 1950 dawned he challenged Kefauver for control of the crime issue. Rebuffed, he turned to something even juicier, the menace of communism in government.

It was around this time that McCarthy had dinner at Washington's Colony restaurant with Father Edmund Walsh, dean of the Georgetown University School of Foreign Service, to whom he confessed his need for a campaign issue. After discussing such unexciting options as the Saint Lawrence Seaway and a Townsend-type pension plan for the elderly, Walsh brought up communism.

McCarthy did not have to be persuaded. "The government is full of Communists," he declared. "The thing to do is hammer at them."

These were the circumstances that would lead to McCarthy's personal rendezvous with destiny in the improbable locale of Wheeling, West Virginia. He was certainly not alone among Republicans in "hammering" at the issue of communism. Three days before he spoke in Wheeling on February 9, at a dinner meeting of the Ohio County Women's Republican Club, party leaders meeting in Washington had adopted a platform for the 1950 congressional elections calling for "a strong policy" against the spread of communism and fascism at home and abroad.

But McCarthy brought to the cause a new passion, which seemed so deep it stirred the emotions of his audiences, along with a willingness to stretch the facts, or if need be invent them to make his point. Exactly what McCarthy did say in Wheeling that night will never be known for certain because the senator himself denied what he was reported to have said. No audio or visual record of the speech survived; a recording made by the Wheeling station that broadcast the speech was erased the next day, and McCarthy had no formal written text that he would acknowledge.

His talk was cobbled together from bits and pieces uttered by other Republicans, Richard Nixon among them. But the key paragraph, which aroused attention and made McCarthy a national figure, as reported on February 10 by *Wheeling Intelligencer* staff reporter Frank Desmond, was this: "While I cannot take the time to name all of them in the State Department who have been named as members of the Communist Party and members of a spy ring, I have here in my hand a list of 205 that were known to the Secretary of State as being members of the Communist Party and who nevertheless are still working and shaping the policy of the State Department."

The derivation of the magic number "205," which McCarthy was to change more than once in the days to come, and which appeared in a draft of the speech handed to reporters in Wheeling, at first was a mystery. Ultimately it was traced to a statement made in 1946 by President Truman's secretary of state, James F. Byrnes. Of 3,000 federal employees screened for loyalty because they were being transferred to the State Department from other agencies, Byrnes said, damaging information had been turned up on 284, 79 of whom had been discharged. That left 205.

What McCarthy did not know, nor did anyone else, was how many of these 205 had since been fired or had quit. Nor was it known what kind of damaging information had been learned about them—they might have been Communists, or fascists, or alcoholics, or sexual deviants.

Two days later, when he arrived in Reno, Nevada, for another speech on the Communist threat, McCarthy had modified the crucial paragraph. In a draft handed to reporters in Reno, the number 205 had been crossed out and replaced by the number 57. That number, though McCarthy did not explain, apparently came from a source similar to the Byrnes statement—a 1948 report of the House Appropriations Committee compiled by former FBI agent Robert E. Lee, which noted that of 108 past and present State Department employees who posed "security problems," 57 were still working there as of 1948.

A few days after his Reno talk, when McCarthy inserted what he claimed to be the text of the Wheeling speech in the *Congressional Record*, he again referred not to 205 but to 57

cases, describing them this time as "individuals who would appear to be either card-carrying members or certainly loyal to
the Communist party."

Whatever it was that McCarthy actually said in Wheeling, the story reached the world by a somewhat circuitous
route. The Associated Press had no bureau in Wheeling; it
was represented there by Norman L. Yost, managing editor of
the *Intelligencer.* It was Yost who took a couple of paragraphs
from Frank Desmond's story and phoned them in to the AP
bureau in Charleston, West Virginia. As the AP night editor
there, Charles Lewis, began writing the brief story, he came to
the number 205 as the total of Communists in the State Department. Lewis phoned Yost back and asked him to confirm
that number. Yost asked him to hold the phone, checked with
Desmond, and then told Lewis that 205 was accurate.

Yet Desmond had never asked McCarthy to see the "list"
he claimed to have in his hand. If he had done so, and Mc-
Carthy had shown him nothing more than the 1946 Byrnes
statement, it seems unlikely that Desmond's story would ever
have created the storm it eventually generated.

Perhaps Desmond was just an overworked, underpaid reporter whose better journalistic instincts had been dulled at
the end of a long day. But what of the Associated Press, the
mighty combine representing nearly every paper of worth
in the country? Why didn't Lewis ask Yost to demand the
list? Apparently the thought didn't occur to him. And so the
number 205 was the figure in the story the AP sent out to its
member newspapers, mainly for the afternoon cycle since it
was too late for the morning run. The AP story was notable for
its length, or rather the lack of it; it was only 110 words.

Contrary to later legend, the story did not create an immediate sensation. Of 129 papers of all sizes across the country
surveyed by Edwin R. Bayley of the University of California,
Berkeley, 18 carried the AP story on February 10, the day

after McCarthy's speech. The largest of these was the *Chicago Tribune*, a paper then devoted to advancing the conservative cause.

But the story picked up momentum thanks to McCarthy's adroitness and journalistic gullibility. In the days following the Wheeling speech the Wisconsin senator made a series of talks on the same theme, with modified facts and numbers, a strategy well designed to keep the story alive. Then on February 20, 11 days after the original speech in Wheeling, McCarthy took the Senate floor to speak at length on "the extent to which Communists have infiltrated into the State Department and are shaping policy." This time, instead of 205 or 57 card-carrying Communists, he addressed himself to "81 loyalty risks" culled from Robert E. Lee's House Appropriations Committee report and proceeded to analyze them one after another. Dissatisfied that only a handful of senators were present—most Democrats stayed away to demonstrate their disdain for the occasion—McCarthy demanded and got a quorum. He did not hesitate to improve upon the evidence in Lee's list. Where one suspect was said to be of "uncertain" health, McCarthy reinterpreted that to be "his *mental* health is unstable." A "typist at the Soviet Embassy" was converted into "an assistant editor." And so on and so forth.

Aware that McCarthy could no longer be ignored, and realizing that the Republicans would demand an investigation of his charges, the Democrats launched a preemptive strike. Majority Leader Scott Lucas of Illinois, who later that year would be politically embarrassed by Kefauver's allegations, offered his own proposal for an inquiry. But Lucas cagily designated the moderate Senate Foreign Relations Committee to chair it rather than the conservative Appropriations Committee, which would have been the Republicans' choice.

The Republicans agreed to support Lucas's initiative, provided the investigation would include previous charges of subversion at the State Department and access to the records of all government employees who had been charged. This last was crucial for McCarthy, who knew he needed more solid information than the skeletal allegations in his speeches if he were to be taken seriously by the investigating committee, which would be headed by Millard Tydings, veteran Maryland Democrat.

McCarthy had only two weeks after the adoption of the Senate resolution to prepare for the Tydings hearings. But he had the eagerly volunteered services of an informal cadre of right-wing Washington reporters who had been covering communism as an issue long before McCarthy discovered its potential value. On traditional political issues, various interest groups such as farmers, business, and labor were represented by lobbyists who, among other things, provided lawmakers with information to buttress their points of view. Anti-communism was too young to have its own lobby, but these militant journalists became an informal one for the sake of McCarthy's career and the cause in which they believed, and for their own ambitions. Some gave him speech material, or wrote his speeches, most notably Willard Edwards, congressional correspondent of the *Chicago Tribune*, and Ed Nellor, an assistant to conservative radio columnist Fulton Lewis, Jr. Others, including ex-Communist Fred Utley, a correspondent for the libertarian weekly *The Freeman*, kept him in touch with fellow Republicans and passed on leaks from federal agencies. It also helped that conservative publishers William Randolph Hearst and Robert R. McCormick made sure that key journalists in their employ chipped in to aid McCarthy with advice and favorable notices.

In addition, McCarthy played another long shot. He let it be known to reporters that he was prepared to name the leading Soviet spy in America, "the boss of Alger Hiss." This evil genius, McCarthy said, was Owen Lattimore, a respected Far

East scholar at Johns Hopkins University and sometime State Department consultant. When Lattimore was called before the Tydings Committee, its members found nothing in his testimony or his government loyalty file to back up McCarthy's charges. Still, McCarthy pressed on. He summoned Louis Budenz, former editor of the *Daily Worker*, among the most prominent and voluble of the many recovering Communists who came forward at the time to recant, repent, and expose former comrades. Budenz testified that during his days at the *Worker* he had been told "to consider Owen Lattimore a Communist." That was enough to satisfy those who wanted to believe in McCarthy.

By the time the hearings concluded, McCarthy had uncovered no Communists previously unknown. The Tydings Committee report in July denounced the Wisconsin senator for perpetrating "a fraud and a hoax," on the American public, denied his accusations, and charged him with deliberate and willful falsehood. But McCarthy's supporters dismissed the committee's indictment as a partisan smear, which further endeared him to his admirers. Far from having his credibility destroyed, McCarthy, with help from his friends in the press, came out of the Tydings hearings as the undisputed leader of America's battle against the menace of domestic communism.

Not surprisingly, McCarthy made as one of his first goals the defeat of Tydings, who faced reelection in Maryland in 1950. Once again he had plenty of journalistic support. The McCormick-owned *Washington Times* gave its enthusiastic backing to Tydings's opponent, Republican John Marshal Butler. It also published a special four-page tabloid section filled with sneers at Tydings's record and featuring a composite photo of Tydings and Communist party head Earl Browder. On election day Tydings, a four-term incumbent, went down to defeat.

But that was not the end of the matter. A month after he lost his seat, Tydings filed charges with the Senate's Subcommittee on Privileges and Elections, denouncing the conduct of the campaign against him as "scandalous, scurrilous, libelous and unlawful," and urging a full-scale investigation. In February the subcommittee began public hearings that extended for three months and in August issued a bipartisan report sharply critical of McCarthy's supporters for conducting a "despicable 'back street' campaign." But the report made no specific recommendations for action.

Among those frustrated by this indecisive outcome was Democratic senator William Benton of Connecticut, a liberal who had been appointed to fill the vacancy created by the resignation of an earlier McCarthy foe, Senator Raymond Baldwin. Benton had little experience in the Senate and little influence there, but he had considerable imagination, honed by his years running the celebrated New York advertising agency of Benton and Bowles. A few days after the filing of the committee report on Tydings's defeat, Benton introduced a resolution in the Senate calling for a broad investigation of McCarthy leading toward his expulsion from the Senate.

Benton's proposal was so drastic that it probably would have died of neglect—except for McCarthy himself. He helped keep Benton's idea alive with attacks on the subcommittee that had investigated Tydings's charges, chaired by Democratic senator Guy Gillette of Iowa. McCarthy's tactics prompted Gillette to give Benton a hearing.

McCarthy responded to this threat by continuing to attack the subcommittee and refusing Gillette's repeated invitations to testify on Benton's charges, conduct which three years later would come back to haunt him. After months of wrangling with McCarthy, the committee finally issued a report in January 1953, the last day of the Eighty-second Congress, which had little to say about McCarthy's tactics in dealing with the

Communist threat. Instead it mostly raised questions about the propriety of the senator's financial activities.

That was no problem for McCarthy. He declared that the report set a "new low in dishonesty and smear," and dismissed critical members of the committee as "left wingers" and "lackeys" for the Truman administration. In the wake of a series of attacks and investigations in the Senate, then under control of the opposition Democratic party, McCarthy emerged stronger than ever. And after the 1952 elections, his own party held now the upper hand both on Capitol Hill and in the White House.

Even before the elections McCarthy had become bolder and more reckless. Perhaps his most vicious attack came against Secretary of State Dean Acheson. Addressing the Senate on May 24, 1951, McCarthy cited Korean War amputee Bob Smith, whose lost limbs were "a tribute to the traitorous Red communist clique in our State Department." With heavy sarcasm and vulgar callousness toward the wounded soldier, McCarthy suggested that when Smith received his artificial limbs, "he first walk over to the State Department and call upon the great Red Dean and say, 'Mr. Acheson, if you want to at long last perform one service for the American people you should remove yourself from this country and go to the nation for which you have been struggling and fighting so long.'"

In June 1951, in the wake of President Truman's dismissal of General Douglas MacArthur, McCarthy claimed that the chief executive was a drunkard. "The son of a bitch should be impeached," he said, claiming that Truman's decision to get rid of MacArthur stemmed from a night of "bourbon and Benedictine." That same month McCarthy declared—in a phrase that became emblematic of his particular brand of demagoguery—that Secretary of Defense George Marshall was part of "a conspiracy so immense and an infamy so black as to dwarf any previous such venture in the history of man."

All the while the press corps did little to challenge McCarthyism. To the contrary, on balance they added to the momentum of his crusade. In part this was due to McCarthy's own skill and shrewdness, but the press's clumsiness and inhibitions also played a role. Another factor was the atmosphere of the times. The conviction of Alger Hiss, the Korean War, and the arrest of the Rosenbergs all made domestic communism seem more menacing and McCarthy appear more the timely messenger of danger.

So it was that McCarthy benefited greatly from "objective reporters" and their unblinking neutrality. John Steele of the United Press, who covered McCarthy for two years, later complained that his job was "*not* to put Senator McCarthy and his work in focus, but to take his speeches, his words and with as much sensationalism and speed as possible—and always with a straight face—spread them as gospel in the name of 'straight' reporting."

William Theis of the Hearst-owned International News Service accused all three wire services of being "so goddamn objective that McCarthy got away with everything, bamboozling the editors and the public." The approach of the wire services was critically important in forming the first public impressions of McCarthy. By one estimate they were the source of almost 85 percent of the news published by newspapers about McCarthy in the crucial month following his Wheeling speech when he became a major force in the nation's political life. The dependence of radio news on the wires was even greater, and for Americans in rural areas, radio was often the main source of news. TV news, then in its rudimentary stages, also relied heavily on the wire services. These wire stories had plenty of flaws to begin with, mainly a lack of background or reasoned interpretation. But they were often weakened further by local editors who trimmed stories, removing explanatory material in favor of a bare-bones presentation.

Throughout his career reporters struggled with the dilemma of McCarthy, trapped by the conventions of their trade. Many journalists, including some distinguished members of the profession, felt that because of McCarthy's position and the attention he had drawn to himself (with the help of the press, of course), the press had no choice but to be a conduit for whatever he chose to say. "McCarthy's charges are news which cannot be suppressed or ignored," wrote Walter Lippmann, the preeminent political columnist of the day but a man who was surprisingly insensitive to civil liberties concerns. "They come from a United States senator and a politician in good standing at the headquarters of the Republican Party. When he makes such attacks against the State Department, it is news which has to be published."

Perhaps. But if what McCarthy said was news, it was only part of the story. The other parts were what evidence he had for his allegations, the political inspiration behind him and his party to make those charges, the reaction of the targets of his attacks, and the overall impact of his attacks on the threat of communism. Some newspapers tried to provide their readers with this perspective. The *Denver Post*'s publisher, Palmer Hoyt, decreed that coverage of McCarthy be presented in a way so that readers could understand how and when his statements were misleading. "The plan of printing only 'straight facts' in the news columns and only opinion on the editorial pages leaves a twilight zone of 'news interpretation' untouched by the newspaper," Hoyt explained. "Newspapers should have no taboos against 'interpretation' when it is necessary to an understanding of any happening." The *Milwaukee Journal* took a similar view, inserting parenthetical corrections and explanations into McCarthy stories. But few reporters on other papers followed along. Most complained along with their publishers that it would take too much time and trouble.

As the 1952 election campaign approached, one thing was clear: McCarthy's decision to build his career upon the battle against communism had worked out splendidly. However controversial his anti-Red crusade was in other parts of the country, it had made him immensely popular in his own Wisconsin. Running for renomination, McCarthy campaigned little. He underwent chest surgery that July and spent most of the summer recuperating. He crushed his opponent, an obscure former county district attorney named Leonard F. Schmitt, by a margin of more than two to one. "Wisconsin people are voting against Stalin," said Schmitt.

The general election still lay ahead, but it was clear that McCarthy was headed for victory. It was in this setting, just after McCarthy's overwhelming victory for renomination, that Dwight Eisenhower, campaigning in Wisconsin for his own election, backed away from his intention to defend the reputation of George Marshall. Eisenhower's admirers later said that he had been talked out of the Marshall defense by his advisers, who feared that it would alienate McCarthy's obviously strong following in the state. Instead Ike denounced subversion in government, which sounded like cheerleading for McCarthy, and then shook hands with the senator.

McCarthy found a way to repay Ike for this indulgence. He made a fierce attack on the Democratic presidential candidate, Adlai Stevenson, eight days before the election at a Republican fund-raising dinner in Chicago. But just as significant was the medium he selected—television. His Chicago speech attacking Stevenson was his first major appearance on national television, and he took full advantage. The thrust of his speech was that Stevenson and five of his key advisers were supporters of communism, a charge that he claimed was supported by public documents. In fact the documents not only did not prove his charges, in some cases they refuted them.

Some in the Eisenhower campaign professed to be embarrassed by the speech. But no one repudiated it. Whatever damage he did to Stevenson, McCarthy seemed to have helped himself. The story of the speech made the front page of nearly every paper in Wisconsin, allowing McCarthy to dominate the news.

Yet his much anticipated election triumph was underwhelming. McCarthy won 54 percent of the vote, compared to 64 percent for the GOP gubernatorial candidate, incumbent Walter J. Kohler, and he ran behind the GOP ticket in most counties. In fact, despite the concern of Ike's strategists about McCarthy's political strength, Eisenhower ran ahead of McCarthy in the state with 61 percent of the vote.

Republican control of the new Congress gave McCarthy a greater opportunity to make a big noise as chairman of the Senate Committee on Government Operations and its investigative arm, the Permanent Subcommittee on Investigations. Helping him exploit this opportunity was the relatively new medium of television, which McCarthy had field-tested in the 1952 campaign with his Chicago attack on Stevenson.

Using his new committee chairmanship as a forum, McCarthy's first target was the Voice of America, the United States' major propaganda arm abroad. He claimed that "subversive" elements were influencing voice programming. After a week of closed hearings on the issue, the administration, seeking to placate McCarthy at the start of Eisenhower's presidency, demoted one official and fired three others. And Voice officials assured McCarthy they had begun banning material by "controversial authors." After screening witnesses at the closed hearings, McCarthy chose some, friendly or otherwise, who he thought would most help his cause at open hearings before television cameras.

The Wisconsin senator soon showed how quickly he had adapted to the new medium. His first significant victim was a

Voice official named Reed Harris, whom McCarthy browbeat mercilessly. Harris was accused of helping the Communist cause by curtailing some broadcasts to Israel. But most of McCarthy's attack focused on a book Harris had written more than twenty years earlier defending the right of professors to teach atheism, communism, and other unpopular ideas. "Now, you wrote a book in 1932," McCarthy said. "I'm going to ask you again: at the time you wrote this book, did you feel that professors should be given the right to teach sophomores that marriage—and I quote—'should be cast out of our civilization as antiquated and stupid religious phenomena'?"

Desperately Harris tried to explain himself. "My feeling is that professors should have the right to express their considered opinions on any subject, whatever they were, sir."

That did not satisfy McCarthy. He went back at the witness.

"All right, I'm going to ask you this question again," he said.

"That includes that quotation," Harris answered. "They should have the right to teach anything that came into their minds as being the proper thing to teach."

Still that wasn't enough for McCarthy. He had Harris in a hammer lock and continued to squeeze. "I'm going to make you answer this," the senator insisted.

Harris gave up. "All right, I'll answer yes, but you put an implication on it and you feature this particular point of the book, which, of course, is quite out of context, does not give a proper impression of the book as a whole."

Such nuances did not interest McCarthy, and he plowed ahead with his interrogation. Finally Harris's indignation exploded.

"I resent the tone of this inquiry very much, Mr. Chairman," he said. "I resent it, not only because it is my neck, my public neck, that you are, I think, very skillfully trying to wring, but I say it because there are thousands of able and loyal employees in the federal government of the United States who have been properly cleared according to the laws and the security practices of their agencies, as I was before."

To make Harris's treatment still more unfair, his response was cut short. Before his turn for rebuttal, other witnesses called by McCarthy took so much time that the ABC network, following its previously announced schedule, ended its coverage after Harris had been on the stand for only a half-hour. "McCarthy is setting a frightening precedent," Jack Gould warned in the *New York Times*. "If he agrees in advance to recess a hearing on cue, then he must do his share to see that all witnesses have their hour upon the stage." But McCarthy had no such qualms. As for Reed Harris, his resignation from the Voice was accepted a month later with a letter of commendation. The Harris case demonstrated that the senator had learned how to manipulate television and its deadlines just as well as he did the print press.

Following his investigation of the Voice of America, McCarthy carried his hunt for Communists to the Government Printing Office, the Central Intelligence Agency, and the Foreign Service, all without demonstrable effect—except to maintain himself as an intimidating presence. Arguing on the basis of alleged softness toward communism, he fought Eisenhower's appointments of Harvard president James B. Conant as high commissioner to Germany and Charles E. ("Chip") Bohlen as ambassador to the Soviet Union. He failed on both counts, but, typically, this did not slow him down. Instead he pushed ahead into even more controversial areas. He took on the United States Army.

In the fall of 1953, McCarthy claimed that a Communist spy ring was operating at the Army Signal Corps Center in Fort Monmouth, New Jersey. "Our entire defense against atomic attack," he said, was in jeopardy as he launched a full-scale probe.

But McCarthy had cast a wider net than the Signal Corps in his quest for flaws in Army security, and he won his biggest head-lines from an incident that had little to do with Fort Monmouth and more to do with military bungling than subversion.

At the center of the case was a New York City dentist, Irving Peress, who in October 1952 had been inducted into the Army and commissioned a captain under the Korean War doctors' draft law. What set Peress apart from most Army dentists was that he had been active in the American Labor party, an important left-wing force in New York State and a favored target of anti-Communists. Accordingly, when Peress was asked to fill out and sign a questionnaire about member-ship in subversive organizations, he simply wrote on the form "Federal Constitutional Privilege."

It was several months before military officials noticed this entry and several months more before they investigated. In June 1953 Army intelligence recommended that Peress be separated from the service. While this recommendation drifted through channels, in October, under an amendment to the doctors' draft law, Peress and seven thousand other Army doctors and dentists were promoted to major based on their civilian medical experience.

Around this time Peress's case came to the attention of Brig. Gen. Ralph Zwicker, a much decorated hero of World War II's Battle of the Bulge and the commandant at Camp Kilmer, New Jersey, where Peress was stationed. Outraged when he learned that Peress was about to be promoted despite his unresponsiveness to Army security procedures, Zwicker demanded that Peress be summarily tossed out of the Army.

Army personnel, well aware of McCarthy's investigation, were eager to sweep the Peress matter under the rug before the senator got wind of it. But Army rules and regulations made this no simple matter. A court-martial was considered but was ruled out: Peress had done nothing wrong under military law. Another possibility was to give him a less than honorable discharge, but Peress could have delayed that procedure for a year or so. With McCarthy breathing down its neck, the Army took what seemed to be the easiest way out: it decided to grant Peress an honorable discharge, effective in March 1954.

Before that happened, McCarthy got wind of the situation and summoned Peress to a closed session of his committee on January 30, 1954. He got little out of it. Peress took the Fifth Amendment, refusing to answer thirty-two questions about his Communist affiliation.

Realizing he might be headed for trouble, on February 1 Peress asked the Army for an immediate discharge, a request the Army approved. That same day McCarthy wrote the Army asking that Peress's discharge be delayed and that he be court-martialed. But the Army honorably discharged him anyway, on February 2.

The case gave McCarthy a new battle cry for his probe of the Army—"Who promoted Peress?"—and a fresh target, General Zwicker. McCarthy knew nothing of Zwicker's protest against the Army's handling of the Peress case. All that mattered to the senator was that Zwicker was commandant of the post where Peress had been stationed. McCarthy summoned the general to appear before his subcommittee on February 18, 1954, in closed session. Confronting Zwicker, McCarthy demanded the names of all officers who had been involved in Peress's discharge. On the advice of the Army's lawyer, Zwicker refused. He was thus put in the position of appearing to protect officers whose handling of Peress's promotion he himself had criticized when he first learned of it.

It was Army Secretary Robert Stevens who revealed to the press the confrontation between McCarthy and Zwicker, hoping to put the best face on it. But, given the circumstances, there was no good way to do that. Zwicker threatened privately to resign, then changed his mind and was ordered by Stevens not to return to testify before the McCarthy Committee.

McCarthy was riding high. As crude as his tactics were, he was winning approval even from his sometime critics, such as *Time* magazine, which cited his grilling of Zwicker as highlighting "a week packed with investigative achievement." "If the millions of Americans who deplore and despise Senator McCarthy want to understand the millions who admire McCarthy, 'despite his methods,' they could ponder McCarthy's record of the week," the magazine added.

Meanwhile President Eisenhower had his own, very different opinion. The White House let it be known that Eisenhower was infuriated—"ripping mad" was the phrase—at McCarthy's assault on his former brother officer. This was enough to assure a large turnout of reporters at the president's press conference on March 3, his first since Zwicker's testimony—and to prompt McCarthy to schedule a press conference of his own to answer what everyone anticipated would be a blistering attack.

But for Eisenhower to take on McCarthy directly and publicly would have demanded that the president abandon the defining principle of his career, his determination to succeed without arousing antagonism. This characteristic was ingrained from Ike's early childhood in Abilene, where he grew up on the wrong side of the tracks, literally and figuratively. Children on the North Side looked down on poorer children like Dwight and his brothers who lived on the South Side. In spite or perhaps because of this disadvantage, Eisenhower was determined to get ahead in life. But he decided at a tender age that ingratiation was often the better part of valor for a poor boy trying to make his way in the world. "I think his grin saved Ike a lot of trouble," a longtime friend said of him as a youth. At West Point and throughout his career in the Army, Eisenhower made it a point to remain controlled in the face of frustration and disappointment. His ability to get along with people, notably U.S. allies, helped him overcome his lack of combat experience and rise to the pinnacle of America's World War II military machine. It was no accident that "I Like Ike" became one of the most potent political slogans of all time. Ike liked to be liked.

When it came to political controversy, Eisenhower's personality traits were reinforced by his background in the military, which helped shape a conservative view of politics that was essentially anti-political. As a soldier he was cut off from most of the social and economic forces that dominated civil life and shaped American politics. More than isolation, Eisenhower developed a disdain for politics that was part of the military tradition. As one of his West Point instructors later declared, "If any convictions were acquired by the cadet they were generally of contempt for mere politicians and their dishonest principles of action." Not surprisingly, Eisenhower had little use for the normal give-and-take of politics. He rationalized his refusal to challenge McCarthy directly by depicting such a confrontation as beneath the dignity of his office. "I am not going to get into a pissing contest with that skunk," he told his brother, Milton.

So it was that instead of the rumble of Ike's anger that reporters had expected to hear at the March 3 press conference, the president delivered scarcely more than a whimper. He promised that the Army would reform the procedures that had failed in the Peress case, praised General Zwicker, and called for more congressional courtesy toward officials of the executive branch. He never mentioned McCarthy's name. Reporters were stunned. In the corridors outside the Oval Office the patrician voice of the columnist Joseph Alsop, a consummate foe of McCarthy's and until then a great admirer of Ike's, could be heard expressing the sentiments of many about the president's behavior. "Why the yellow son of a bitch!" Alsop exclaimed.

But if the president sought to avoid a harsh conflict, McCarthy had no such intention at his own session with the press, which drew not only a crowd of print reporters but the cameras of the TV networks. They all got their money's worth. McCarthy ripped into Zwicker, whom he called "stupid, arrogant or witless," and patronized Eisenhower. Seizing on the president's pledge to tighten its procedures on potential security risks, he said, "Apparently the President and I *now* agree on the necessity of getting rid of Communists."

In effect McCarthy had answered a popgun with a howitzer, and had emerged all the better for it. As James Reston of the *New York Times*, certainly no admirer of McCarthy's, wrote, the senator's counterblast "was a perfect illustration of his mastery of mass communication techniques. He knows the importance of timing and violence in a political fight. As a result the McCarthy image and McCarthy melody lingered on the TV screens tonight, long after the President had gone to bed."

From the moment he first burst into the national consciousness with his Wheeling speech, McCarthy's rise had been aided and abetted by the mass media. This was particularly true of television, which had gained steadily in importance as McCarthy grew in prominence. With its insatiable appetite for fresh red meat and its disregard of nuance, television was perfectly suited to McCarthy's hit-and-run style of political debate.

From the start, McCarthy demonstrated a notable instinct for anticipating the needs of the networks and the cameras. "He'd say, 'We're going to have a hearing, and we're going to have so-and-so, who's a Communist, there—what day do you want us to do it, Fred?'" recalled Fred Friendly, Edward R. Murrow's producer and partner at CBS. "And up to a time we did it that way."

So it went, and so McCarthy surged. But now, for the first time in his four years of tumult and paranoia, McCarthy had overplayed his hand and given his enemies an opening. Quick to take advantage was Adlai Stevenson, who had been a prime McCarthy target during the 1952 campaign. Following the one-sided exchange between Eisenhower and McCarthy on March 3, Stevenson condemned Eisenhower for his failure to denounce McCarthy and depicted the Republicans as a split party, "half McCarthy and half Eisenhower."

McCarthy immediately demanded equal time from the networks to reply. But now at last President Eisenhower, whom McCarthy had so recently mocked, took the opportunity to even the score. At a closed-door meeting in the Oval Office with GOP congressional leaders, Eisenhower laid down the law: McCarthy must no longer be allowed to play the role of party spokesman. Instead Eisenhower made certain that Republican National Chairman Leonard Hall, not McCarthy, would respond to Stevenson. And then Ike assigned the spokesman's task to his vice president, Richard Nixon, celebrated among foes of communism for his unmasking of Alger Hiss.

Other trouble for McCarthy was brewing from within the administration he had so readily defied and challenged. While McCarthy undoubtedly thought he had gotten the best of Eisenhower in the wake of his tiff with General Zwicker, the Army itself had not called it quits. Events already in train would lead to one of the last things McCarthy wanted, a televised confrontation on Capitol Hill. For once he did not relish the public exposure, because he knew that this time he would be on the defensive.

Even as his feud with the Army headed toward a full-scale legislative hearing, McCarthy now faced another formidable adversary whom he thought he had cowed into silence. This was the acknowledged master of the television medium that had helped vault McCarthy to the top—Edward R. Murrow of CBS.

5

St. Ed and the Dragon

Ever since his initial attack on the State Department, McCarthy had successfully counted on fear to silence his enemies. But in the case of Ed Murrow, the tactic backfired. Murrow felt so threatened by McCarthy that he struck back.

Until March 1954 Murrow had never challenged McCarthy directly. When asked about it by friends, he blamed his inaction on the restrictions of broadcasting—nervous sponsors, timid network executives, inflexible federal regulators. His reticence was notable because other journalists—not only print columnists but also broadcast commentators like Martin Agronsky and Elmer Davis—had spoken out against McCarthy. Because of this, in fact, Agronsky began to lose sponsors from his ABC network show. He was summoned to meet Robert Kintner, the network president, who told Agronsky that some of the affiliate stations complained he was treating McCarthy unfairly.

"They suggested I should talk to you about the way you're reporting McCarthy," Kintner said, or so the story goes. "Are you going to change?"

"No," Agronsky said flatly.

"That's what I thought you'd say," Kintner said. "Keep it up."

Murrow despised McCarthy, or so he told his intimates. He had presented programs on civil liberties that challenged the concepts of McCarthyism, and had taken some sly shots at the senator. In an admiring documentary on George Marshall, Murrow had asked former President Truman about McCarthy's assault on Marshall's patriotism. "The man who made that attack isn't fit to shine General Marshall's shoes," Truman responded. In closing that program, Murrow, referring to Truman, had said, "We have not always seen eye to eye with him, but certainly we do on the subject of General Marshall." And then he had added with a grin, "And we are also obliged to applaud his choice of shoeshine boys." McCarthy's name was not mentioned, but no one needed to be told that the senator was the target of Truman's ire and Murrow's quip.

There were enough samples of Murrow's work to make clear where he stood. One *See It Now* program focused on the American Legion's campaign to prevent the American Civil Liberties Union from organizing a chapter in Indianapolis. The Legion was foiled when a Roman Catholic priest offered his church basement to the ACLU as a meeting room.

But Murrow's most powerful defense of civil liberties stemmed from the case of an air force reserve officer, Lt. Mike Radulovich, who was being pressured by his superiors to resign from the service because his sister and father had been secretly accused of radical beliefs. The elder Radulovich had immigrated from Serbia more than forty years earlier, served in World War I, and made his living in coal mines and auto plants. His sin in the eyes of the air force was that he read a Serbian-language newspaper sympathetic to Marshal Tito, the Communist ruler of Yugoslavia. At the time, however, Tito had broken with Stalin's Soviet Union and was trying to pursue an independent course with the help of loans from the

United States, eager to exploit any chink in the Iron Curtain. The lieutenant's sister was alleged to be a Communist, though no evidence had been shown to her brother.

Perhaps the most dramatic moment of his program on the Radulovich affair was Murrow's interview with the father, who explained in broken English how he had written to President Eisenhower seeking justice for his son. Murrow also interviewed the sister who, without discussing her own views, condemned the idea that her brother should be punished for her beliefs. Concluding the broadcast, Murrow said he could not judge the charges against Radulovich's father and sister because the air force had not disclosed that evidence. "We believe that the son shall not bear the iniquity of the father, even though that iniquity be proved, and in this case it was not." *Variety* called Murrow's program "the most important broadcast of the year."

In November 1953, a month later, Air Force Secretary Harold Talbott, went on *See It Now* to announce that the air force had decided it wanted to keep Lieutenant Radulovich in its ranks after all. "He is not, in my opinion, a security risk," Talbott declared.

It was around this time that McCarthy's probe of subversion and spying at the Army Signal Corps headquarters at Fort Monmouth, New Jersey, was in full swing. In October he had told reporters that he had already uncovered "the earmarks of dangerous espionage." Simultaneously the dispute between McCarthy's chief aide, Roy Cohn, and the Army over the treatment of newly inducted private David Schine was picking up heat. Yet McCarthy noted Murrow's program on Lieutenant Radulovich, which had gotten under his skin. He dispatched one of his aides, Don Surine, to contact *See It Now* reporter Joseph Wershba. Surine caught up with Wershba on Capitol Hill, where he was researching a story.

Surine first grumbled about the Radulovich story, which he referred to as the "Radwich junk." Ignoring the butchering of the lieutenant's name, Wershba tried to brush him off, but Surine had something else on his mind. Putting his hand on Wershba's arm, he said, "What would you say if I told you Murrow was on the Soviet payroll since 1934?"

Wershba was stunned. Whereupon Surine took him to McCarthy's office and produced a photocopy of a nineteen-year-old story from the Hearst-owned *Pittsburgh Sun-Telegraph* linking Murrow, and other far more prominent persons, to an educational organization sponsoring a summer seminar for American students and teachers at Moscow University. The story suggested that these students were being trained to be "adept Communist propagandists." Surine explained to Wershba that the project had been backed by a Soviet cultural agency called VOKS, whose real mission, Surine contended, was international espionage.

"I'm not saying that Murrow is a Communist himself," Surine added charitably. "But he's one of those goddam anti-anti-Communists, and they're just as dangerous." "Let's face it," Surine said, offering one of the favorite metaphors of Red hunters, "If it walks like a duck, talks like a duck and acts like a duck, then goddamit, it's a duck."

Wershba responded that Surine and his boss were stretching their case, more than a little. He pointed out that in Churchill's war memoirs, then being serialized, the former prime minister had seemed to criticize the Allied commander Dwight Eisenhower for allowing the Soviets to seize Berlin before U.S. and British forces got there. "You're not going to say that Eisenhower sold out too," he chided Surine.

But the McCarthy aide was not fazed. His response indicated the elevated importance that McCarthy and his staff enjoyed, at least in their own eyes. "In our 1952 campaign we never gave a blank check in our support of Eisenhower's candidacy," Surine said.

By this time Wershba had gotten the Surine/McCarthy message: Murrow had better watch his step. As tenuous as the charge about the Moscow University seminar might seem, Wershba realized that McCarthy had already done serious damage to government officials and others with fragments of information like that contained in the 1935 *Sun-Telegraph* story. On the night after Surine issued his none-too-subtle threat, Wershba alerted Murrow, just after his evening newscast.

The broadcaster was not having a good night to begin with. Struggling against a heavy cold, he looked pale. But after reading the copy of the clip that Surine had presented to Wershba, his face reddened. Given the Radulovich program and his "shoeshine boy" comments, Murrow could hardly have been surprised that McCarthy would find a way to strike back. Now he grinned weakly, with the mixture of relief and anxiety that comes with learning the specific nature of long-awaited trouble. "So that's what they've got," he muttered.

Wershba who knew Murrow well enough to tease him, tried to lighten his mood. "Mr. Murrow," Wershba said, with mock pomposity, "you've had a long and honorable career, enough to enable any man to retire to the role of country gentleman."

But Murrow saw no humor in the situation. He scowled and proceeded to vent to Wershba about the chilling effect of McCarthy's tactics on discussion of public issues in general, and particularly in the media. "I haven't even been able to talk about the whole problem of relations with Communist China," he complained. It struck Wershba that this was the first time he had ever heard Murrow acknowledge the impact of McCarthy, not just on the whole country but on his own work. To Wershba at that moment, Murrow seemed like a man who was played out.

But the next day, when Murrow approached Wershba to pursue their conversation, his normal high-energy level had returned. His cold was gone and his color normal—his temper, however, was near the boiling point. There was no longer any doubt about what he would do; the only issue was timing. "The question now," he told Wershba, "is when do I go up against these guys?"

To those who knew Murrow well, the brooding and apparent anguish that preceded his ultimate decision were part of a familiar pattern of introspection and soul-searching in his life and career. In this situation the stakes were high. Murrow had covered the biggest stories in the world for the past fifteen years, from the prelude to World War II through the opening decade of the cold war, first on radio and now on television. His own ascent paralleled the rise of broadcast journalism and embodied, as many people believed, the very best of that still developing craft. If Murrow were to tilt against McCarthy and break his lance, it would be a setback to his entire profession and to the hopes of McCarthy's foes.

Anyone might have hesitated before placing such prominence in jeopardy. But in Murrow's case the risk was greater because of the effort it took to get where he was. He had to blaze a trail through an uncharted domain of journalism, and his own convoluted personality had added to inevitable stresses and strains.

At first glance Murrow might have seemed like a sure bet for success. To begin with there was his striking good looks—not the bland visage of a movie star but a craggy face with a few moles that he was careful not to conceal, helping make his handsomeness rugged and credible. Then there was his baritone—rich, powerful, unsettling and reassuring at the same time, redolent with authority. As Howard K. Smith, one of his colleagues, put it, "Ed could say 'twenty-six' and it sounded like the most important declaration ever made by a man." The face and the voice, along with his tall, well-muscled physique, were fused to create an impression of elegance tempered with straightforwardness, sobriety laced with cutting wit, the end product being a man whom women fawned over and men sought as a comrade.

But the strengths Murrow drew on for success often had obverse aspects which got in his way. And the pros and cons of Murrow's character would be mirrored in the medium he pioneered and whose dominant role he helped establish. He was idealistic yet deeply pessimistic, with a darkness of outlook that seemed to lend a sense of urgency to his pursuits. Although gifted with breadth of vision, his actions were often narrowed by selfish concerns. Passionate in pursuing principle, at times he seemed coldhearted and shortsighted in seeking the means to an end. He impressed all who knew him with his intellectual integrity; but what thrust him to the top of his field as much as anything else was a formidable flair for theatricality and self-dramatization.

Murrow was born and christened Egbert Roscoe in 1908 at a place called Polecat Creek in North Carolina. This was not even a town but a stream cutting through the piedmont near Greensboro. The boy's father, Roscoe, raised a little tobacco but mostly corn and hay on 120 acres, land given him by his father. Roscoe Murrow was six feet tall and husky in appearance, good-natured in temperament. His even disposition was challenged frequently by his wife, Ethel, a demanding woman who imposed on her husband and three sons strict rules of conduct stemming from her Quaker faith and the puritan outlook that dominated her life. Her fond wish was that one of her sons would enter the ministry, and she named her youngest, Egbert, after a pastor she admired.

Roscoe, helped by his three sons even before they entered grade school, scraped out a meager living from the land. Some comfort could be taken from the fact that everyone they knew endured much the same circumstances. But there was a limit even to Roscoe's patience. In 1914, when Egbert was six, Roscoe Murrow moved his family to Washington State where he took up residence in a town called Blanchard, in the Puget Sound area. There he improved his fortunes somewhat by working in logging camps and then as a railroad brakeman. His sons, including young Egbert, followed him into the logging camps, working summers. Amid those rough-and-ready surroundings, Egbert decided that the name Ed would be more suitable to a young man trying to make his way in the world.

Although the youngest of the Murrows seemed to prefer the company of grown-ups, this did not prevent him from doing well among his peers. His record at Blanchard's Edison High School was the first in the string of success stories that marked Ed Murrow's life. He starred in the school play and in nearly everything else. He was elected president of the senior class and also of the student body, and voted most popular student. He went on to Washington State University, somewhat reluctantly because of its "Cow College" reputation based on its emphasis on courses in farming, mining, and veterinary medicine. But his financial situation left him no choice, and Murrow certainly made the best of it. Guided by a brilliant speech teacher, Ida Lou Anderson, who took a shine to him, Murrow had an even greater impact on the Washington State campus than on Edison High School.

As a sophomore he played the male lead in the drama faculty's production of the Pulitzer Prize–winning play *Craig's Wife*. Praise from a local critic anticipated comments that years later would be made about his broadcasting performances. "He spoke calmly and with wonderful control," the reviewer wrote. "But beneath the calmness there was a depth of emotion superbly expressed." His appearance marked a personal milestone: the playbill listed him as Edward R. Murrow, the first time Egbert's new name had appeared in print.

By the spring preceding his junior year, using contacts among fellow members of an influential secret society, he contrived to get himself elected president of the student body, the same honor he had gained at Edison High. This office served as his admission ticket to the annual conference of the Pacific Student Presidents Association. There he won election as president of the association, a post that would serve as an important springboard to his postcollegiate life.

Amidst all these laurels, Murrow was often bothered by fits of depression. "The outlook at present for me isn't too bright," he wrote a former college girlfriend. In another lugubrious note, he added, "The doctor claims my nerves are shot all to pieces," sounding a refrain that would become a familiar accompaniment to his future exertions to the edge of exhaustion and sometimes beyond in pursuing one goal or another.

He left college trailing glory. He had used the Pacific Student Association presidency to scale even greater heights, winning the presidency of the National Student Federation of America. It was June 1930, and the country every day was sinking deeper into what would become known as the Great Depression. But even in these bleakest of times, Murrow's special gifts once again led him to good fortune. The National Student Federation, which had elected him to serve another year as its president, agreed to send him to New York to run its national office, with what at the time seemed like a munificent sum, $25 a week, as living expenses in lieu of a salary.

Considering the times it was a remarkable opportunity, and Murrow took maximum advantage. His first move was to attend the congress of an international amalgam of student associations in Brussels. The trip abroad took on added significance when he applied for a passport. Because Polecat Creek issued no birth certificates, his mother submitted an affidavit attesting to his birth. After first writing in "Egbert," she crossed that out and scribbled his name as Ed R. Murrow. The document served as a legal name change.

At the Brussels conference, as almost everywhere else, Murrow's combination of charm and substance won him a new legion of admirers and a new friend, Lewis Powell, the future Supreme Court justice. The two young men toured Europe together after the conference, and years later Powell would recall Murrow's pervasive seriousness, his taking international problems so personally that he referred to countries as "we" and "they," along with his habitual gloominess even in the face of his own good fortune. Murrow's pessimism, Powell came to believe, was "genetic."

Meanwhile good breaks kept coming his way. In 1932 his record at the National Student Federation helped him win a job as head of a new organization, the International Institute of Education. It set for itself the lofty and optimistic goal of encouraging intellectual and cultural exchange among students around the globe. It was Murrow's first real paying job and in those times a very good one—his salary was $5,000 a year.

This financial security put him in a position to marry a young woman named Janet Huntington Brewster. The couple had met while she was a Mount Holyoke student and both were attending a National Student Federation conference. Beautiful, well organized, efficient, and popular, she came from conservative Republican stock. But as with many others of her generation and background, her conscience was stirred and her outlook transformed by the upheavals of the times. Before she met Murrow her goal was to go to New York to become a social worker. That never happened. Instead she married Ed Murrow in the fall of 1934 and went on to become the mother of his son and carve out a career for herself as a journalist.

At first, marriage seemed to brighten Murrow's outlook. "I have unlimited confidence in us," he wrote his bride-to-be shortly before their wedding. "We shall make of our lives a real work of art." But his customary dark side soon reasserted itself, a tone change that must have bewildered his future wife. "It's really a pretty rotten world, isn't it?" he wrote her. "I have no confidence in the future, and little pride in the past."

For all his dreary ruminations, Murrow himself was doing quite well. At age twenty-five, his energy and precocious assurance earned him election to the ultimate establishment stronghold, the Council on Foreign Relations, most of whose members were old enough to be his father. Murrow's work at the Institute also led to his involvement in the Moscow seminar, which two decades later Senator McCarthy would seize upon as ammunition against him. At the suggestion of the director of the Institute, Stephen Duggan, Murrow negotiated with officials of the Soviet Union to organize a summer session of courses at Moscow University for American students who wished to learn about that country. To oversee the program he created an advisory council of prominent American educators, including himself, and worked hard to convince the seminar's hosts to emphasize education rather than propaganda. This was easier said than done; the Soviets balked nearly every step of the way. Finally, after approving seminars in 1933 and 1934, they canceled a third that had been scheduled for 1935, the one that caught the attention of the *Pittsburgh Sun-Telegraph*.

Although Murrow took full advantage of the openings for career advancement offered by the Institute, as time went on he seemed to face diminishing returns. In 1936, feeling himself at a dead end, and without great forethought, he made a decision that would shape the rest of his life: he went to work for the Columbia Broadcasting System. He started at CBS not as a broadcaster but as an impresario of sorts, finding speakers to fill the many hours the network devoted to public affairs.

Ahead of him lay fame to a degree that he could never have imagined, arising in the context of world-shaking events. The first of these epochal moments was the onset of World War II, the conflict that established Murrow as one of the leading journalists in history. In 1937, soon after he joined CBS, the network sent him to London as its European representative, which ideally positioned him to exploit the opportunities the war offered. At first he replicated his job at home, lining up distinguished speakers to air their views on CBS. Murrow used that position to make friends with a range of personalities, from the Tory Winston Churchill, already an historic figure, to the dynamic socialist leader Harold Laski. All of them would later enrich the work of Murrow the correspondent.

It was a heady existence for the young man, not yet thirty. He moved with ease among the British social and intellectual upper crust, impressing nearly everyone he encountered. One British journalist observed of him, "He just knows what is really happening in Washington, but so modest is he that no one would suspect him of having met most of the people who really matter anywhere."

Not everyone agreed. After hearing Murrow address the Royal Institute of International Affairs, a BBC executive found "a tinge of histrionics in his character." Others detected more than a tinge. Murrow's theatrical inclinations were as much a part of him as his pessimism, so that most people didn't object. To burnish his image as a dashing young cosmopolite, he found a tailor on Saville Row and developed a taste for clothes with an English cut. Along with double-breasted suits he wore a rakish wide-brimmed hat and black gloves.

Coincidentally it was around this time that Murrow had his first look at television. Far ahead of U.S. networks, the BBC had inaugurated a television service, one hour a night, five nights a week, reaching some fifteen hundred receivers within seventy miles of London. Given a set by Murrow's British colleagues, for a while he and Janet watched the drama, news, and sports on the six-inch screen avidly. After viewing a play with a visitor, Eric Sevareid, who would become one of the most renowned of "Murrow's boys," the crew of young men whom he recruited for CBS in its early, brilliant days, Murrow told Sevareid, "That's the wave of the future right there."

Then, as the novelty of TV paled, Murrow stopped looking at it. He had more urgent things to deal with. The European crisis transformed him from a contact man whose voice would be heard on CBS only when he was introducing the speakers he had lined up, into a full-fledged correspondent. For this he had Hitler to thank. The Fuhrer's first conquest, the bloodless seizure of Austria in 1938—the *Anschluss*, as it was called—marked Murrow's debut as a correspondent and indeed the birth of CBS News as an international medium. As Hitler marched on Vienna to claim his prize, CBS correspondents hastily recruited by Murrow went on the air via shortwave to the United States to give Americans the reaction direct from European capitals, with Murrow himself broadcasting from Vienna.

"This is Edward R. Murrow," he announced. "Everything is quiet in Vienna tonight. There is a certain air of expectancy about the city, everyone waiting and wondering where at what time Herr Hitler will arrive." It was the first CBS News Roundup, a format that was repeated the next night as the first German troops arrived. The news roundups became a CBS trademark as Europe and then the United States itself plunged into World War II, helping establish the network as supreme in the field and Murrow as its rising star.

During the 1940 Blitz, when Hitler's Luftwaffe attempted to bomb Britain to its knees, Murrow was stationed in London. His calm, understated description of the Nazi onslaught and the stoic British response, broadcast nightly, came to epitomize for American audiences the steadfastness of the British. The controlled impression he created for his audience, established by his signature opening, "This is London," contrasted with the tension that seized him as he delivered his report. Underneath the table on which his microphone was perched, his foot tapped continuously and perspiration poured down his face. He could hardly wait for the broadcast to end to light a cigarette. He was now consuming three packs a day to soothe his jangled nerves. It was a habit that would continue for the rest of his life and ultimately bring on his death from lung cancer.

When Allied bombers began pounding Europe in preparation for D Day, Murrow insisted on going along on one of the raids, "so I can know a little better how the pilot feels when the tail is shot off." His bosses at CBS objected to the risk, but in December 1943 the RAF agreed to let him and four other correspondents hitchhike on Lancaster bombers attacking Berlin. It was not a milk run. The RAF lost fifty Lancasters, and two correspondents did not make it back. Murrow won a Peabody Award, radio journalism's highest honor, for the broadcast he did on his return. More important, he survived the raid and the rest of the war. In 1945 he returned to the United States, seeking to match his wartime success with postwar CBS.

That turned out not to be easy, at least at first. Murrow allowed himself to be talked into an off-air executive position as vice president of news, education, and discussion programs, something similar to his first job at the network. Predictably unhappy without the opportunity to get to a microphone, he abandoned the executive world in two years and returned to broadcasting with a nightly news and commentary show.

Then came television, a medium that Murrow, like most radio journalists, viewed with considerable skepticism, as his standoffish attitude toward CBS's coverage of the 1948 conventions demonstrated. The Kefauver crime hearings helped bring him around. "The television performance has been fascinating, the audience fantastic, perhaps because the midgets in the box have been real," Murrow said afterward.

The shape of the future could not be denied. CBS had now set up a separate division for television under its news department. In 1951 Murrow and a new partner, producer Fred Friendly, decided to transfer their prizewinning radio documentary series, *Hear It Now*, to television and call it *See It Now*.

The next year Murrow launched yet another television show, *Person to Person*, a kind of video celebrity magazine featuring interviews with stars of entertainment, sports, and politics, ranging from Marilyn Monroe to Roy Campanella. The critics were testy. "Substandard Murrow, marked by aimlessness and a degree of silliness," complained *Time*, citing Murrow asking one of his first guests, the conductor Leopold Stokowski, whether his piano was in tune. But the public loved it, and so did advertisers. And the ad revenues helped cover the costs of *See It Now*, which never made money for the network, and in Murrow's mind this was justification enough. After five weeks on the air *Variety* had awarded *See It Now* a special citation as "the most original, informative and entertaining type of journalism now riding the video waves." It was Murrow's pride and joy, and it was the program that attracted the attention and roused the ire of the senator from Wisconsin. This weapon, the most powerful in his arsenal, Murrow now proposed to use against McCarthy.

Murrow's career had long before become entangled in the tensions of the cold war, both the shooting part of it abroad and the Red-hunting dimension at home. In both arenas this "twilight struggle" was more nuanced and frustrating for him than the battle against the Axis. When the Korean War exploded in 1950, Murrow, like an old warhorse, could not resist returning to the scene of combat. After six weeks at the front he returned to the States and prepared a blistering condemnation of military leaders who he charged had launched a costly offensive mainly because "they decided we needed a victory" to boost their prestige at home. But higher-ups at CBS killed the broadcast because it violated an order by Gen. Douglas MacArthur forbidding reporters to criticize command decisions. This rejection was a particular blow to Murrow because his final appeal to air the broadcast was turned down by the board chairman William S. Paley, Murrow's godfather and sheltering spirit during both their careers at CBS. Murrow was deeply hurt, Paley recalled later. "He, Ed Murrow, the great man, the man who could never do anything unfair or unjust, was being made out to look like a guy who didn't live up to his word. The hurt just stood out on his face."

At home Murrow had taken a shot against the new Red Scare soon after it began in 1947. "The right of dissent—or, if you prefer, the right to be wrong—is surely fundamental to the existence of a democratic society," he said in challenging the House Un-American Activities probe of Hollywood. He also reminded Americans of a quote from Adolf Hitler: "The great strength of the totalitarian state is that it will force those who fear it to imitate it."

Murrow himself was no reasonable person's idea of a Communist or even a fellow traveler. He blamed the Soviet Union for inspiring the Korean War and joined a group called the Committee for the Present Danger, which sought to rally the public against the threat of Soviet aggression. His personal response to the swirling currents of anti-communism was cloaked in caution. When the blacklist and loyalty oaths came to CBS, Murrow did not resist. "You have to choose your battles," he told one friend in the midst of the internal soul-searching at CBS about the loyalty oath, which he himself signed. That was February 1954. But Murrow was already planning to go to battle against McCarthy, not so much out of choice but rather out of necessity. And it was a battle he was determined to win.

Planning for a program answering McCarthy had been going forward since Wershba's initial encounter with Surine in

November 1953. Murrow left the early groundwork to Fred Friendly, his producer and trusted collaborator. By March 2 Murrow was confident enough of the work so far that at the conclusion of that Tuesday night's *See It Now* he told his viewers that the next program would deal with the climate of "unreasoning fear in America." He did not mention McCarthy's name. On Sunday, March 7, Murrow called Friendly and told him to get the film ready: "Fred, I've been thinking over a lifetime. And I've come to a decision." Friendly took that as the final go-ahead.

That evening the staff gathered to watch a preview of the film clips Murrow would be working with on Tuesday. Then Murrow, in a rare act of humility, asked everyone present what they thought. The cameramen were high on the product, the reporters much less so. Many felt, as Wershba later told Murrow, that the film did not do enough—that it merely recorded what McCarthy had said and done, and would give heart to his supporters. Murrow seemed unshaken. He pointed to the darkened screen and said, "The terror is right here in this room." As the preview was ending, a woman film editor asked, "But isn't the White House ever going to do something about McCarthy?" Murrow's face reddened with anger. The man who rarely used profanity, particularly in the presence of women, replied, "The White House is not going to do and not going to say one goddam thing." His tone reflected his exasperation that because of Eisenhower's passivity, Murrow had been forced to take on this risky task.

The day before the broadcast, Murrow and Friendly asked CBS to buy an ad in the *New York Times* to run on the day of the broadcast. But the network refused to pay for the ad or even allow its logo to be used in connection with the show. So Murrow and Friendly arranged for the ad themselves and dug into their own pockets to pay for it. Three columns wide by seven inches high, it announced that *See It Now* would present "a report on Senator Joseph R. McCarthy" that night. Along with the copy was a photo of Murrow, cigarette in hand.

Whatever the reasons for his early reluctance to take on McCarthy, no one who watched the show that evening could accuse Murrow of pussyfooting. He began straightforwardly enough with a quote from McCarthy, speaking seventeen months earlier in Milwaukee, warning that if the fight against communism became a fight between the nation's two political parties, "one of those parties will be destroyed and the Republic cannot endure very long as a one-party system." Then came the punch line right out of McCarthy's mouth from the audiotape of a speech delivered the previous February in Charleston, West Virginia: "The issue between the Republicans and Democrats is clearly drawn. It has been deliberately drawn by those who have been in charge of twenty years of treason. The hard fact is—the hard fact is that those who wear the label, those who wear the label Democrat wear it with the stain of a historic betrayal."

Murrow then took aim at the conflict between McCarthy and the leader of his party, President Eisenhower. *See It Now* showed Ike promising during his campaign for the White House that the executive branch of the government was up to the task of ridding the government of subversives. Next came McCarthy speaking that same night. Having met with Eisenhower the night before, McCarthy announced that he was convinced that Ike "will make a great President, an outstanding President." But then came the "but." "But I want to tell you tonight," McCarthy declared, "tell the American people as long as I represent you and the rest of the American people in the Senate, I shall continue to call them as I see them regardless of who happens to be President."

Murrow went on to deal with the controversy over McCarthy's treatment of Eisenhower's old wartime comrade, General Zwicker, depicting the senator mocking his critics: "And wait till you hear the bleeding hearts scream and cry about our methods. But they say," McCarthy continued with a flourish, brushing his hand through his hair in a mock effeminate gesture, "'Oh, it's all right to uncover them, but don't get rough doing it, McCarthy.'"

Next Murrow showed McCarthy, in his televised response to Eisenhower's tepid protest the week before, gloating over the way he had treated Zwicker as a witness before his committee. "If a stupid, arrogant or witless man in a position of power appears before our committee and is found aiding the Communist Party, he will be exposed," McCarthy said. "The fact that he might be a general places him in no special class as far as I am concerned."

In that press conference McCarthy was portrayed as giving the back of his hand to Eisenhower. "Apparently, the President and I now agree on the necessity of getting rid of Communists," the senator said. "We apparently disagree on how we should handle those who protect Communists. When the shouting and the tumult dies, the American people and the President will realize that this unprecedented mud slinging against the committee by the extreme left-wing elements of press and radio was caused solely because another Fifth Amendment Communist was finally dug out of the dark recesses and exposed to the public view."

Another vignette showed McCarthy striking a low blow at Adlai Stevenson, calling him "Alger," and then correcting his allusion to Alger Hiss with a giggle. "I mean Adlai," he said, a thrust that drew the anticipated burst of laughter from his audience.

Murrow's viewers also got a taste of McCarthy performing the role on which he had built his reputation, grilling an already intimidated witness before his committee, in this case, Voice of America official Reed Harris. During his questioning of Harris, Murrow pointed out, McCarthy twice stated that the American Civil Liberties Union was listed as a subversive front. This was plainly untrue, Murrow emphasized. "The Attorney General's list does not and has never listed the ACLU as subversive, nor does the FBI or any other federal government agency. And the American Civil Liberties Union holds in its files letters of commendation from President Truman, President Eisenhower and General MacArthur."

Murrow, who had once said he favored "ringing a bell every time a newscaster is about to inject his own view," concluded with a slam of McCarthy that could have set church bells pealing around the land. "It is necessary to investigate before legislating," Murrow declared. "But the line between investigating and persecuting is a very fine one, and the junior Senator from Wisconsin has stepped over it repeatedly." "His primary achievement," Murrow said of McCarthy, "has been in confusing the public mind, as between internal and the external threats of Communism. We must not confuse dissent with disloyalty. We must remember always that accusation is not proof and that conviction depends upon evidence and due process of law. We will not walk in fear, one of another. We will not be driven by fear into an age of unreason."

In sum, what Murrow had done was to treat McCarthy much as McCarthy might have treated Murrow, had he commanded a television program. Having surveyed fifteen thousand feet of film, Murrow had selected a series of clips that showed McCarthy at his very worst. As one conservative critic complained, Murrow offered "a compendium of every burp, grunt, stutter, nose probe, brutish aside, and maniacal giggle the senator had ever allowed to be captured on film."

It wasn't only conservatives who were offended by Murrow's manipulative selectivity. Two of McCarthy's dedicated foes in the press, John Cogley of *Commonweal* and Gilbert Seldes of the *Saturday Review*, both voiced their misgivings. Seldes claimed that Murrow had made a serious mistake by underestimating McCarthy. "I got the impression that the giant Murrow had been fighting a pygmy." He noted that the program was billed as a report but that in fact it was an attack followed by an editorial appeal for action. "In the long run," Seldes argued, "it is more important to use our communication system properly than to destroy McCarthy."

But such was the sentiment in liberal circles that the editors of the *Saturday Review* imposed a rare footnote below Seldes's column, stating that "it had caused considerable discussion and debate among the staff," thus none too subtly separating the magazine from their columnist's point of view.

Like Seldes, Cogley took a long view, contending that Murrow had "set a bad precedent" with his heavy-handed selectivity. "Certain other commentators might make a totally different selection of film which would turn Senator McCarthy into a man on a shining white steed—infinitely reasonable, burdened with the onus of singlehandedly cleaning out subversives in the face of violent criticism, wholly without self-interest." Viewers could be shown, Cogley argued, "the friendly political opponent who debated Congressman Eugene McCarthy and consistently called him 'Gene' as if they were bosom buddies disagreeing over some abstruse point," and "the playful McCarthy who threw his arm around Senator Flanders after the Vermont Republican lambasted him." Cogley's assessment concluded with a somber warning: the same liberals who were cheering Murrow's assault on McCarthy might some day have cause to regret the damage done by someone with a different point of view wielding the same weapons.

But such critics made up a distinct minority. "Praise Pours In on Murrow Show," was the *New York Times* headline two days after the broadcast. Of more than twelve thousand phone calls and telegrams CBS received—the largest response the network had ever seen—those cheering Murrow outnumbered critics by about 15 to 1. Local stations around the country reported similar reactions. That same day's edition of the *Times* carried a hosanna from Jack Gould: "An exciting and provocative examination of the man and his methods. . . . Crusading journalism of high responsibility and genuine courage." So swept away was *Variety*, the mainstay of the trade press, that it called the date of Murrow's McCarthy attack "Good Tuesday," thus endowing it with semi-religious significance and almost sanctifying Murrow.

What all these admirers overlooked was the main fault with Murrow's broadcast—not so much what he had put in— though much of this was so one-sided it violated the standards of good journalism—but rather what he left out: the environment in which McCarthy operated and flourished. Murrow touched on this but only briefly, at the very end of his commentary: "The actions of the junior Senator from Wisconsin have caused alarm and dismay amongst our allies abroad, and given considerable comfort to our enemies. And whose fault is that? Not really his. He didn't create this situation of fear; he merely exploited it—and rather successfully. Cassius was right. 'The fault, dear Brutus, is not in our stars, but in ourselves.'"

This was a major criticism, not of McCarthy but of politicians in both parties and other prominent Americans who had tolerated McCarthy's excesses, if not approved them. It was an indictment that deserved to be explained and analyzed in far greater detail than the few sentences Murrow allotted to it.

Murrow seemed to want to benefit from the grandeur of his language, with its Shakespearean allusion and Delphic tones, without assuming the burden of providing specifics. In a sense he was trapped by his own eloquence, which screamed out a question he did not choose to answer: Who did he mean by "ourselves"? He certainly could have mentioned the Eisenhower administration, including the president himself, along with the media in general for their mindless "objectivity." And he might have uttered a brief *mea culpa* for his own delay in taking on

McCarthy. All told Murrow had thirty minutes of time, less a few minutes for commercials, for his report on McCarthy, an eternity on television; it would have taken no more than a minute or two to answer the question his peroration begged. His failure as TV news's most prominent and supposedly courageous voice to say more on the fundamental issue of the enablers of McCarthyism was an ill omen for television's coverage of the Army-McCarthy hearings that would soon begin.

As compelling as it seemed at the time, Murrow's broadcast did not immediately change the attitude of those who preferred to keep their distance from McCarthy. While the critics may have anointed Murrow as the patron saint of television news, his bosses at CBS restrained their enthusiasm. Murrow heard not a word from Bill Paley. The day after the broadcast, Friendly rode down on the elevator with the president of CBS Network television, Jack Van Folkenburg. They made small talk, but Van Folkenburg notably had nothing to say about the program that was standing the world of television on its ear.

McCarthy took his time striking back. On the night of the broadcast Murrow's crew, anticipating a counterblast, waited for hours but heard not a word. McCarthy's response came on the radio show of Fulton Lewis, Jr., a scourge of the New Deal and liberalism in general, on March 11, two nights after the Murrow show.

McCarthy had his hands full that night. Denied the right to be the official GOP spokesman to reply to Adlai Stevenson's Miami speech, he used Lewis's program for that purpose. In response to Stevenson's charge that McCarthy was dividing the Republican party and the country, McCarthy shot back that it was better to have some healthy disagreement, like the GOP, than to be pressured as Democrats were to agree with one another. He also defended himself against Vermont Republican senator Ralph Flanders, an early critic who had become increasingly public in his disapproval. On March 9, the same date as Murrow's broadcast, Flanders had risen in the Senate to deliver the sharpest denunciation of McCarthy yet heard from a fellow Republican. Flanders's main complaint was that McCarthy's inflamed rhetoric aimed at the internal threat of subversion was distracting the country from greater dangers abroad. But McCarthy now sought to refute the idea that the great risk to the nation's security came from without, not from within. He cited a Lincoln quote to the effect that all the foreign armies combined could not "make one track on the Blue Ridge" if there were not weakness within America. "If danger ever reaches us," Lincoln said, according to McCarthy, "it must spring up among us."

As for Murrow's program, McCarthy knew that most of Fulton Lewis's audience would be in his camp, so his comments were in the form of a sermon to the choir. "I must say, Fulton, that I have a little difficulty answering the specific attack he made, because I never listen to the extreme left-wing bleeding-heart element of radio and television." Then McCarthy fulfilled Don Surine's implied threat by reading aloud the nineteen-year-old story about Murrow's involvement as an adviser to the 1935 Moscow University seminar. "This may explain why Edward R. Murrow week after week feels he must smear Senator McCarthy," the senator said. "Maybe he is worried about the exposure of some of his friends. I don't know."

An old political adage admonishes against getting into a public brawl with a newspaper journalist: "Never pick a fight with someone who buys ink by the barrel." In the electronic age that axiom could be extended by adding the phrase "or has a daily radio show." On March 12, one night after McCarthy's blast, on his regular CBS broadcast, Murrow explained that he was one of only twenty-five members of the advisory panel to the Moscow seminar. Among the others were John Dewey, University of Chicago president Robert M. Hutchins, and University of North Carolina president Frank Graham. He also pointed out that the seminar had never met in 1935—because it had been abruptly canceled by Soviet officials. He did not mention the 1933 and 1934 seminars that *were* held, but McCarthy evidently was unaware of them. And for good measure, Murrow tossed in a response to McCarthy's use of a quotation from Lincoln. Murrow chose to quote the paragraph following the passage McCarthy had relied on, in which Lincoln had warned of "the growing disposition to substitute the wild and furious passions in lieu of the sober judgments of courts."

The next evening, March 13, McCarthy got the back of the hand from someone in his own party and supposedly on his side—Richard Nixon, who had been assigned by Eisenhower to answer Stevenson on behalf of the GOP. But Nixon's nationally broadcast speech that reached ten million Americans was aimed right at McCarthy. The vice president decried the "reckless talk and questionable methods of Congressional 'Red hunters.' When you go out and shoot rats you have to shoot straight because when you shoot wildly, it not only means that the rats may get away more easily, but you might hit someone else who is trying to shoot rats, too."

On April 6, four weeks after Murrow's initial "report" on McCarthy, came the senator's big moment in his duel with Murrow—the equal time he had demanded that CBS grant him so he could respond to Murrow's attack. If McCarthy was distracted, it was understandable. His feud with the Army over G. David Schine, which had begun the previous fall, was steadily escalating. The Army had made public its side of the argument on March 11, just two days after Murrow's onslaught. McCarthy had hit back, but now he faced a Senate hearing on the feud, which was turning into the most serious controversy of his controversial career.

Nevertheless he plowed ahead with his response to Murrow, though his remarks appeared to be those of a man whose mind was directed elsewhere. Although McCarthy had his talk produced by Batten, Barton, Durstine and Osborn, one of Madison Avenue's leading ad agencies, and filmed at Agency Fox Movietone News, the result was still much like a drab studio appearance.

The *New York Times'* account of the program headlined McCarthy's charge of a deliberate delay in the U.S. development of the H-bomb. He wanted to know whether this was caused by "loyal Americans or traitors." "If there were no Communists in our government," McCarthy demanded, "why did we delay for 18 months—delay our research on the hydrogen bomb, even though our intelligence agencies were reporting, day after day, that the Russians were feverishly pushing their development of the hydrogen bomb." The reason for the delay, as would later become clear, was concern among U.S. officials about the loyalty of nuclear physicist J. Robert Oppenheimer, an issue that would become the center of prolonged public controversy. But since McCarthy did not provide that information, his charge had little impact on his dispute with Murrow except to contribute to confusion.

Murrow "as far back as twenty years ago" was engaged in Communist propaganda, the senator claimed, an apparent reference to the Moscow seminar. Murrow had belonged to the Industrial Workers of the World (IWW), listed as subversive by the attorney general, McCarthy claimed. The British scholar Harold Laski, whom McCarthy described as a Communist propagandist, had dedicated a book to Murrow. And Owen Lattimore, the alleged master spy, had mentioned Murrow favorably in one of his books. All these illustrated McCarthy's familiar tactics—innuendo, insinuation, and half-truths.

Before the night was over Murrow had issued a statement denying membership in the IWW, pointing out that Laski was a socialist, not a Communist, and that the book dedication was in tribute to Murrow's reporting of the Battle of Britain during World War II. As for Lattimore, Murrow had never met him.

McCarthy, wrote Jack Gould in the *New York Times*, had unwittingly confirmed the thrust of Murrow's criticism of him as a reckless purveyor of smears. "Mr. Murrow only reported as best he could" on McCarthy's tactics. "The Senator on the other hand gave the expert's own authorized version."

The next morning President Eisenhower was asked his view of the Murrow-McCarthy exchange. "No comment," said Ike. But he did add that Edward R. Murrow had been his friend since Murrow had covered the war Eisenhower had fought in Europe a decade earlier. *Newsweek* pointed out that "Murrow said nothing that some newspapers haven't said before. But Murrow said it on television, and the week's events proved the significance, if anyone had any lingering doubts, of what he had to say."

It was *Billboard* that read the greatest importance into the event. Where major newspapers attacking McCarthy had failed to stir much public indignation, "a single 30-minute TV show may well go down as the lance that pricked and completely deflated the McCarthy balloon." But this was a bit too much. Murrow did not finish off McCarthy. But he was surely the banderillero who set up McCarthy for the fatal blow that he was to inflict on himself in the Senate caucus room.

6

At War with the Army

It would have been hard to find any happy Republican senator among the four members of the Senate Permanent Subcommittee on Investigations as the argument between the U.S. Army and Senator McCarthy blew up in their faces. Each had been around long enough to realize that no benefit for his party could come from such an affair. But it was easy to spot the most unhappy of all the GOP lawmakers. That would be Karl Mundt of South Dakota, who as senior Republican would have to assume the role of acting chairman of the subcommittee in an investigation of the affair.

The South Dakota senator, then serving his first full term in the Senate and about to turn fifty-four, was an acknowledged leader in the struggle against what he liked to call "Godless Communism and Red Fascism." He had first made his mark as a backbencher in the House of Representatives when, after returning from a postwar trip through Eastern Europe in 1947, he introduced legislation that established the Voice of America to combat Communist propaganda behind the Iron Curtain.

He soon made bigger headlines in 1948 when he teamed with a young California congressman named Richard Nixon to sponsor the Mundt-Nixon Bill, which among other things required all Communist organizations, and labor unions suspected of Communist taint, to register with the Department of Justice. The Mundt-Nixon partnership became even more famous when it spearheaded the House Un-American Activities Committee probe into the background of State Department official Alger Hiss, resulting in Hiss's conviction on perjury, one of the great causes célèbres of the early cold war.

But Mundt did not allow his enthusiasm for the hunt to blind his judgment or erase his interest in other goals besides the struggle against the Red menace. For all the stereotypical view of him held by Eastern liberals as some form of Midwestern troglodyte, Karl Mundt was in reality a man not without intellectual credentials and a certain suppleness of intelligence. Starting out as an elementary schoolteacher, he developed an early interest in rhetoric, leading him to found the National Forensic League in 1925 and edit its journal, *The Rostrum*, for the next fifteen years. He rose to become a college professor of social sciences along the way, acquiring a master's degree in economics from Columbia University.

A staunch isolationist in his early years in Congress, Mundt was converted to internationalism by Pearl Harbor. He was quick to promote U.S. involvement in the United Nations. The United Nations Relief and Rehabilitation Administration (UNRRA) and the United Nations Educational, Scientific and Cultural Organization (UNESCO) both received his strong support at their inception. Conservation was also a cause high on Mundt's agenda. He had been a leader on South Dakota's Game and Fish Commission before coming to Washington, and on Capitol Hill he fought to raise water-quality standards. In addition to being a tireless speaker, he was a prolific writer of magazine articles on a broad range of public issues.

All of these were facets of Mundt's image as a public man, creating a somewhat different picture from the narrow-minded witch-hunter depicted by his liberal critics. But now Mundt saw his reputation jeopardized by the storm brewing over the committee. Not just his image but also his very political life was at stake, for in November 1954 he would be seeking his second term in the Senate. Mundt had been around Capitol Hill long enough to sense when events were taking a troublesome turn, and he grasped that this was happening because of the row between McCarthy and the Army. Mundt wanted to maintain good relations with McCarthy and his supporters, his comrades in his own crusade against communism. But his ties to these forces now seemed to put him at odds with a fair number of other Republicans who were finding McCarthy, as useful as he had been in his way, increasingly hard to take. On top of this list was the leader of the party, Dwight Eisenhower. Mundt did not see how the hearings could avoid exacerbating an already nasty conflict between the two factions, thus jeopardizing his own future.

No wonder then that, like others in his own party, Mundt would have preferred to let the bitter feud between McCarthy and the Army wither away from neglect and inattention. But the Army itself had made that impossible. On March 11, 1954, the Army had brought its weeks-long feud with McCarthy to a head by releasing a searing report on its troubles with the Wisconsin senator. The most sensational charge in the thirty-four-page indictment was that McCarthy and his top aide Roy Cohn had threatened to "wreck the Army" in an attempt to get special treatment for Pvt. G. David Schine, Cohn's close friend and erstwhile colleague on the McCarthy committee staff. The strong implication was that much of the Army's recent trouble with the McCarthy committee had come about because the Army refused to give Cohn what he sought on behalf of Private Schine.

Specifically the Army report stated that in late October 1953, shortly before Schine's induction, John G. Adams, counsel to the Army, told Cohn that "the national interest required that no preferential treatment be given to Mr. Schine." Two months later, in January 1954, after Schine had been inducted and was completing basic training, Adams told Cohn that like most inductees, Schine was likely to be shipped overseas. That piece of information, according to the Army's report, led Cohn to declare that such treatment would "wreck the Army" and cause Robert Stevens "to be through as Secretary of the Army."

Although these and other allegations in the Army report were not officially made public until March 11, the Army shrewdly arranged for some copies of the report to reach what it hoped would be sympathetic hands on Capitol Hill two days in advance, on March 9. One of the early copies came to Michigan senator Charles Potter. The senator was a bona fide war hero, having lost both legs in World War II, but a humdrum legislator. Nevertheless the usually bland Potter was incited to action by the Army's charges, and his response to the leaked report fulfilled the Army's fondest hopes. Grasping the document with one hand and one of his canes with the other, Potter collared two other Republican members of the committee, Mundt and Everett Dirksen of Illinois, and demanded that the committee meet at once and fire Roy Cohn.

But any such meeting required the permission of the chairman, Senator McCarthy, and he unsurprisingly rejected the idea, insisting that he talk to Cohn first. Next day he told his colleagues, "Roy denies everything categorically. You haven't seen the other part of the story."

And so on Friday, March 11, when the Army report was released, Cohn and McCarthy held a joint press conference and countered the Army's indictment with a blast of their own. This amounted to eleven intra-office memos, purported to have been written in the last six months by McCarthy or Cohn or the subcommittee's executive director, Francis Carr. Probably the harshest of the countercharges amounted to what Mc-Carthy, quoting from one of Carr's memos, called "blackmail." According to Carr, at a December 9 meeting with John Adams, the Army counsel repeatedly referred to Schine as "our hostage," leading Carr to conclude that the Army "will keep right on trying to blackmail us as long as Schine is in the Army."

Just about as damaging, if it was to be given credence, was the Carr memo about Stevens's attempt at a November 6 meeting in his Pentagon office to divert McCarthy to another path. Fearful that he would be forced to resign by the revelations McCarthy was expected to produce about the Army, Stevens allegedly suggested that the subcommittee "go after the Navy, Air Force and the Defense Department instead." Told that the subcommittee had no evidence justifying such an inquiry, Adams supposedly advised McCarthy's aides "not to worry about that because there was plenty of dirt there, and they would furnish us with leads." In a similar vein, according to a December 9 memo, Adams offered to trade "specific information about an Air Force base where there were a large number of homosexuals" for information on what Army project the committee planned to investigate next.

Some of the memos, coincidentally or not, carried the same dates as entries in the Army's report. Thus on January 14, the day the Army said Cohn promised to "wreck the Army" if Schine were sent overseas, a Roy Cohn memo to Senator McCarthy said that Adams had come to the committee office and threatened that if McCarthy continued his probe of the Army, "he will fight us in every way he can."

The congruence of the dates in the Army's report with those in the McCarthy-Cohn response caught the attention of Army officials. It gave them reason to suspect that the memos had not actually been written on the dates they carried but rather cooked up afterward to rebut the Army's charges. But this was an issue that would not arise until later. In the meantime

Stevens denied these charges as "utterly untrue" and "fantastic," though he did not deny telling McCarthy he feared he might have to resign.

The release of these two public assaults—the Army denouncing McCarthy and Cohn, and McCarthy and Cohn firing back at the Army—made clear, to the regret of Karl Mundt and his GOP colleagues, that the Senate would have to take responsibility for cleaning up this mess. And that would be hard to do because the conduct of both parties to the dispute, and their eagerness to wage their battle in public, reflected discredit on both sides. If there was any truth to the counterattack by McCarthy and Cohn, the Army, by trying to ward off McCarthy's probe, had seriously embarrassed itself.

As for McCarthy, he found himself in the most serious trouble of his Senate career. As *Time* pointed out, what was most threatening to McCarthy about the Army report was that "it had drawn a careful bead on the one-man subcommittee's real brain," Roy Cohn, whom McCarthy had come to regard as indispensable. Particularly revealing was what the report indicated about the relationship between McCarthy and Cohn and former committee aide Schine, the center of the prolonged battle between the Army and McCarthy's committee.

According to the Army, in mid-October, early in the struggle over Schine's impending induction, McCarthy told John Adams that Schine was of no help to the committee but was mainly interested getting his picture in newspapers. Indeed, McCarthy said, Schine had become something of a pest. This was after Cohn had urged the Army to assign Schine somewhere in the New York area so that he could be available for consultation by the committee. A few days after he had described Schine in these unflattering terms, McCarthy told Adams that he did not want Cohn to know of his views.

Yet McCarthy seemed to go this way and then that way on the Schine issue. On December 17, 1953, according to the

Army's statement, while riding in a car with Cohn and Adams, McCarthy asked Adams to ask Secretary Stevens if the secretary could find a way to assign Private Schine to New York. But less than a week later, on December 22, McCarthy wrote Secretary Stevens a letter stating that his committee had no further interest in Private Schine and that he hoped Private Schine would be treated the same as other soldiers.

All of this was bound to add to the gossipy speculation about the ties that seemed to bind Cohn to Schine, and perhaps to McCarthy too. Already the usual off-color jokes were making the rounds in Washington, as in the quip "Bedfellows make strange politics." Even coarser was the mock song lyric that nightclub comic Joe E. Lewis had added to his routine: "I'm gonna love you like nobody's loved you, come Cohn or come Schine."

But despite the jokes, no one friend or foe was making the mistake of not taking Cohn seriously. *Time* labeled him a "hazel-eyed dynamo" and acknowledged that his energy was channeled by a keen mind and innate political cunning. A relentless, seemingly nerveless interrogator, at age twenty-seven Cohn was contemptuous of all senators on the subcommittee save McCarthy, who described his aide as "the most brilliant young fellow I have ever met," a judgment Cohn would certainly not have challenged. "Roy has deserved a spanking since he was a child," an old friend of the Cohn family said. "But I doubt if he ever got one in his whole life."

Given Cohn's upbringing, it was easy to understand why he often looked down on most of the rest of the world. An only child, he was the son of Dora Marcus and Albert Cohn, a justice in the Appellate Division of the New York State Supreme Court and a onetime protégé of Tammany boss Ed Flynn, who wielded substantial power in the Democratic party. Cohn was a child prodigy of sorts. His gift was not in the arts or sciences but rather in politics, and not as taught in school but instead as practiced in the Bronx County courthouse where his father held forth. Here the lodestar was the "favor bank," where balances were built on IOUs and contracts for favors given and promised.

Cohn had no childhood to speak of. From the earliest years of memory he was treated and conducted himself like an adult in miniature. "I didn't hang around arguing with my buddies about whether DiMaggio was better than Mel Ott," Cohn later recalled. His idea of a good time was debating with his father the significance of interesting cases that had come before his court. He claimed he was only eight when his already hard-boiled reasoning permanently altered the judge's assessment of eyewitness testimony. And at twelve he bawled the old man out for a major favor-bank defalcation, allowing his conscience to prevent him from ruling on an important case in order to suit the needs of another judge whose finagling had gotten the elder Cohn his judgeship.

Cohn was bright enough to make his own way in the world. But family connections helped him gain ground even faster and go farther. At fifteen, using the connections of an uncle, Bernie Marcus, he brokered the purchase of New York radio station WHOM to Generoso Pope, a political power in New York's Italian community, and earned a $10,000 commission. Cohn didn't squander the money; he kicked back a portion of it to a lawyer for the Federal Communications Commission who had helped him close the deal. He liked to impress his friends by telephoning famous family friends such as "Bill"—Mayor William O'Dwyer—on the spur of the moment to make small talk, all of which made his parents brag all the more about how clever their offspring was. More purposefully, he would call a police precinct to fix a speeding ticket for one of his high school teachers.

As he matured he continued to rely on his unsurpassed combination of brains, chutzpah, and clout. At eighteen, in the last year of World War II, Cohn avoided the draft by having himself nominated to West Point three times in a row by a friendly congressman and failing the academy's minimum strength and endurance tests three times in a row. But by this time the war and the draft were both over.

Not having been in service did not stop Cohn from using speed-up programs designed for veterans, to earn both his undergraduate and law degrees at Columbia in three years. Out-of-school contacts once again helped him, landing him a job as a clerk typist in the office of the U.S. attorney for the Southern District of New York, a strategic place for him to await his twenty-first birthday and admission to the bar. That came in May 1948, three months after he turned twenty-one and the same day he was sworn in as an assistant U.S. attorney at $3,397 a year.

The cold war and the new Red Scare were just getting under way. But Cohn, with an instinct for the main chance, saw which way things were heading and made sure he got in on the ground floor. Quickly establishing himself as a specialist in subversion, he played a major role in the trials that marked the path of the anti-Communist crusade, notably the Rosenberg case. On his upward path Cohn demonstrated an ability to leave colleagues in the dust while he himself gained the confidence of his boss. The head of the U.S. attorney's office in New York was Irving Saypol, and in 1950 Saypol made Roy Cohn, then all of twenty-three years old, with two years' experience, his confidential assistant, allowing the young man to play a starring role in the Rosenberg case.

In New York City, where Big Media was rife, Cohn could never be accused of hiding his light under a bushel. He cultivated a coterie of conservative journalists, mostly Hearst staffers, including the syndicated columnists George Sokolsky and Walter Winchell. They all shared his fixation on the Red threat and were glad to promote Cohn's achievements in return for inside information from the U.S. attorney's office.

When Cohn was transferred to Washington as a special assistant to U.S. Attorney General James McGranery in September 1952, he made sure his friends in journalism were informed so that they could give his arrival in the capital its proper due. No sooner did he reach Washington than he was assigned a task that would inevitably bring him to the attention of his future patron, Senator McCarthy. He was entrusted with preparing a perjury indictment against Owen Lattimore, whom McCarthy had labeled the top Soviet espionage agent in the United States. The seven charges that Cohn assembled got nowhere in the legal system. Two were dismissed by the court, and the Justice Department dropped the others. But his work earned Cohn the admiration of McCarthy.

Cohn made an even stronger personal impression, for better and for worse, in his next important assignment, testifying before a House subcommittee investigating alleged lethargy by the State and Justice departments in probing American Communists on the United Nations staff. None too subtly, Cohn indicated to the committee that most of his superiors at Justice had opposed his efforts to make public the criticism of the two departments. The subcommittee ultimately exonerated Attorney General McGranery and his staff but noted with a candor striking in such a report: "Cohn left the impression that he is an extremely bright young man, aggressive in the performance of his duties." And, the report added artfully, "probably not free from the pressures of personal ambition."

In 1953, with the Democrats who had installed him out of power, and with the new attorney general, Herbert Brownell, blind to his virtues, Cohn turned from the executive branch to Capitol Hill. There McCarthy installed him as chief counsel to the Special Subcommittee on Investigations. That did not go over well with another young lawyer, Robert Kennedy, who had been hired by McCarthy in January 1953 to serve on his Permanent Committee on Investigations. This was a favor to the Kennedy family patriarch, Joe Kennedy, the retrograde onetime New Dealer who had contributed generously to McCarthy's reelection campaign. The senior Kennedy wanted his son to be named chief counsel. But because Robert Kennedy's only work experience since graduating from law school less than two years before had been to manage his brother John's victorious 1952 campaign for the U.S. Senate, he had to settle for assistant counsel with Roy Cohn as his boss. Adding to Kennedy's resentment, Cohn was eighteen months younger than he. Cohn peeved the future attorney general even more by treating him like an errand boy, sometimes dispatching him for sweet rolls and coffee. Kennedy would leave in six months, privately complaining about the sloppy investigating style of McCarthy and Cohn. He would later return as counsel to the Democratic minority, thus serving as an aide to Senators John McClellan, Stuart Symington, and Henry M. Jackson during the Army-McCarthy hearings.

Young Kennedy's feelings did not disturb Cohn one bit. He had hired his own assistant, a young man named G. David Schine, the son of J. Myer Schine, the multimillionaire owner of a string of hotels and theaters. Cohn's old boss, Irving Saypol, had brought Schine and Cohn together at a luncheon in downtown Manhattan in 1952. Schine was pleasant in demeanor, handsome in an oily kind of way, well turned out, and had plenty of money to throw around. To be sure, Cohn was no pauper himself; he earned $20,000 a year in salary from the McCarthy Committee and had family money behind that. The two twenty-five-year-olds soon were seen almost everywhere that counted among Manhattan's hot spots.

But what cemented their friendship was that Schine wanted to be an investigator of Communists, which of course was Cohn's consuming interest. Schine's vitae presented little by the way of experience, but he had written a pamphlet called "Definition of Communism," copies of which were distributed in the rooms of the Schine hotel chain along with the Gideon Bible. A month after Cohn took command of the committee staff, he hired Schine as an unpaid consultant on psychological warfare. Two months later the new team made its investigative debut as they swept through U.S. Information Service posts in Europe in eighteen days "to see if there's waste and misman-agement and to pin down responsibility," as Cohn put it.

The European press jeered, depicting the pair as incom-petent postadolescents. Theodore Kaghan, in the U.S. High Commissioner's Public Affairs Division, joined in the mock-ery, labeling the pair as "junketeering gumshoes." Two weeks later he stopped laughing after Cohn unearthed the fact that in 1939 Kaghan had signed a nominating petition for a Com-munist party candidate for the New York City Council. He was recalled by the State Department and fired.

Back in the States Cohn and Schine continued to live life to the fullest, flying down to Washington from New York on Monday and taking adjoining rooms at the Statler Hotel for the week. On Friday nights they headed back to Manhattan to cram in as much high life as they could in such elegant hang-outs as the Stork Club's Cub Room. Cohn, a premier insider, did his best to share his privileged access with his friend. At McCarthy's wedding in September 1953, Cohn pushed Schine into a family wedding picture, a courtesy that irked the groom no end.

But this happy-go-lucky state of affairs was gravely dis-turbed by word that Gerard David Schine was about to be drafted into the United States Army. Cohn appeared to regard Schine's imminent induction as a test of his will and influence. He did what he could to get Schine a post at the Central Intel-ligence Agency, or, failing that, a direct commission. When the CIA would not oblige, and when the Army ruled that Schine did not have the qualifications for a commission, Cohn sought to make sure that Private Schine was shielded from the normal stresses and strains of military life.

Orders went out from the Secretary of the Army's office to the commanding general at Fort Dix that Pvt. David Schine was to receive regular night and weekend passes during his eight weeks of basic training. This was an unheard-of privilege for trainees, part of whose indoctrination was to be sufficiently humbled to accept their often unpleasant duty as soldiers, including the possible need to sacrifice life itself. Only once did Schine pull KP duty. One afternoon his squad leader hastily called a group of GIs to clean stoves. After the detail was formed, the squad leader reputedly groaned: "Oh, my God! I've picked Schine! What in hell am I going to do?" Later he apologized: "Aw gee, the light was bad," he told Schine. But after a while the military brass decided that the more they did for Schine, the more Cohn and McCarthy demanded. And so the Army finally called a halt to this losing game, leading to the public eruption of charge and countercharge in mid-March.

That in turn forced the McCarthy Committee, though without McCarthy at its helm, to decide unanimously to conduct full-scale public hearings into the imbroglio. Although no senator dissented from the final vote, which took place during an executive session of the committee on March 16, the agreement was not all that easy to reach. The debate, the minutes of which were later released, reflected the partisan tensions in the committee that became more apparent during the public hearing that followed.

For the Republicans on the committee as well as in the Senate generally, the battle between McCarthy and the Army represented a bad case of bad news. The dispute pitted a leading Republican senator, who many in the GOP regarded as a vital political asset, against the executive branch of the government, which happened to be headed by the first Republican president in twenty years. The Democrats would have been less than human if they did not take some satisfaction out of the furor. For the better part of four years McCarthy had been a problem for the Democrats, impugning their patriotism and putting their leadership on the defensive. Meanwhile few in the GOP had done anything to deflect McCarthy's attacks. Now McCarthy was a Republican problem, a development that suggested the Democrats might at long last enjoy some relief. Still, circumstances were not so simple that Democrats could afford to relax and observe the spectacle of internecine Republican warfare. That sort of stance, suggesting they were hoping to benefit from an argument that appeared to threaten the national interest, would not sit well with the public. And besides, given McCarthy's unpredictability and the explosiveness of the issues of national security and subversion, and the uncertainty of where the truth lay in the dispute between the Army on one side and McCarthy and Roy Cohn on the other, no one could tell whose ox would finally be gored.

Thus in the executive session both sides showed an inclination to tiptoe rather than be stampeded into battle, an attitude manifested most clearly by Senator Everett Dirksen of Illinois, who was already emerging as one of the great weathervanes in Senate history. "Most politicians shift with the wind, but Mr. Dirksen shifts with a zephyr," the *New York Times* observed in the midst of one of Dirksen's course changes. While Chairman Mundt may have ranked first among McCarthy's Republican peers by virtue of the title vested in him, among Senate Republicans Dirksen was in some ways a more significant and potentially at least more influential figure. Then fifty-eight, Dirksen was undergoing the second of several metamorphoses that would eventually help him gain a prominent place in history.

In his early years on Capitol Hill as a key Republican on the powerful House Appropriations Committee and then as chairman of the Republican National Congressional Committee, Dirksen had been considered one of the ablest members of the Republican delegation. He positioned himself near the ideological center of his party, usually supporting President Harry Truman's foreign policies. But in 1950 when he ran for the Senate, he turned sharply to the right, becoming a conservative isolationist and ardent backer of Senator McCarthy. This earned him the support of the *Chicago Tribune*, then the voice of right-wing Republicanism in Illinois and indeed throughout the Midwest. Dirksen first became known nationally to Americans at the 1952 Republican National Convention where he backed the conservative hero, Senator Robert Taft of Ohio, for the presidency and strenuously opposed the nomination of Dwight Eisenhower. Among the most vivid memories of that convention was Dirksen at the podium wagging his finger at New York governor Tom Dewey, the party's unsuccessful standard-bearer in 1948 and 1952 and the generalissimo of the Eisenhower forces. "We followed you before, and you took us down the path to defeat," Dirksen reminded Dewey.

Of course the Dewey-Eisenhower path did not lead to defeat but instead to a great victory, which challenged Dirksen's dexterity at adjusting to changes in the political environment. As a Taft supporter who still relied heavily on the good opinion of the mighty *Tribune*, it was awkward for him to desert his old allies and causes, notably McCarthy and the crusade against communism. But he was too shrewd a political realist to cut himself off from the power and patronage of the White House and the new Republican president.

All of this figured in his response to the now open warfare between the Army and Senator McCarthy. Dirksen's initial instinct was to do what came naturally to him: he sought to sweep the whole thing under the rug—under the guise of statesmanship—demonstrating his tendency never to use ten words to make a point when he could think of a hundred to utter. The committee's first priority, as Dirksen explained to his colleagues, was "to ascertain what can be done to reestablish the credibility and public confidence that is necessary in the case of any committee that has a useful and constructive function." Would public hearings help the committee reach that goal? Dirksen asked himself and the other committee members. It was a question he had no difficulty answering in the negative. No one knew for sure exactly what public hearings might produce, but Dirksen for one could see the dangers clearly.

"Would a public hearing or even a private hearing accomplish anything in getting this thing back into focus and into proper perspective?" Dirksen asked rhetorically. "I have grave doubts about it," he said, once more responding to his own question. "I think by the time you got over the whole agenda of witnesses that might have to be heard, we would have to give several weeks to this business. When it was all through, we certainly would not have been pursing the basic purposes and objectives of the committee." Considering the fuss that had already been made, Dirksen wondered why more sound and fury was needed. Why couldn't the committee simply say, "All right, everybody has had his say in public. Let's forget about it and start with a clean page"?

This notion was presented with such benign innocence that some would find it attractive. But not crusty John McClellan of Arkansas, the ranking Democrat on the committee whom Lyndon Johnson had entrusted with the stewardship of Democratic fortunes in these proceedings. If McClellan seemed hard-bitten, he had a right to be. The son of a tenant farmer who somehow had made himself a lawyer, and a mother who died when he was three weeks old, McClellan was raised in Grant County, one of the poorest counties in Arkansas, itself one of the poorest states in the union. He went to the local schools, simultaneously studying law in his father's office. At age seventeen he was admitted to the bar by a special act of the Arkansas legislature. McClellan did not pretend to credentials he did not possess. "I am an uneducated man," he would tell interviewers.

But he had enough book-learning so that when he joined the Army in the Great War he was commissioned a second lieutenant in the Signal Corps. Afterward, in civilian life, he prospered in the law and then turned to politics, moving up the ladder from city attorney in Malvern to state prosecuting attorney, then to two terms in the U.S. House of Representatives where he backed Roosevelt's economic policies but opposed anti-lynching legislation. In 1942 McClellan made it to the Senate, where his record fit the profile of other conservative Southern Democrats of the time: staunchly anti-Communist and internationalist in foreign policy, against the goals of labor unions, and strongly opposed to efforts to erode the racial barriers of the South. But while he would never have been invited to join the board of the American Civil Liberties Union, he was a stickler for adhering to certain legal procedures. As a member of the McCarthy Committee, his attitude had not infrequently brought him into conflict with its chairman.

A good deal had been said by both sides in the Army-McCarthy dispute, he pointed out. "I do not know whether any of these statements are true, or which are true or which are not, and so help me I haven't any fixed opinion about it," he insisted. "But it is before the public, and this committee cannot afford to do anything that would look like we are trying to hush things up." Here McClellan bluntly reminded McCarthy and the others that the committee had not spent much time worrying about the reputations of the persons it had chosen to interrogate in the past. "You bring these folks in here and you put them before the television, and you portray them and present them to millions of people and then you cite them for contempt because they refuse to answer questions." Now the committee was confronted with a raging argument involving a number of high-level officials. He did not believe, McClellan made clear, that the committee could command public respect if it did less than bring these higher-ups before the committee "and let the public hear them testify, just like you do anybody else against whom accusations are made."

Two other Democrats, Symington of Missouri and Jackson of Washington, supported McClellan's call for a public airing of the dispute, and so did Republican Charles Potter. In order to make the idea of public hearings more palatable, Potter contended "it can be done expeditiously and without being prolonged." With notable prescience he added, "I share Sen. Dirksen's view that the longer it goes on the worse it is going to be, as far as the public impression of our committee is concerned and the Army and other people that are involved."

Dirksen, who was nothing if not a realist, now realized that the tide was running against him and acted accordingly. He folded his cards and went along, adding the cautionary note that steps should be taken to "make sure that it does not become a Donnybrook Fair and it is kept on sound and orthodox lines."

But here Chairman Mundt, the most reluctant of all those present, sounded a cautionary note. "This is going to take some time," Mundt said. "We might as well face up to that. Ten days or two weeks is a minimum." It was a point well worth making, but events would demonstrate just how low Mundt's guess of a minimum was.

But Mundt had another issue to bring up, of particular importance to him personally. And this was to relieve the committee, and not incidentally himself as its chairman, of what he called "this very distasteful job." The committee, Mundt contended, was "not the proper forum before which to try these charges and countercharges." Whatever the committee reported, people might say, "of course the committee did it that way because they were prejudiced, or because of their connection with a member of the staff who was under investigation, or because the chairman of the committee was involved." The most prudent course, Mundt argued, was to turn the job over to "some committee which is not in any way suspected of having leanings one way or another."

But Senator Dirksen, among others, did not think much of that idea. Having earlier in the meeting tried to shield the whole affair from public light, Dirksen now stood up for accountability and responsibility. "What a dismal confession it would be to the country that seven members of the United States Senate who are confronted with a problem had to throw it in the laps of other Senators who have only equal prerogatives on committees and in the United States Senate," he declared.

Symington, his Democratic colleague, pointed out that there was no precedent for such a transfer of responsibility. And he added, pertinently, his fear that "the public would get the wrong impression"—which actually would have been the correct impression. So like Mundt himself, though to a lesser extent, the rest of the committee was trapped; they could not get out of doing this "distasteful job."

Although his efforts to find an escape route had been frustrated, Mundt had still another suggestion for a way to ease the public discomfort he so dreaded. What about revisiting the procedure used for the Senate inquiry into President Truman's firing of Gen. Douglas MacArthur in 1951? For those hearings the Senate Foreign Relations Committee had met in closed session in the caucus room, then released transcripts of the proceedings hourly to the press waiting outside. "That gets away from your motion picture cameras and the TV and things of that kind," Mundt explained. "I thought it was a rather dignified hearing, and I don't like to see this thing get to be a public brawl."

But by this time a majority of the committee, spearheaded by McClellan, had clearly accepted the need to hold public hearings. And so Mundt's attempt to avoid a "brawl" went nowhere.

Despite the eventual unanimous agreement to conduct hearings, it was more than a month before the proceedings actually began. For one thing the committee, having decided to sideline its regular chief counsel, Roy Cohn, for the occasion, had to find a substitute. That was Mundt's job, and he did not have an easy time with it. This assignment promised to be a thankless task for a lawyer interested in his future, with the potential for doing more harm than good. Among those who came in for early consideration were William P. Rogers, then deputy attorney general, and William Jameson, president of the American Bar Association. Both declined. After two frustrating weeks Mundt found a man who actually wanted the job—a Massachusetts lawyer named Samuel Sears who had lobbied both senators from his state for their help in getting the appointment. That alone should have been cause for suspicion.

Mundt asked Robert Kennedy, himself a Massachusetts man, to check on Sears's credentials and objectivity. Perhaps young Kennedy was in too much of a hurry to note that Sears had raised campaign funds for Senator McCarthy and had publicly praised his work in getting "the pinks and commies out of the government." Or maybe his own family's admiration for McCarthy clouded his judgment. In any event, Kennedy gave Sears a clean bill of health, after which Mundt publicly announced his selection. But when word of Sears's affinity for McCarthy became known, Mundt's colleagues turned thumbs down. "He's got to go," was the way John McClellan put it. And he did.

Soon thereafter Mundt settled on Ray Howard Jenkins, a politically ambitious criminal lawyer from Knoxville, Tennessee, recommended by Everett Dirksen. If Jenkins harbored strong views one way or another on Senator McCarthy, he had never uttered them in public.

Amidst the hubbub over Sears, it went almost unnoticed that the Pentagon had announced the selection of another Boston lawyer, Joseph Nye Welch, a senior partner in the well-respected firm of Hale and Dorr, to represent the Army in the hearings. Welch was unknown to political Washington, and for the present he chose to stay out of the limelight. Asked his views on McCarthy and McCarthyism, he said simply, "I'm a registered Republican and a trial lawyer. I'm just for the facts."

But matters were not to be as simple as that, as Welch soon discovered. Just after his appointment was announced, he drafted two young lawyers from his firm, James St. Clair, who would later represent Richard Nixon in the Watergate scandal, and Fred Fisher, who would also achieve public recognition but in a very different and unwelcome way.

St. Clair and Fisher had just begun doing preliminary research on the controversy when Welch decided to vet them both as they talked over drinks in the cocktail lounge of the Carlton Hotel. "Boys, we're in the kind of lawsuit that is different from anything you've known," Welch told them. "Everything will go—even the lawyers will be on trial. If there is anything in any of your lives that might be embarrassing to you, it better come out now."

St. Clair had nothing to report, but Fisher did. This would have surprised anyone with even a cursory knowledge of the young man's background. He had been born on Patriot's Day, April 18, 1921, to a prosperous middle-class family in Wollaston, Massachusetts, just outside Boston. His mother's family had come to this country in the 1600s to live in a Puritan settlement. The forebears of his father, Fred George Fisher, Sr., had arrived in the mid-nineteenth century, fleeing political turmoil in Germany. Fred Fisher, Jr., grew up in comfortable surroundings but with a bent toward striving, inherited from his father who made his mark in the business world as a salesman of folding boxes. Fred Jr. starred at fullback for his high school team and was remembered long after his graduation for a spectacular touchdown run in the big game of his senior year. He went on to Bowdoin where he pledged that most white shoe of all white-shoe fraternities, Delta Kappa Epsilon.

Fisher was not yet twenty-one when the Japanese bombed Pearl Harbor. No sooner did he finish college than he enlisted in the Army's Signal Corps. Before he was shipped overseas he did two things at his father's behest: applied for Harvard Law School and married his sweetheart, Natalia Marie Benz, whom he had met while doing preenlistment schooling for the Signal Corps. Fisher emerged from the war with first lieutenant bars and the urge to make up for lost time. He started Harvard Law in March 1946, less than a week after the Army mustered him out.

In his second year at Harvard he made a decision that he now felt obliged to account for to his mentor, Joe Welch. Seeking help in learning more about the profession he was about to enter, he joined an organization called the National Lawyers Guild. Nationally the Guild was a fervently left-wing organization founded amidst the social and political ferment of the 1930s. It was created to provide what its founders billed as "a progressive" alternative to the American Bar Association, which then—even more than now—could always be found on the side of the status quo. For one thing, the ABA did not accept black members.

Nationally the Guild crusaded for a variety of unpopular causes, some of which later became more popular, such as civil rights, and others which did not, such as defending radicals faced with criminal prosecution. Some of its four thousand members defended some of the Hollywood Ten and helped in the Rosenberg defense. It also defended some of the Communists charged with violating the Smith Act, a 1940 law which all but made the Communist party illegal and whose key provisions were ultimately overturned by the Supreme Court.

But on a local level the Guild's makeup and priorities varied from chapter to chapter. At Harvard its members included liberal and moderate lawyers, some like Fisher himself, and members of the Republican party. Most of them were veterans and were more interested in forging careers for themselves after graduation than in left-wing politics. It was the only professional organization open to law students as the ABA had no chapter on the Harvard campus.

After graduating from Harvard in 1947, Fisher helped organize a Guild chapter in Suffolk County, Massachusetts, working with a man named Greenberg, who was allegedly a full-fledged member of the Communist party. But after that episode, as Fisher became more aware of the controversy surrounding the Guild's ideological leanings and as the Red Scare heated up, he resigned from the Guild. He joined the ABA, eventually becoming president of its Massachusetts chapter, and relied on the Republican party as the outlet for his political interests.

Presented with this information, Welch immediately feared that McCarthy would get hold of it somehow and use it to undermine his presentation of the Army's case. "The only controversy was whether the damage to the Army's case would be more severe if I left than I remained," Fisher recalled later. Welch and Fisher, along with St. Clair, Assistant Secretary of Defense Struve Hensel, and another Pentagon official, Fred Seaton, consulted with Jim Hagerty, Eisenhower's press secretary.

Hagerty's initial inclination was to hang tough and brazen it out. But the more he thought about Fisher's connection with the reputed Communist Greenberg, and how troublesome that could be made to appear, the more his resolution weakened. "It was decided Fisher to drop out," Hagerty scribbled in his diary. "Too dangerous to give McCarthy opportunity to brand Fisher as Red and smear up Army defense. Tough decision but necessary."

Fisher, having no choice in the matter, returned to Boston and to Hale and Dorr while Welch and St. Clair remained in Washington to carry on for the Army. Attempting to comfort Fisher, Welch suggested he was the luckiest of the three because no one could tell how the case would end. Then he brightened up and said, "What a case! A million dollars wouldn't buy all the publicity."

But what sort of publicity? That question understandably gave Welch concern. Now he feared that McCarthy would learn about the Fisher case and disclose it, making as much of a scandal of it as he could. To preempt McCarthy, Welch revealed the story himself, to the *New York Times*. On April 16 the *Times*, at the tag end of a story about preparations for the hearings that would begin in six days, reported in two brief paragraphs that Fisher had been dropped from Welch's staff because of his previous membership in the National Lawyers Guild. The story went on to say that the Guild had been listed by the attorney general as a Communist front organization. This was incorrect, as the Guild later indignantly pointed out. Brownell had in fact sought to list the Guild as subversive, but the Guild had successfully petitioned the U.S. Court of Appeals to prevent him from doing so. The *Times* never acknowledged its error.

McCarthy did what he could with the information Welch had provided for the *Times* story. In a statement filed with the subcommittee just before the investigation got under way, McCarthy charged that "a law partner" of Welch who had belonged to an organization described by the House Un-American Activities Committee as the "legal bulwark" of the Communist party had been slated to participate in the hearings but was discharged "only when his communist front connection became publicly known." McCarthy did not name Fisher or the Guild, and his reference to the episode went largely unnoticed.

Now, before the hearings began, attention turned to a final difficult question: McCarthy's role in the proceedings. The senator had agreed to step aside as chairman—he had already made up his mind on the issues involved, he told his colleagues—but he wished to remain a member of the committee. That was too much even for Eisenhower. In keeping with his customary neutral stance on McCarthy, the president was struggling to keep his distance from the controversy with the Army, but on this issue he could not resist a pointed comment. "In America, if a man is a party to a dispute, directly or indirectly, he does not sit in judgment on his own case," he declared. Forced to give up his vote, McCarthy appointed as his substitute Idaho senator Henry C. Dworshak, a man known chiefly for his admiration of his colleague from Wisconsin. And McCarthy did persuade the committee to allow him to cross-examine witnesses, though no such privilege had been given to witnesses before the committee when McCarthy was leading its investigations.

At the last moment McCarthy made one more effort to confuse and intimidate when he accused Struve Hensel, the assistant secretary of defense, of having masterminded the Army's effort to discredit McCarthy and Cohn. Hensel's motive, McCarthy charged, was to prevent an investigation of a conflict of interest on his part which amounted to "serious misconduct" and possibly illegality. In fact the charges of misconduct to which McCarthy referred, stemming from Hensel's job as a navy procurement officer during World War II, had long ago been investigated and found groundless. McCarthy had called attention to the alleged conflict of interest in the hope of pressuring Secretary of Defense Charles E. Wilson to get the Army to back off its case against him. But he also wanted his enemies to realize just how dangerous it would be to get on the wrong side of Joe McCarthy, a point he would underline time and again under the glare of television lights in the Senate caucus room.

One issue that surprisingly did not become a major bone of contention was the role of television. Lyndon Johnson had passed the word to committee Democrats through John Mc-Clellan of Arkansas, the senior Democrat on the committee: whatever other concessions they might make to Republicans in agreeing on ground rules for the hearings, the Democrats should insist the proceedings be televised. If the Republicans had objections, they did not voice them publicly. They may have felt that to deny access to the cameras would have made it appear that they were trying to hide the proceedings from the public. And they apparently had forgotten the Kefauver hearings three years earlier and the storm they created.

In any event, there was only one brief reference to television in the March 16 executive session. Mundt, urging the committee to adopt a format like that used for the MacArthur hearings, indicated that he regarded television as less of a potential problem than newsreel cameras. "The TV is all right," he said, adding, "The motion picture cameras on occasion just shoot a little sketch and they don't get the full picture, and this is something where the country should have the full picture and get the full text, and no expurgations."

So when the hearings began, three networks, NBC, ABC, and DuMont, had their cameras at the ready. Only CBS was absent, having decided it did not wish to lose the revenue from its regular daytime commercial broadcasts. NBC would reach the same decision after only two sessions that cost it $125,000 in revenue; it joined CBS in broadcasting late-night summaries.

ABC, prodded by its news editor, Fritz Littlejohn, with veteran correspondent Bryson Rash as its anchor, stayed on the scene, as did DuMont. With gavel-to-gavel coverage, both networks made sure that the public got the "full picture" of the proceedings Mundt had desired. But at times this turned out to be a much fuller picture than Mundt and his Republican colleagues would have preferred.

7

The Soldiering of Private Schine

Some might have thought that Edward R. Murrow's *See It Now* assault, followed by the White House–sanctioned put-down from Vice President Nixon, and then by the thirty-four-page broadside fired by the U.S. Army might have slowed Joe McCarthy's charge and softened his voice. But anyone who reasoned that way was disabused of the notion at the very start of the hearings into the senator's bitter quarrel with the Army. Although he had been forced to give up his seat on the committee, McCarthy's presence at the hearings was conspicuous. He sat next to Roy Cohn at the end of a long table, protected by two bodyguards assigned by the FBI. And his voice was loud enough to drown out Ray Jenkins, the committee's new counsel, just as he was preparing to call the first witness. "Point of order, Mr. Chairman," McCarthy cried, uttering a refrain that was to become the hallmark of the hearings. "Mr. Chairman, may I raise a point of order?"

Rather than a legitimate point of order, McCarthy's aggressiveness displayed a point of political pedantry. He complained that while the Army's brief to the committee was labeled "filed by the Department of the Army," it expressed the views of only a "few Pentagon officials" who had no business representing themselves as the Department of the Army. McCarthy added that he had heard from many people in the military—from generals with long combat records to recently inducted privates—all of them resentful "that a few Pentagon politicians, attempting to disrupt our investigation, are naming themselves the Department of the Army." To cure this affront against the Army's dignity, McCarthy demanded that Secretary Stevens, counsel Adams, and Assistant Secretary Hensel, the principals in the controversy, list themselves merely as individuals instead of passing themselves off as the Department of the Army.

Before McCarthy raised this issue, Chairman Mundt, intending to reassure the viewing public and the rest of the country who might be concerned about the conduct of the proceedings, had offered a sweeping pledge. "It is our joint determination to conduct these hearings with a maximum degree of dignity, firmness and thoroughness," he said in his best rhetorical mode. "We enter our duties with no prejudgment as to the verities in this controversy. We propose to follow the evidence wherever it leads and to give every party to this dispute the equitable treatment and consideration to which he is entitled." As the ranking Democrat, Senator McClellan seconded the sentiment. The senators would conduct this inquiry seeking the truth, McClellan affirmed, "without regard to any personalities that may be involved."

But no sooner were these words spoken than McCarthy challenged Mundt's seriousness of purpose with his quibbling point of order. The chairman might have squelched this protest simply by pointing out that the "few officials" McCarthy complained about happened to have been appointed by the president to run the Department of Army. But that was not the way Chairman Mundt chose to play his new role as McCarthy's supernumerary. Puffing on his pipe, he announced that his ruling would be deferred until Army Secretary Robert Stevens, the highest-ranking of the Pentagon officials involved, had his turn on the witness stand. Thus Mundt made evident to McCarthy that regardless of his technical exile from committee membership, he would be free to pound away at his adversaries as he pleased.

The senator took full advantage of the license Mundt had given him when it was his turn to cross-examine the very first witness, Maj. Gen. Miles Reber. Now assigned to the Army's Western Europe command, Reber had been unfortunate enough to have been the Pentagon's legislative liaison while McCarthy and Cohn had been waging their campaign to get David Schine a direct commission in the U.S. Army. The very model of a modern major general, crisp in appearance and manner, Reber was clearly trying not to pick a fight. Asked about his dealings with McCarthy and his chief aide, he denied feeling intimidated. Asked if Senator McCarthy had acted improperly, he answered in the negative. But Reber did testify that he had been called by Senator McCarthy and also by Cohn on behalf of Schine, on the average of two or three times a day during the two-week period in July 1953 when Schine's credentials were being considered. Many people called him in such situations, Reber said, but the frequency of Cohn's calls was "unusual."

At this point Army counselor Welch had his first chance to question the witness and tried to probe a little deeper. "Disregarding the word 'improper,' do you recall any instance comparable to this under which you were put under greater pressure?" Welch asked. Reber provided the answer Welch was hoping for. "To the best of my recollection," the general said, "I recall of no instance under which I was put under greater pressure."

It was Senator McClellan who put the issue of pressure in sharper focus when he questioned Reber. For someone to support an applicant for a direct commission who possessed the necessary qualifications would not amount to a request for preferential treatment, would it? No, General Reber agreed, it would not. But, McClellan continued, if an applicant failed to possess the requisite qualifications, as the Army had ruled in Schine's case, and someone insisted that he be commissioned anyway, as Roy Cohn did in Schine's case, that would be a request for preferential treatment, would it not?

Reber had no trouble answering. "Yes, sir," he said.

Still, that was probably the most damage he could do to McCarthy's cause. Another man in McCarthy's position might have been content to let the matter rest there, but that was not the way McCarthy operated. When it was his turn to question General Reber, he suddenly injected the name of the general's brother, Sam, a retired foreign service officer and former acting U.S. high commissioner for Germany. McCarthy asked if the general knew that Sam Reber had been the boss of Theodore Kaghan, the official in the high commissioner's office who was fired after Cohn and Schine had targeted him during their Red-hunting tour of Europe. Furthermore, McCarthy demanded, did General Reber know that Sam Reber had "repeatedly made attacks on Cohn and Schine?"

In truth the attacks were nothing more than Sam Reber's defense of Kaghan after he was attacked by Cohn and Schine for having signed a petition for a Communist party candidate. But before Reber could respond to this new line of attack, Ray Jenkins interrupted and challenged the relevance of the question. McCarthy backed off but first made his point—that General Reber was biased in his testimony about McCarthy and Cohn because of his brother's experience with the Cohn-Schine trip to Europe. "If I cannot show bias, Mr. Chairman, and prejudice on the part of a witness, then that is a violation of every rule of law that I know of."

In the afternoon session McCarthy returned to the attack with a vengeance when he took another shot at Reber, this one aimed well below the belt. "Are you aware of the fact that your brother was allowed to resign when charges that he was a bad security risk were made against him as a result of the investigations of this committee?" he asked the general. Once again Jenkins interrupted before Reber could reply, claiming the question was irrelevant. Senator McClellan objected on other grounds. "There has been no testimony that the statements that the Senator makes as fact are true, and until they are established in this record as facts, then the question is incompetent," he argued in his lawyerly fashion. "Let us have a ruling on this," he urged Chairman Mundt, "because we may be trying members of everybody's family involved before we get through."

Finally Jenkins reworded McCarthy's question to ask simply whether Reber's brother had resigned because of the findings of the McCarthy Committee. Before anyone could object, Reber, obviously eager to answer, replied, "I do not know and have never heard that my brother retired as a result of any actions of this committee. My answer is positively no to that question."

After more bickering among the lawyers, Reber managed to gain the floor again. "A very serious charge has been made against my brother in this room," he told the committee. "I would like to answer publicly that charge right now." But McCarthy objected, demanding the right to cross-examine the general if he made any such statement. And Ray Jenkins, whose comments by now were making it clear toward which side in the conflict he was leaning, agreed with McCarthy. "General Reber I think is in error in stating that a serious attack has been made on his brother," Jenkins said in a notable display of legal pigheadedness. "Questions were asked with reference to his brother, but no proof or statement has been introduced with respect to his brother."

That was not the way they practiced law back in Snohomish County, Washington, when Senator Henry Jackson was the D.A. there. "The statement has been made in this room and is apparent to millions of Americans, that General Reber's brother was dismissed as a security risk," Jackson said. "The statement cannot be stricken from all the newspapers tonight, or from the television audience and radio audience," Jackson reminded everyone. "And I think in fairness he should be given the opportunity to answer the statement limited to the charge that his brother was dismissed as a security risk."

Jackson's own statement wasn't completely accurate; McCarthy had said Sam Reber "was allowed to resign," not dismissed. But Jackson was close enough to the truth to force Jenkins to back down and allow General Reber to speak his piece. "I merely wanted to say that, as I understand my brother's case, he retired as he is entitled to do by law upon reaching the age of 50," said Reber. "That is all I want to say. I know nothing about any security case involving him."

Later that day the State Department issued a statement that Sam Reber had retired voluntarily on July 31, 1953. That made it official. Prompted by the storm in Washington, Sam Reber himself told reporters that he had decided to retire when he had just passed his fiftieth birthday, the statutory retirement age. He accused McCarthy of a "deliberate diversionist movement" in bringing his name into the testimony.

Of course no one except Sam Reber himself could know how much the unpleasantness following the Cohn-Schine trip to Europe had influenced his decision to retire. This sort of ambiguity was a consequence of the world McCarthy had created and testimony to the passiveness of others who stood by and allowed him to commit his mischief. Meanwhile McCarthy had to be pleased with himself. At the outset he had thrown mud at his adversaries and diverted attention from his own difficulties—just the sort of thing he had been doing successfully for four years. The difference now was that 45 million people

were watching. It remained to be seen how much, if any, difference that would make.

The answer would depend in part on the testimony of
the next and most important witness, Secretary of the Army
Robert Stevens. Early indications were not encouraging for
the Army's side. Although Stevens's role was to lay out the
Army's case-in-chief against McCarthy, he soon found himself on the defensive, in part because of his own clumsiness.
He had behind him a long and successful career in business,
the military, and government, but nothing in his experience
had prepared him for contending with Senator McCarthy
and his allies.

Born just before the turn of the century, Stevens had devoted most of his adult life to the successful stewardship of the
J. P. Stevens Company. The giant textile manufacturer had been
founded early in the nineteenth century by Nathaniel Stevens,
and its leadership had passed from father to son on into the
twentieth century. Robert Stevens and his elder brother, John
Jr., took direction of the company on October 27, 1929, two
days before the stock market debacle that heralded the Great
Depression. Amidst the chaos, Franklin Roosevelt found a post
for Bob Stevens in the New Deal as a director of the Federal
Reserve Bank of New York. Despite hard times, the company
grew steadily and expanded by absorbing other textile firms.
Stevens was hailed for his skill in managing and reorganizing
a corporation that at one time had fourteen divisions running
twenty-nine mills, each operating as an independent company.
Stevens melded the fourteen divisions into three, each set up
to manufacture a different kind of fiber.

As war threatened in 1940, Roosevelt summoned him
again, this time making him head of the National Defense
Advisory Commission. After Pearl Harbor, Stevens, who had
been a second lieutenant in the field artillery in World War I,
became a colonel handling textile procurement for the Army.

His service won him a host of honors including the Medal of the Legion of Merit and the Distinguished Service Medal.

After the war Stevens returned to his textile company and became its chairman as it continued to dominate its industry in the South. When Eisenhower won the White House and began assembling an administration staffed mainly by businessmen, it was only natural that he should turn to Bob Stevens. Stevens was the former chairman of the Business Advisory Council, a talent pool from which presidents going back to Calvin Coolidge had always recruited. And the Army, to which Stevens felt a strong attachment because of his service in two world wars, was a natural place for him to be posted. His new boss, Secretary of Defense Charles E. Wilson, was a friend from the Business Advisory Council.

As Army secretary, Stevens prided himself on not being deskbound. In little more than a year on the job he had already clocked 74,000 miles on trips to Korea and other parts of the world on Army matters. This followed the pattern he had established in the textile business of keeping an eye on local plants scattered around the country. But he was to find out that the Army, especially after Senator McCarthy began to investigate it, and the world of Washington politics were both very different from the J. P. Stevens Company and the business world.

Before he was sworn in to testify at the hearings, Stevens's conduct in relation to the dispute with McCarthy had already given reason to question his judgment and his fortitude. In part the problem arose from his inexperience and naiveté. Having heard that Senator McCarthy had discovered security problems in the Army, he assumed that McCarthy would be glad to have his help, which he eagerly offered, in finding a solution. He did not realize that what McCarthy valued was the problem, not a solution. The last thing he wanted was the Army's help in solving the Army's problem.

But blame for Stevens's innocence could not be laid on his shoulders alone. There had been no one in the administration, least of all Stevens's old commander, now resident in the White House, to offer him guidance, to advise him that unless he stood up to McCarthy's bullying, the bullying would become unbearable. And so in September 1953 when Stevens first got wind of McCarthy's investigation, the secretary asked to meet with him in the hope, he later explained, of trying to resolve McCarthy's concerns about the Army's supposed security weaknesses. All that came of that idea was a suggestion from McCarthy, accepted by Stevens, to attend a dinner given by G. David Schine's parents at a New York hotel. In November Stevens met with McCarthy again, this time flying to see him in New York where the senator was conducting hearings, in another effort to "get together with him." Stevens then flew McCarthy and his aides to Fort Dix where they visited with Schine—and where Stevens, in a lapse of judgment that would soon be widely advertised, had his photo taken with Schine.

In February, following McCarthy's investigation of the case of Major Peress and the senator's denunciation of General Zwicker, Stevens got an earful from Army chief of staff Gen. Matthew B. Ridgway. Just as it was the first duty of an officer in uniform to protect his men, so that same obligation fell upon the civilian leaders of the Army, the former commander of the Eighty-second Airborne instructed Stevens. His backbone stiffened by Ridgway, Stevens now called McCarthy and threatened to prevent other officers from appearing before the committee.

"Just go ahead and try it, Robert," McCarthy told him. "I am going to kick the brains out of anyone who protects Communists. I will guarantee that you will live to regret it."

But Stevens was determined. That same day, Saturday, February 20, 1954, he ordered General Zwicker and two other officers whom McCarthy had subpoenaed to appear before him on Thursday, February 25, not to testify. That Monday, Washington's birthday, when he was honored by the Freedom Foundation at Valley Forge, Stevens won a standing ovation and was hailed with a new nickname, "Fighting Bob." But none of the Republicans on the McCarthy Committee were applauding. They feared what McCarthy might do in response.

That Wednesday, February 24, at the behest of Vice President Nixon, Stevens lunched with Senators Dirksen and Mundt in the Capitol. Because fried chicken was on the menu, the gathering inevitably and irrevocably became known as the "chicken lunch." When the meal was finished, so was "Fighting Bob's" defiance of McCarthy. He reversed his earlier stand and agreed to allow Zwicker and others to testify and to grant McCarthy carte blanche.

Stevens apparently did not fully understand what he had agreed to. On the day following the luncheon, when he read the headlines—"STEVENS BOWS TO McCARTHY" proclaimed the *New York Times*—he broke down and cried, then called Nixon to tell him he had decided to resign. But Eisenhower thought it was too late for that. The president's staff prepared a statement for Stevens which the secretary duly read to the press, vowing he would never allow Army officers to be "browbeaten or humiliated" by a congressional committee, and declaring that he had received assurances from McCarthy that that would not happen. But the impact of this pledge was considerably diluted when Senator McCarthy said the idea that he had given Stevens such assurances was "completely false." Two weeks later the Army issued its thirty-four-page report condemning McCarthy's efforts on behalf of Schine. The fat was in the fire.

The scars Stevens suffered from that episode would never fully heal. Now two months later, testifying before McCarthy's committee, with McCarthy himself more or less sidelined,

Stevens had a chance to redeem his reputation. But this experience would turn into another and more prolonged ordeal.

Things started off smoothly enough. Stevens finished his prepared testimony on the first afternoon of hearings, concluding: "The United States Army does not coddle Communists. The Committee knows that, the American people know that." The next day he continued to offer his account of the dispute, this time in response to questions from counsel Jenkins. Stevens seemed more at ease than he had been on the first day, even injecting a bit of humor into his testimony when he told of G. David Schine's direct bid to help his cause with the Army. In October 1953, when Schine, prior to his induction, was driving Stevens to hearings that McCarthy was conducting in New York, he mentioned to Stevens, as the secretary told the story on the witness stand, "that I was doing a good job ferreting out communists. He thought I could go a long way in this field. And that he would like to help me. He thought that it would be a much more logical plan for him to become a special assistant of mine to assist in the communist-seeking program than being drafted into the Army."

"Was that your statement or his?" Jenkins wanted to know.

The spectators in the hearing room burst into laughter as Stevens explained the statement had been made by Schine. Then as if not to appear to be taking matters too lightly, Stevens sounded a sober note. "I said to him that one of the best things that ever happened to me in my life was my opportunity for serving in the U.S. Army in two world wars," he testified. In the same vein he recalled telling Schine "that if he would face up to his forthcoming induction, and approach it in the right way, that he would look back on it all his life as one of the greatest experiences that he had, and that if for any reason he did not take his military training, in my opinion he would regret it for the rest of his life."

Stevens did not say what Schine's response was, if he had any. But given this reluctant soldier-to-be's sybaritic lifestyle and high self-regard, it seems difficult to imagine that the concept of service, in the military or anywhere else, was a notion to which he could easily relate.

Things stopped going smoothly for Stevens when he referred to the transcript of a phone conversation on November 7 with Senator McCarthy about Schine's status in the Army. Testifying from memory, without referring to the transcript, Stevens said: "Now in that conversation Senator McCarthy said that one of the few things he had trouble with Mr. Cohn about was David Schine. He said that Roy thinks that Dave ought to be a general and operate from a penthouse on the Waldorf-Astoria or words to that effect." McCarthy added, Stevens went on, that "he thought a few weekends off for David Schine might be arranged, or words to that effect. Perhaps for the purpose of taking care of Dave's girl friends." That drew laughter from the spectators and an outraged protest from McCarthy. He called the monitoring of his phone conversations without his knowledge "one of the most indecent and dishonest things I've ever heard of."

That was a bit like Claude Rains being "shocked, shocked" to learn that gambling was going on at Humphrey Bogart's Casablanca cabaret. In accordance with procedure common in the Pentagon and many other federal offices in the capital, telephone conversations had been routinely monitored by Stevens's appointment clerk, who took shorthand notes of what had been said. When the committee learned that somewhere between fifty and a hundred of Stevens's conversations dealing with McCarthy, his committee, and his staff had been monitored, Senator Jackson demanded that the transcripts of all of them be subpoenaed immediately.

Army counsel Joseph Welch thought that was a fine idea. "Nothing will delight the Army more than to make every such

telephonc conversation available," he said. But he acknowledged there was a serious legal problem because of a section
of the Federal Communications Act which banned the disclosure of an intercepted phone conversation. (The law treats a
monitored conversation like a wiretap intercept if one party is
unaware of the monitoring.) The revelation of the monitored
conversations touched off a three-hour argument which dis-
rupted the testimony and then dragged on for weeks in the
background as the hearings continued. It was a dispute, the
Army claimed, that created a serious hindrance to its efforts
to prove its claims against McCarthy. Ultimately many of the
transcripts were released after the persons overheard had given
their permission without bringing noticeable benefit or harm
to either side in the controversy.

After a weekend break, Stevens returned to the witness
stand on Monday, April 26, the third day of hearings, and was
again questioned by Ray Jenkins. But this was a very different
Jenkins from the one who had in lawyerly fashion led the secretary through his direct testimony. "My position is a peculiar
one," Jenkins explained to Stevens, with a full measure of the
self-importance that seemed a part of him: he was required
both to help the witness present his case, then challenge it as
fiercely as he could. So Stevens was now confronted by what
amounted to a different breed of attorney. Instead of the bland
interrogator who had taken his direct testimony, he had to face
Ray Jenkins the cross-examiner, who turned into a Southern
version of Torquemada.

Although Jenkins made a point of saying that he did not
represent either the Army or Senator McCarthy, it had not
been difficult to guess from his questioning of General Reber
which way he was leaning. First he had suggested to Reber
that the "vital work" in which Schine was engaged should be
considered in evaluating the conduct of McCarthy and Cohn,
a proposition that Reber rejected. Then Jenkins had sought to

prevent General Reber from responding to McCarthy's slander of his brother.

As a criminal trial lawyer in Tennessee, Jenkins was used to concentrating on one objective, getting his man off. In more than thirty years of practice he had defended six hundred murder defendants without having a single one pay the ultimate penalty. The key to his success, he once said, was getting the jury "so damned mad at the victim that they want to dig up the body and kill the SOB all over again." In the early years of his practice he took on the defense of a Knoxville bondsman charged with shooting a local press photographer who had offended the bondsman by taking his photo. The photographer offered the photo, which had won him a prize in a journalism competition, as evidence to bolster his case. After gaining some delays to let things cool off, Jenkins brought his client into court on a stretcher, contending that he was physically and mentally ill, and charging that the photographer had in effect brought on the shooting by harassing and goading the bondsman. The defendant got off with a light fine and a sixty-day sentence in the workhouse, small potatoes for felonious assault with a deadly weapon, documented by a photograph.

Jenkins was born in a town called Unaka, on the North Carolina side of the Great Smokies. By the time he was eleven his father, Columbus Sheridan Jenkins, known to his friends as "Lum," a country doctor, moved his family across the mountains to Tellico Plains, Tennessee, in the wild-boar country. From his early boyhood Jenkins always wanted a job of some kind, though his family did not need the money. At times his enterprise was embarrassing to the comfortably situated Jenkins clan. When Grandfather John Canada Jenkins, known as "Can," a revenuer, visited Tellico Plains with his second bride, young Ray had a flourishing shoeshine business in the center of town, where the newlyweds would surely pass on their way to the Jenkins home. The boy was ordered to take that day off because Can didn't want his bride to know she had married a man whose grandson shined shoes. Reluctant to give up a whole day's profits, Ray worked until he heard the train whistle, then folded his stand and waited around the corner for the bride and groom to go by, when he went back to work.

As Jenkins grew older he gave up his shoeshine stand but never stopped hustling, though his eye was on more than nickels and dimes. The law, he ultimately decided, was his true calling. He skipped undergraduate school and went directly to the University of Tennessee law school. There he demonstrated an aptitude early, winning first prize for scholarship along with his degree. As a top-ranked trial lawyer, most of his income—about $60,000 a year—came from civil litigation. But it was the criminal law on which his reputation was based.

Despite his prestige in the profession, whether by natural inclination or calculated design Jenkins's demeanor at fifty-seven still reflected the rough-hewn manners and mores of the Tennessee hill country. "He is the sort of lawyer who completely dominates a case and a court," wrote the Knoxville correspondent of the *New York Times*. "Rising with square jaw set and fire in his eyes, he'll unbutton his collar, loosen his coat, untie his tie and go to work. He reminds one of a boxer dog, when he sets his jaw."

Jenkins had more than a passing interest in politics. He lost a bid for Congress in 1939 when local Republicans picked another candidate. In 1940 he managed the Senate campaign of an up-and-coming young Republican named Howard Baker. Baker lost that year but eventually won election to the House of Representatives. More important to Jenkins, his son and namesake married the daughter of Senator Everett Dirksen, a connection that paved the way for Jenkins's appointment as counsel to the McCarthy Committee. His friends in Tennessee viewed that post as a springboard to higher political ground, most likely as a challenger to the Democratic incumbent, Senator Estes Kefauver, whose term would be up that November. But for the moment Jenkins was still trying to get his footing in this unfamiliar territory. This hearing room, in the cauldron of Washington politics, was a much more nuanced situation than the challenges he faced in the criminal and civil courts of Tennessee. Jenkins had a strong will, but his mind lacked the subtlety that his Army counterpart, Joseph Welch, displayed. He was unprepared for surprises while Welch had shown himself ready to turn the unexpected to his advantage. Thus when the issue of the legality of the monitored phone transcripts arose, Jenkins seemed completely stumped and rendered mute. Welch was quick to jump in and urge the admission of all the disputed transcripts.

But the task of cross-examination, which now presented itself, was the one part of Jenkins's assignment that he found most comfortable. He began his interrogation of Stevens by returning to an earlier theme: Senator McCarthy's work, and thus, David Schine's too, was of such overriding importance that both should be excepted from normal standards of behavior. In making this point, Jenkins was either unaware of or chose to ignore McCarthy's comments describing Schine as a publicity hound and a pest. In appraising the propriety of the efforts made on Schine's behalf by McCarthy, Jenkins asked Stevens, should not consideration be given to Schine's work for the committee, and the committee's overall task?

At first befuddled by the question, Stevens finally answered "that the time and place to do that was prior to his being drafted. Once the selective-service process worked it was then incumbent upon Senator McCarthy and his staff not to make calls such as you referred to, to the Army."

But Jenkins brushed that argument aside and began to zero in on McCarthy's case against the Army and the fundamental weakness of the Army's defense. The Army's sin, it became apparent to neutral observers of these proceedings, was not that it had refused to make Schine an officer, or get him a job with the CIA as Roy Cohn demanded, presumably on McCarthy's behalf. No, the Army's real transgression lay in all the concessions it had made and privileges it had granted to David Schine.

The simplest answer for this was that Stevens and the Army had treated McCarthy like the rest of the Eisenhower administration did—by temporizing and retreating and placating, tossing morsels in his path as if he were a python with an ever-active appetite. But the other explanation that McCarthy and Cohn provided, at least by implication, and that Jenkins sought to advance, was more sinister. It went beyond mere cravenness and approached criminal behavior. The gist of it was that catering to Schine the Army was trying to buy off McCarthy so he would abandon his investigation.

Jenkins began off slowly to pursue that point. "Is it not a fact," he asked Stevens, "that you did make concessions to David Schine with reference to leaves of absences, passes and so on?"

Yes, Stevens agreed, the Army had made concessions. But the reason was that "we did not want, or I did not want, the Army to be in the position of obstructing the work of a committee of Congress that at that time was engaged in investigating the Army."

Jenkins let that answer rest on the record for a bit while he pursued his view of McCarthy's investigation at Fort Monmouth. Would Stevens agree that McCarthy's committee "had done an important piece of work that enhanced the national security?"

Stevens conceded that McCarthy had helped to speed up action in some cases. But he added, "I think it would have been far more effective if he had not pursued the publicity tactics that went with this investigation. I think that did a lot of harm in a lot of ways."

Now Jenkins saw the opening he had been searching for. "And Mr. Stevens, you wanted it stopped, didn't you?"

Stevens rushed into the trap. "Yes, sir," Stevens replied.

"And consequently you wanted Senator McCarthy's investigation stopped, didn't you?"

"No, sir, I didn't want it stopped," Stevens insisted. But at this point he would have had trouble convincing anyone outside his immediate family that he meant what he said.

Ray Jenkins then set out to show that Stevens had tried to use Schine to halt the McCarthy investigation. He recalled that Stevens had visited Schine's apartment in New York and later had been the guest of Schine's parents at dinner. These events, which occurred after the Army had been pressured and importuned by McCarthy and Cohn—or so the Army had claimed in its March report—had been cited by McCarthy and Cohn as evidence of "bad faith" on the Army's part.

Now Jenkins, armed and prepared by Roy Cohn, presented the most damning evidence of this bad faith, as damning in its way as the photo of Jenkins's bondsman client shooting at a photographer. Had there been a photo of Schine "taken with you alone at your suggestion, anywhere?" he asked the secretary.

Stevens was uncertain whether that had happened or not.

"Let me show you a picture, Mr. Stevens, for the purpose of refreshing your recollection," Jenkins offered unctuously. Whereupon he produced a photo that Stevens acknowledged was a picture of him and Schine, then a private in the Army, taken at McGuire Air Force Base, adjoining Fort Dix, New Jersey, on November 17, following a meeting with Senator McCarthy.

"I would say that this is a picture, undoubtedly of David Schine, and a rather grim-looking Secretary of the Army,"

Stevens offered. Except that in the photo Stevens did not look at all grim. Instead he looked like a middle-aged father might look, gazing proudly upon his son in uniform. Moreover this photo had been taken at a time when Stevens claimed to be outraged at the demands McCarthy was making on Schine's behalf. Why then would he pose for such a photo, except that even at this late date he was fawning over McCarthy? Grim or smiling, it did not make for a pretty picture.

Stevens had gone to see McCarthy to see "if we could get together" on the investigation of Fort Monmouth, he explained.

"You went up to make peace with Senator McCarthy, didn't you, to stop this investigation?" Jenkins demanded.

"No, sir, I didn't go up there to stop the investigation."

But Jenkins ignored the denial. "Now getting back to Schine, Mr. Stevens, isn't it a fact that you were being especially nice and considerate and tender of this boy, Schine . . ."

Stevens started to interrupt, "Wait, wait, wait, wait," he cried.

But Jenkins cut him off and then finished his allegation, ". . . in order to dissuade the senator from continuing his investigation of one of your departments?"

"Positively and completely not," Stevens sputtered, and insisted he treated all privates in the Army the same.

This was pretty rich, Jenkins suggested, and rolled his eyes in disbelief.

Finally Stevens was able to get his own rationale onto the record. In meeting with McCarthy ten days before the picture-taking incident, he had objected to the "constant hammering of the army in the press." This was giving the public the impression of a serious espionage problem, he complained. He wanted to handle the problem himself, Stevens said. And he would report on his progress to McCarthy. "And if we weren't doing the job right, I assumed that he would come back into the picture." So in his own words he basically confirmed the thrust of Jenkins's allegation, that he wanted McCarthy to cease and desist.

Lost to public attention in the hubbub over Stevens's motives for meeting with McCarthy were some mundane but crucial facts Stevens had provided in response to Jenkins's questioning. Before McCarthy launched his probe of Fort Monmouth, six civilian employees had been suspended for "security reasons." These suspensions, Stevens emphasized, did not stem from hard evidence of disloyalty but rather from allegations that created suspicion and required investigation.

Since then the Army had suspended twenty-nine more employees.

"As a result of the McCarthy investigations?" Jenkins asked.

No, Stevens said, though he conceded that McCarthy's probe may have hastened the suspensions. More important, thirteen of the thirty-five had already been reinstated because "no charge of sufficient substance" had been brought against them. Most of the rest either had hearings or were awaiting hearings. Even more important, Stevens said, "There has been no case in which anyone of these 35 people has pleaded the fifth amendment or refused to answer any questions that have been put to them."

The perspective that Secretary Stevens thus provided to the committee seemed beyond the ability of the participating senators to grasp. They might have asked of themselves and of Senator McCarthy in particular: What are we all doing here? Where is the threat to the Republic? But no one raised such questions. Neither committee members nor television broadcasters were willing to look beyond the petty trivia on which the attention of the committee, the press, and the country had focused.

Also overlooked was a statement released on the day before Stevens's appearance by a leading scientific group, the

Federation of American Scientists, as part of a 30,000-word study charging that "substantial damage" to defense research had resulted from the investigations at Fort Monmouth. The report noted that more than two score civilian employees had been suspended or suffered loss of clearance, though none of them had been accused of espionage and McCarthy had turned up no evidence of espionage at the base. "Of over 120 charges against 19 employees which were analyzed in detail, only six involved Communist membership or affiliation, five of which were denied under oath," the report stated. "The sixth was an admission of attending Communist meetings with the employee's mother at the age of 12 or 13."

At the conclusion of Stevens's testimony that day, Jenkins asked, "Was the investigation of Fort Monmouth an unfair treatment of the Army, considering the results obtained?"

Said Stevens: "It was not fair to the American people, to create in the minds of the public and of the services the idea that there was a lot of current espionage going on at Fort Monmouth when such was not the case." But fair or not, if the public had that impression, the first three days of hearings, and certainly Secretary Stevens's testimony, had done nothing to dispel it. Something had to be done to save face for the Army. And it was just that challenge that the Army's freshly minted counsel from Boston now undertook to meet.

8

Turning the Tide

After three days of hearings McCarthy had every reason to be pleased with himself. With his boldness and relentlessness he had dominated the first day. "It is clear that Senator McCarthy will use every weapon at his command—and they are numerous—in this case in which he is one of the accused as well as accuser," James Reston wrote in the *New York Times* about McCarthy's opening-day performance. And for the next two days it was not so much his aggressiveness as the boneheadedness of his adversaries that kept him on top.

It was on the fourth day, April 27, that Joe Welch struck back, with the swiftness and cunning of a mongoose, and began the process of slowly but steadily stealing the hearings from McCarthy. "Mr. Chairman, I don't know what it is, but it is a point of something," Welch began with a sly allusion to McCarthy's favorite parliamentary weapon, his innumerable "points of order." Welch's "point of something," as he explained, was that "a doctored photograph" had been presented to the committee. It was a bold charge to make, and if Welch's accusation did not hold up it would be bad news for him and for his client, the Army. But Welch was not running as much of a risk as it might seem. Late the previous evening, while he was still pondering how to respond to the photo of Stevens and Schine introduced by Jenkins, which had caught him off guard, the day was saved by a phone call from the official Army photographer at McGuire Air Force Base. He was incensed because the photo he had taken of three people had been altered to make it seem like a photo of two people, Stevens and Schine.

Welch immediately had the authentic photo flown to Washington the next morning, and breathed a sigh of relief. The next day he sought to exploit his good fortune. "I show you now a photograph in respect of which I charge that what was offered in evidence yesterday was an altered, shamefully cut-down picture, so that somebody could say to Stevens, 'Were you not photographed alone with David Schine?' when the truth is he was photographed in a group." The "group" turned out to be two other persons besides Schine and Stevens, a Col. J. T. Bradley, the commander of McGuire Air Force Base, and Frank Carr, executive director of the special committee, who was only partially visible. It may have been a small group, but it was certainly not, as Ray Jenkins presented it, the Army secretary and the private in *pas de deux*.

With this surprise thrust, forcing Ray Jenkins and the McCarthy side of the controversy on the defensive, Joseph Nye Welch announced his presence as a figure to be reckoned with in the hearings. If his gambit with the controversial photo was a surprise, so, to most of the outside world, was Welch's emergence as a force. After all, his experience as a Boston lawyer specializing in anti-trust and estate law was as far removed from the various forms of connivery being examined in the hearing room as were Welch's humble origins, a long way from his exalted status in the New England legal community.

He was the son of English parents, his mother a housemaid and his father, William, a runaway who had enlisted in the

Royal Navy at fourteen. William Welch's wanderlust eventually took him to the American Midwest and to his brother's farm in Illinois, where his future wife, Martha, was the hired girl. Although a decent fellow, William had developed during his years at sea a weakness for strong drink. His bride, to preserve the young couple's chances of survival, moved her family to a farm in Iowa near the town of Primghar, a name derived from the initials of its first settlers. Primghar's great virtue to Martha Welch was that within its borders saloons were unknown. It was in Primghar, in 1890, that Joseph, the youngest of William and Martha's seven children, was born.

Welch's father had a hard time earning a living from the Midwestern soil and worked as a handyman to make ends meet. In the soothing flow of later memory, young Joseph recalled "the blessing of being poor and totally unaware of it." Prodded by his mother, he threw himself into his schoolwork while clerking for two years in a real estate office to help his family get by. He occasionally sought relief from this drudgery at, of all places, the local courthouse, where the give-and-take of the adversarial legal system fascinated him. "I was impressed by the fact that a lawyer could say something and then say, 'Strike it out,'" Welch later recalled. "That seemed to me to be a particularly godlike quality."

With $600 in savings he headed off to Grinnell College where he pursued the same demanding work ethic, waiting on tables in the campus dining rooms during the school year while during vacations selling maps door to door to Iowa farmers for $1.95, of which he was able to keep the dollar for himself. He graduated from Grinnell with a Phi Beta Kappa key and then won a $600 scholarship to Harvard Law School. The night before he left home for Harvard, his father inquired whether Cambridge was near to Iowa. Told its actual location, William Welch dug into the little grey box on the living room shelf and handed to his son the $19 that represented his lifetime savings. "He gave me all a father could, all he had," Welch recalled years later.

At Harvard, Welch did his parents and himself proud, finishing second in his class. Graduating in 1917 after marrying a Georgia girl he had met while she was attending Boston's Emerson College, he enlisted in the Army and was selected for officers training school; but the war ended before he was commissioned. Now he sought a job at the prestigious Boston firm of Hale and Dorr. His record at Harvard helped him but so did his background as a door-to-door salesman. The managing partner reasoned that selling maps to tightfisted farmers in the flat, precisely laid-out counties of Iowa was akin to selling iceboxes to Eskimos—and took him on. By 1936 Welch had become a senior partner and head of the firm's trial department.

His rise in his profession was of course accompanied by a significant enhancement in his financial status. One way he compensated for the privations of his youth was to turn himself into a latter-day Beau Brummell. He admitted that his closets held 18 suits and 18 pairs of slacks, but his greatest weakness was for bow ties. He owned 150 of them, a number that seemed even to him somewhat disproportionate. When Welch's house in Walpole, Massachusetts, was looted while he was on vacation and his entire wardrobe stolen, he told police that he was missing 75 ties because he was abashed to admit he owned 150.

Although his courtroom skills won him a national reputation in legal circles, Welch was little known outside the profession. He had shrugged off questions about his view of McCarthyism by claiming, "I'm just for the facts." *Time*, profiling him early in the hearings, reported, "Welch has never been active in politics or civic affairs."

But there was more to Welch than he let on. In the 1920s he had been caught up in the Sacco and Vanzetti case, which not only embroiled the Massachusetts courts but provoked worldwide controversy. Welch had once lived in Braintree, site of the payroll robbery and murders for which the two anarchists were convicted and executed. He was close to Herbert B. Ehrman, one of the defense lawyers, and knew Judge Webster Thayer, who sentenced the defendants to death, and on whose stubbornness Welch blamed the outcome of the trial. Later he told associates that he was deeply disturbed by the result and felt that justice had been overshadowed by popular passions and political expediency. Indeed, by some accounts he saw a parallel between that case and the excesses of McCarthyism.

But these feelings Welch confided only to a few people close to him. The public saw only the patrician Boston lawyer, in his custom-made three-piece suits and button-down oxford shirts, who insisted on writing out everything in longhand and treating one and all with consummate courtesy. He was aided in his practice, as he would be during the committee hearings, by an engaging, self-effacing courtroom style. This unprepossessing manner would prove to be a devastating weapon when he was confronted by Washington figures who were untroubled by a sense of humility. Too late Roy Cohn would discover that Welch had "an unerring instinct for the jugular."

One person who did recognize this quality long before Cohn was Bruce Bromley, one of the eminences of the New York bar. Bromley was a former New York appeals judge and a legendary litigator. But more important, when it came to matters touching on politics he enjoyed the full confidence of the governor of New York, Thomas E. Dewey, no mean shakes as a lawyer himself. Twice defeated as a GOP presidential candidate and in 1954 in his third term as governor of New York, Dewey was the man probably most responsible for the presidential nomination of Dwight Eisenhower over the bitter opposition of Republican conservatives.

A highly self-contained personality, Dewey had turned back a range of feelers from Eisenhower about presidential appointments, including the chief justiceship of the Supreme Court. He had already achieved plenty of glory in his life, yet he knew that nothing he gained could erase the sting of the humiliation he had suffered in 1948 when Harry Truman denied him the presidency everyone thought he had as good as won. After his defeat, Dewey reacted with grace and humor, traits that surprised most people and would have served him well had he exhibited them to the voters in his ill-fated campaign. Bidding farewell to loyal supporters, Dewey remarked that his circumstance reminded him of the successful wake at which a mourner overdrowned his sorrows, passed out, and was placed in a handy coffin to sleep it off. He awoke at dawn with a lily in his hand and wondered, "If I am alive what am I doing in this coffin? And if I am dead, why do I have to go to the bathroom?"

Dewey had watched the president he had helped install in the White House struggle with the problem of McCarthy for more than a year. With the Army-McCarthy hearings about to begin, he could not have been greatly surprised when the president's aides turned to him for help in selecting legal representation for the Army. Realizing that Eisenhower needed an extraordinarily adroit lawyer on his side, Dewey sought the advice of Bruce Bromley, whom Dewey had appointed to the bench. And Bromley suggested Joe Welch.

So it was that in April 1954, as Welch was in his Boston office talking with a widow about a will, he was interrupted by a phone call from Bromley, an old friend. Bromley strongly suggested, to put it mildly, that Welch fly to New York and meet him at his private New York club. Welch took the next plane. When he arrived at his assigned destination he found Bromley with a man whom even a political outsider like Welch had no trouble recognizing, Tom Dewey. Together this pair pressed upon Welch the idea that it was his duty as a citizen and a member of the bar to represent the Army, now faced with the most critical peacetime challenge in its history.

Welch protested, pointing to his supposed inadequacy for the job. "I told them I would not know how to comport myself in the presence of television and radio," Welch later recalled. "It didn't seem to make much impression—they said they still wanted me to represent them." Welch inevitably assented, agreeing to take the job *pro bono*, and Dewey was obviously appreciative. When Welch summoned to Washington the two lawyers he had asked to assist him, James St. Clair and the unfortunate Fred Fisher, Dewey saw to it that both men were given his private phone number if they needed help when they arrived in Washington.

In the same modest vein with which he stressed his deficiencies in talking to Bromley and Dewey, Welch would later claim to have been terrified by his first glimpse of the Senate caucus room: "So many cameras, so much television, those movies, that bank of lights." But whatever timidity he actually felt he soon overcame, as he demonstrated with his exposure of the altered photo.

No one was more shattered by this revelation than the unwitting perpetrator of the fraud Welch had revealed, Ray Jenkins. The day before, when Jenkins had emerged seemingly triumphant in his duel with the hapless Stevens, his own hopes for the U.S. Senate had presumably risen. Now he found himself in the position of being a dupe.

What's more, Welch did not exactly help Jenkins's situation when he addressed his counterpart directly. "Mr. Jenkins, I would like to say with all of my power, sir, I know you would never participate in a trick like this, but I suggest to you that you were imposed upon."

All Jenkins could do was to aver that the now controversial photo had been presented to him "by one of the parties in interest in this case, and I might say an adverse party of interest to Mr. Stevens, as being the genuine authentic photograph. And I presented it in good faith as authentic."

But before Jenkins could make further efforts to explain, McCarthy broke in with another of what had by now become his inevitable points of order: "The point of order is this: That Mr. Welch under the guise of making a point of order has testified that a picture is doctored. And he makes the completely false statement that this is a group picture and it is not."

But on this occasion Ray Jenkins, who had been letting McCarthy have his way, apparently felt less kindly disposed toward the senator, having been misled by one of his aides. Jenkins whispered in Chairman Mundt's ear, whereupon Mundt interrupted McCarthy. "Counsel advises the chair that the Senator is engaging in a statement or cross-examination," he said, "rather than a point of order."

McCarthy did not take kindly to this refinement. "I am getting rather sick of being interrupted in the middle of a sentence," he complained.

This was too much for Democrat Stuart Symington, who was to be the most confrontational of the Democratic committee members. "I would like to say that this is not a point of order," Symington interjected, "it is out of order."

"Oh, be quiet," McCarthy characteristically retorted.

But Symington, unlike Chairman Mundt earlier in the proceedings, stood his ground. "I haven't the slightest intention of being quiet," Symington replied evenly. "Counsel is running this committee, and you are not running it."

Suddenly within the cavernous caucus room itself, and in millions of living rooms around the country, it became apparent to everyone watching—to the committee members and their aides, the opposing counsel, the press, the spectators in Room 318, and the television viewers in their homes—that the chemistry of the hearings had been transformed. Mc-

Carthy had been forced to abandon his customary accusatory stance and instead to find ways to fend off Joe Welch. This Harvard-trained lawyer with the genteel demeanor had suddenly turned into the most formidable adversary McCarthy had ever faced. The hearings, as Welch and his colleagues acknowledged—only to themselves for the moment—had passed a turning point. And Joe Welch was only beginning to drive his advantage home.

McCarthy did have a chance to get his oar in with a question for Secretary Stevens, who remained on the witness stand. "Let me say that whether you had your picture with Schine alone or with another colonel, doesn't concern me. And I don't think it improper at all. I think you are entitled to have your picture taken wherever you want to. But do you think that having another colonel in the picture standing on the other side of the private, does that decrease or increase the significance in any way?"

It was a fair question, and for once Stevens gave the best answer possible for his side. "I think it increases the significance of what is happening here tremendously," he said. "Because it shows that somebody has taken it upon themselves to edit the information that is going to come before the committee." The question and the answer neatly summed up the argument, which reflected credit on neither side. On the one hand was the inappropriateness of Secretary Stevens being photographed with a private soldier who was the central figure in a controversy swirling around the Army and an investigating committee of the United States Senate. On the other hand was the deceit involved in altering the photo to heighten its impact.

But who had altered the photo? This was the question that Ray Jenkins, struggling to redeem his own reputation, now pursued as Stevens was excused and Roy Cohn took the witness stand. Jenkins demanded to know the pedigree of the controversial picture. From the start, as he later acknowledged,

Cohn hurt his cause, and McCarthy's, by his self-assurance, bordering on arrogance: "At the outset may I have the record indicate that I am not represented by counsel and that none of the various persons here as aides represent me in any way. I am here myself and I am here to answer any questions which Mr. Jenkins might have to ask of me."

Visibly upset, Jenkins referred to a conference he and Cohn had had five days earlier as Jenkins prepared for his cross-examination of Stevens. Had not Cohn told him that on November 17, 1953, in the midst of this controversy with Mc-Carthy over the treatment of Schine, Stevens had asked to be photographed with David Schine?

Cohn confirmed that. And he went on to claim that the photo was proof that Stevens had acted in bad faith in charging that Cohn had been guilty of "improper inducement and persuasions" on behalf of David Schine. Refuting those charges, Cohn now argued, was the fact that long after this improper pressure had supposedly been brought, "Mr. Stevens was not only most solicitous of Private Schine, but was in his company, not only once but twice and had asked that he be photographed with Private Schine. That is what I told you, sir, and that is the fact." At Jenkins's request, Cohn had asked a member of his staff to send a copy of the photo of Schine and Stevens to Jenkins, "a blown-up copy," he added. "I now find on inquiry a member of the staff saw some third person who was not recognized standing to the side. They thought the third person had no relevance and that the picture wanted was the picture of Stevens and Schine. That is what was blown up and that is what was sent up to you."

Had Cohn ever said anything to him, Jenkins, about a third person in the photo? Jenkins asked.

No, Cohn said. "I think it makes not the slightest bit of difference, sir," he added. Regardless of Colonel Bradley's disappearance from the photo, "this is a picture of Secretary Stevens and Mr. Schine looking at each other, taken on an occasion when Mr. Stevens flew down to see Mr. Schine after he claims he had been threatened and improperly persuaded and induced."

Jenkins gave up and dismissed the witness.

Of course Cohn was right that it should have made no substantive difference that others were in the photo with Stevens and Schine. Their presence did not alter Stevens's fundamental folly in having himself photographed with Schine at a time when he supposedly felt himself greatly imposed upon by Senator McCarthy and his staff. Not to mention that having arranged the plane trip to McGuire Air Force Base for McCarthy and Cohn, and then chauffeuring them to Fort Dix before the picture-taking, Stevens had then insisted that they take his plane to their next destination, Boston, while he headed back to Washington "some other way." There was no reasonable purpose that could be construed for his doing that except, as Cohn suggested, to fawn upon McCarthy and persuade him to postpone or abandon his inquiry into the Army.

But Cohn's career was built on taking maximum advantage of any opportunity open to him. In this case he had seen the chance to worsen the harm the secretary of the Army had inflicted upon himself by making it appear that Schine and Stevens were a twosome, not just part of a quartet. And he had asked his staff to produce a photo of Stevens and Schine, not a photo of Stevens and whoever else happened to be there. By doing so, however, he had presented an opportunity to Joe Welch. And Welch now set about deflecting attention from the clearly indiscreet behavior of the secretary of the Army to the question of how and why falsified evidence had been presented to the committee. This was an issue bound to stir memories of Senator McCarthy's past, memories that he would prefer be forgotten, including the use of a phony photograph by McCarthy's allies in the campaign to unseat Senator Millard Tydings in 1950.

Welch's best opportunity to emphasize the altering of the photo came after Cohn had submitted to further grilling by committee members. Finally it was Welch's turn to confront Cohn directly. In accordance with the committee's rules of procedure, he was given only ten minutes. But they may have been the longest ten minutes of Roy Cohn's life.

Welch began on an amiable note. "Mr. Cohn, I assume you would like it understood that although you and I sit at the same table, I am not your counsel," he said.

All Cohn had to do was accept this gentle tease. But Cohn had already demonstrated his inability to let well enough alone, and he could not do that in this case. Instead he fell back on his flair for gratuitous remarks. "There is not a statement that has been made at this hearing with which I am in more complete agreement, Mr. Welch," he said. Perhaps he would be fortunate if Welch were his counsel, Cohn said, though it was clear he did not really think that for a moment. "Roy Cohn is here speaking for Roy Cohn, to give the facts," he declared. "I have no counsel and I feel the need of none."

Inwardly Welch must have licked his chops. Outwardly, though, he continued the light banter. "In all modesty, sir, I am content that it should appear from my end that I am not your counsel."

Still Cohn would let him have the last word. "I might say that you are certainly not going to get any fee from me, Mr. Welch."

Welch now focused on the controversial photo, the original of which hung on the wall of David Schine's office in New York, which he still maintained as a link to his happier days as a civilian. Cohn had described the photo as showing Stevens smiling at Shine. "It is a grim smile on Stevens's face," Welch suggested.

Cohn went along. "If you want to call Mr. Stevens's smile a grim smile, sir, I fully accept what you say." In any case, Cohn said, it was a photo of Stevens and Schine. "They are standing next to each other. They are looking at each other."

But Welch insisted that in the photo Stevens was looking to his right, and to his right was not only Schine but also Colonel Bradley. So maybe, Welch suggested, Stevens was looking at Bradley, not Schine. "It would take someone with clairvoyance to know at whom Secretary Stevens is looking, would it not?"

"No, sir, I don't think so," Cohn replied. He was not about to give ground. "It would take somebody with common sense who can look at a picture and see what is in it."

Welch ignored the rebuff. "I think I observe on Colonel Bradley's face a faint little look of pleasure. Do you, sir?"

Cohn had yet to learn to be sufficiently wary of Welch. So he unwisely offered a quip. "I would say I know that Colonel Bradley had a good steak dinner shortly afterward. Maybe he was anticipating that."

Once again he had set up Welch, who responded without a moment's hesitation. Alluding to the look of self-satisfaction on Schine's face, he retorted, "If Bradley is feeling good about a steak dinner, Schine must be considering a whole haunch of beef." The spectators roared with laughter.

When Welch's time ran out, Cohn was saved from further harassment by Welch. But he was not spared the scorn of his own boss. As Cohn and McCarthy walked to the elevator together during the lunch-hour recess, McCarthy told him, "You were about the worst witness I ever heard in my life," and then proceeded to explain his judgment in detail.

Just then Senator Symington, coming up behind the two men, could not resist a quip. "Don't be too hard on him, Joe," Symington said. "I'll give you fifty dollars for his brain any day." For once Cohn could think of no reply. Later he admitted that at the moment he thought Symington would be overpaying.

But the end of Cohn's testimony did not mean that Welch was prepared to drop the issue of the altered photo. He pursued the matter through the week until on Friday, April 30, the seventh day of the hearings, James Juliana, a former FBI man and an investigator on McCarthy's staff, testified that he was responsible for altering the photo but denied any attempt at deception. As Juliana told the story, the original photo, which showed three persons—Schine, Stevens, and Colonel Bradley—had been sent to Roy Cohn in Washington because Jenkins asked for the photo so he could confront Stevens with it. Cohn asked Juliana to have copies made, and Juliana turned that task over to another McCarthy aide, also a former FBI agent, Don Surine, the very same person who had conveyed McCarthy's threat to expose Edward R. Murrow.

At the mention of Surine's name, ears pricked up in the hearing room. Although no one there knew of Surine's role in trying to intimidate Murrow, Surine had made his mark in another controversy. He had come under the scrutiny of the Senate Elections Subcommittee that had investigated McCarthy's role in the defeat of Tydings in 1950. The subcommittee had criticized the contents of an anti-Tydings campaign tabloid which included among other material a composite photo showing Tydings listening to Earl Browder, the onetime leader of the American Communist party. The campaign manager for John Marshall Butler, the Republican candidate who defeated Tydings, took responsibility for the tabloid and was fined for violating Maryland election laws. But in its report the subcommittee investigating the election found that some of the photos used in the tabloid were provided by members of Senator McCarthy's staff, "including particularly Don Surine."

The report also cited conflicts in Surine's testimony before the subcommittee, notably his claim that he had "voluntarily" resigned from the FBI. That assertion was later contradicted by FBI chief J. Edgar Hoover, who explained that Surine had been fired because of his disregard of Bureau regulations. Although the FBI would not say, he was suspected of having sexual relations with a prostitute involved in a white-slavery probe conducted by the FBI.

Mindful of this background, Welch probed deeper with Juliana. "Did you turn to Mr. Surine for assistance on the picture because you considered him peculiarly adept in dealing with pictures?" he asked.

"No, sir," Juliana said.

But Senator Jackson wanted to know more about why Surine was chosen to copy the photo.

Juliana's answer was that Surine had more experience on Capitol Hill. "What do you mean, experience?" Jackson asked.

"He has been working in the building here a lot longer," was Juliana's not very illuminating reply.

Having dodged that issue, Juliana went on with what he claimed to be a perfectly innocent explanation for the altered photo. In response to Juliana's request, Surine had produced two sets of photos, one of the three men, and the other of only Schine and Stevens. Juliana then chose the photo that showed only the two men, mounted it on white cardboard, and turned it over to Jenkins and subsequently to the pages of history. The reason he chose this picture, and not the photo of the threesome, he said, "is because that is what I was led to believe you wanted in the hearings."

Senator Jackson asked if Juliana did not think his choice of photos was significant because of the emphasis in Jenkins's interrogation of Stevens as to whether the secretary had ever been photographed "alone" with Schine. The word "alone" meant nothing to him at the time, Juliana testified.

But Jackson pressed him. "Didn't you know from what you read in the papers that night?" the senator asked.

"I have not read the papers in two weeks," Juliana said.

Juliana's professed indifference to current events got him through to the lunch break but did not spare him further grilling, this from Welch. The counsel for the Army wanted to know if Juliana had been asked for something different than the photo of the three men that hung on the wall of David Schine's New York office. "I never knew what hung on Schine's wall," Juliana responded.

But Welch pushed harder. "You did know what hung on Schine's wall when that was handed to you," he told Juliana.

But Juliana, who saw ignorance as his best defense, did not budge. "I did not know what hung on Schine's wall."

Welch seemingly incredulous, let his imagination roam. "Did you think this came from a pixie?"

Juliana remained his stolid self. "I had no idea," he said.

But his boss was struck by Welch's terminology, and like Cohn, having not yet learned not to push Welch too hard, picked up on the expression "pixie."

"Will the counsel for my benefit define—I think he might be an expert on that—what a pixie is?" Senator McCarthy asked.

Once again Welch never hesitated. "Yes, I should say, Mr. Senator, that a pixie is a close relative of a fairy. Shall I proceed, sir? Have I enlightened you?"

The audience burst into laughter once again while Roy Cohn sat in glum silence. McCarthy could only weakly respond. "As I said, I think you may be an authority on what a pixie is."

In the wake of this exchange, with its unmistakable allusion to the suspected sexual preference of his chief counsel, McCarthy tried to forestall further damage to Don Surine. The Democratic members of the committee wanted to call Surine to testify about the photo, which would open an old can of unattractive worms, and McCarthy objected strenuously. He argued that the committee had heard all that needed to be heard on the matter of the disputed photo. No purpose would be served by calling Surine, whom McCarthy described as only "a messenger" carrying out instructions from Cohn and Juliana.

Hard-pressed, McCarthy now reached into his bag of tricks. He had agreed to step down as chairman of the committee, he contended, only because he had accepted the ground rules the committee had adopted. "But if there were any change in the ground rules during the proceeding, then I would insist upon resuming my place on the committee," McCarthy said. No one on the committee could recall any such pact. But Mundt was not prepared to meet McCarthy's challenge, and Surine was not called, saving McCarthy from further embarrassment, at least for the moment.

Even so, Welch had done considerable damage. Now, though, as Stevens resumed his testimony, it began to seem that while Welch could handle McCarthy and Cohn fairly well, his own client was a more serious problem. Stevens's next difficulty as a witness centered on Maj. Gen. Kirke B. Lawton, the commandant at Fort Monmouth, the Army Signal Corps research center in New Jersey and the focal point for McCarthy's Army spy hunt.

Lawton had made himself a problem for Stevens the preceding November. While giving a series of lectures to selected officers and key civilians at the post, he had credited McCarthy with forcing Stevens to tighten Army rules governing subversives and had asserted that any witness taking the Fifth Amendment was *ipso facto* a Communist. For good measure Lawton added that certain universities, notably the City College of New York, Columbia, and Harvard, fostered leftist ideas among their students. These lectures followed Lawton's closed-door testimony before McCarthy's committee the month before, during which by implication he had favorably contrasted McCarthy's vigor in pursuing subversives with the apparent indifference shown by Stevens. To Stevens, all this added up to a case for removing the general from his hypersensitive post, a move that would seem justified by the norms of military behavior such as obeisance to the chain of command.

But the secretary, since McCarthy had thrust himself into his life, appeared no longer capable of making a decision, let alone carrying it out. His main motivation as Army secretary now seemed to be to shield himself and the institution he led from McCarthy. Accordingly, he had dispatched John Adams, his counsel, to McCarthy to sound him out about deposing Lawton.

It was bad enough that Stevens was forced to admit to having done this, under close questioning by Roy Cohn and Ray Jenkins. Even worse, his confession had to be almost literally dragged out of him. Cohn went at the matter directly. "Did you on November 24 send John Adams to New York to talk to me and talk to Senator McCarthy to ask whether Senator McCarthy would agree not to make a public issue if you relieved General Lawton of his command at Fort Monmouth?" he asked Stevens.

In his first of many attempts to evade answering the question, Stevens said he thought Adams had gone to New York to attend the hearing McCarthy was holding there. Cohn came back at him, reiterating the question and pressing for an answer. Stevens responded with a ramble during which he mentioned how much he disliked going into "the personal situation of a fine professional soldier." But he also acknowledged his concern about Lawton's statements and his judgment in suspending some Fort Monmouth employees suspected of links to subversive activity. What he did not do was answer the question.

That brought Ray Jenkins into the fray to try his hand. Was Adams's assignment to get McCarthy's assurances that he would not admonish Stevens for removing Lawton? he asked Stevens.

"No," said Stevens, "I wanted to inform Senator McCarthy of the fact that I had that matter under consideration."

So Cohn tried again, with his original question, and got the same nonresponsive answer that Stevens had just given to Jenkins. He had asked Adams to inform McCarthy that he was considering removing Lawton, Stevens reiterated, and that was all the secretary would say.

Jenkins pushed again, seeking a yes or no answer, and did not get it. Back to Cohn, who tried a different tack. Did Stevens remember that after talking to McCarthy, Adams had passed on to his boss the "bad news" that McCarthy would not promise to stay silent if Stevens dumped Lawton?

Stevens did not remember that exactly, but he did recall Adams telling him McCarthy was distressed, because Lawton had cooperated fully with his committee.

Jenkins kept pressing. Why inform McCarthy? It was Secretary Stevens's responsibility to keep Lawton or remove him.

"Because of my policy of continued cooperation with the committees of Congress," was Stevens's feeble effort to make a virtue of his equivocation.

As the afternoon drew to a close, Jenkins tried to sum up what Stevens had claimed to be the case: Lawton had been kept at his post, Stevens was contending, because "he was the right man to continue there," and the fact that McCarthy would have disapproved of his removal had nothing to do with it.

"Absolutely not," Stevens said, again affirming Jenkins's interpretation and imposing on the credulity of his listeners. "I settled it on the merits."

A week had passed, and so far the hearings had reflected little credit on anyone involved. They had generated little mail except to the senators directly involved, and some of them were beginning to question the value of their work. At one point Arkansas's John McClellan asked Stevens to calculate the number of man-hours involved in preparing for his testimony, a figure which Stevens had trouble getting around to providing, possibly because it would have been embarrassingly high.

Chairman Mundt reported receiving about four hundred letters, one-third pro-McCarthy, one-third against the senator, and the rest demanding an early end to the hearings. Likewise, Republicans Potter and Dworshak also reported hearing from constituents who wanted the proceedings stopped.

Democratic Congressman John Blatnik of Minnesota said of the letters he received about the hearings, most were from citizens who were "upset and disgusted."

Indeed the tedium, bickering, and pettiness had a way of drawing attention even as it got under the skin of many people. Dr. Charles Mayo, chief of the renowned Mayo Clinic, said the hearings were "so far below the dignity of this country that it is almost not understandable" that they threatened to raise blood pressures around the country. "I will look at it, but I don't agree that it should be happening."

At his press conference, President Eisenhower was asked what he thought about all the fuss over the privileges granted a private soldier. "I trust I will be excused for declining to talk about something that . . ." In his indignation he did not finish his sentence. Flushed and glaring he said, "I mean the whole business. I do not think it is something to talk about very much." Privately he was more forthcoming. "The McCarthy-Army argument, and its reporting are close to disgusting," he wrote his boyhood friend Edward "Swede" Hazlett. "It saddens me that I must feel ashamed for the United States Senate."

Some others might have seen at least an equal cause for shame among the leaders of the Army, not to mention those in the White House. But this did not occur to the president.

The reaction from editorial writers at home and abroad could only add to Ike's distress. The *New York Times* contended that McCarthy had done "grave damage to the safety and security of the United States." But the *Times* also condemned the Senate which "while wishing he weren't around has failed to accept the responsibility for McCarthy." The *Philadelphia Inquirer* called the hearings "a circus spectacle," which is "diverting and dividing the people of the United States when they should be united and concentrating on the grim threats of peril from the outside world."

Indeed, even as Welch and Cohn bickered about the altered photograph of Stevens and Schine, the long-developing crisis in Indochina was worsening. Two weeks before the hearings began, President Eisenhower had declared the defeat of Communist aggression in Southeast Asia to be vitally important to the United States and had outlined the "domino theory" of the Communist threat. "You have a row of dominoes set up," Eisenhower said, referring to the several nations of Southeast Asia. "You knock over the first one and what will happen to the last is that it will go over very quickly."

Nevertheless Eisenhower refused French pleas for direct U.S. military aid in Indochina. And on May 7, 1954, as the Army-McCarthy hearings were starting their third week, the French garrison at the beleaguered stronghold of Dienbienphu surrendered to Viet Minh Gen. Vo Nguyen Giap, presaging the end of French rule in the region.

The seriousness of the Communist surge in Asia heightened the incongruity of the Army-McCarthy hearings in the view of America's World War II allies and partners in the cold war struggle. In Britain the *Manchester Guardian* scolded, "The activities of Senator McCarthy and others like him have left people—both in the United States and abroad—astonished that the Senate can allow them to act in its name." Echoing the contention of the Federation of American Scientists, the

Guardian wrote that McCarthy's probe of Fort Monmouth "must have done immense damage to the working of a vital defense research establishment and it did not uncover espionage or subversion—and yet the Senate did nothing." Cassandra, the widely read columnist for the racy London tabloid the *Daily Mirror*, used more pungent language, describing the hearings as "this steamy miasma of muddy incompetence. The stink, the stench and the stain can only be counteracted by an even bigger stink and stench and stain."

Everett Dirksen did not need Cassandra to tell him the hearings were verging on a fiasco for his party. Dirksen had not wanted the hearings in the first place, fearing just such an embarrassment. But this was a case where being right gave him no satisfaction. Instead, at a closed session of the committee following the weeklong furor over the altered photo, Dirksen sought to persuade his colleagues to call the whole thing off, except for the testimony of Stevens and McCarthy. "Serious consideration" was being given to such a course of action, he told reporters.

But Democrat Symington promptly contradicted him. "No serious consideration was being given to limiting the hearings to only two of the principals," Symington insisted. Speaking for his fellow Democrats, Symington said all six principals should be heard—the others being Adams, Hensel, Cohn, and Carr.

Republicans, however, did not give up on the idea of putting an end to the affair. Some on the committee offered a convoluted remedy: speed up the hearings by reducing television coverage. "If the hearings are not televised they would be expedited materially," contended Michigan's Potter. And Senator Dworshak, McCarthy's supernumerary, supported hastening the pace. A cutback on television might help, he argued, "if only by discouraging some who otherwise might want to use what should be a news medium for publicity purposes."

Who these publicity hounds might be, Dworshak did not say. He certainly could not be accused of grandstanding or doing much of anything else in the hearings, including supporting McCarthy the way the senator had expected him to. Indeed, McCarthy had already publicly expressed his regrets at having chosen Dworshak, explaining that he had done so only because his first choice, Republican senator John Marshall Butler of Maryland, was ill. "I now wish he had been feeling well," McCarthy said.

When it came to grandstanding, by far the most obvious culprit was McCarthy, with his constant points of order and his discursive questioning of Stevens and other witnesses, leading Welch to accuse him of "filibuster by cross-examination." But Dworshak did not single out his sponsor for blame, thus avoiding putting himself even further in the senator's bad graces.

The political reality of the hearings was best summed up by Republican senator H. Alexander Smith of New Jersey, who at age seventy-four, with ten years in the Senate behind him, did not shrink from candor. "The Republicans in the Congress are casting discredit on the Administration because of these hearings," he declared. "I think this spectacle will hurt the Republican Party while the Democrats are feasting."

The damage was twofold, as lawmakers privately acknowledged. On the one hand the Eisenhower administration was depicted as weak-kneed and hypocritical because of the behavior of Army Secretary Stevens. On the other hand McCarthy was being hurt too. As the syndicated columnist Thomas L. Stokes wrote, "The bully in the Senate comes out plainly as he tries to take over an investigation in which he himself is on trial. The sly trickster in him, so well known here, comes out as he seeks to divert the testimony from the issue and as he smugly resorts to innuendoes and half-truths." Damaging McCarthy's prestige threatened to deny Republicans a weapon they had relied on heavily for four years in partisan combat.

Others in both parties preferred to avoid discussing the political impact and to issue their criticism from a lofty perch, based supposedly on their concern for civic health. Democratic Congressman Henderson Lanham of Georgia called the hearings "the sorriest spectacle of our generation." Referring to the siege of Dienbienphu, he warned that the hearings were obscuring the fact that "Indo-China and all of Southeast Asia are being lost to the Free World." The hearings "are harming the country," said Senator Burnet R. Maybank of South Carolina. "The charges ought to be investigated, but I'm against doing it in a televised vaudeville show."

The paradox of such criticism was that in some ways the television networks covering the hearings might have been happier with vaudeville than with the pomposity and trivia that so often clogged the proceedings. The problem for television was cost and content. For both reasons, though primarily the first, NBC had dropped coverage after two days. "It cost us a lot of money last week" and might cost the precious goodwill of advertisers, a network spokesman told the *New York Times*. An idea of just how much money was provided by the trade publication *Broadcasting/Telecasting*, which estimated that continued coverage of the hearings by NBC, ABC, and DuMont, and by radio, would cost about $10.5 million in airtime, labor and equipment costs, and losses from cancellation of regularly scheduled commercial programs. It was just that sort of red ink that scared CBS away at the outset, though it continued to provide daily summaries each evening, as NBC now began to do.

"George Herman and I were assigned to monitor daylong hearings and prepare a summary for half-hour specials every night," recalled the veteran broadcast journalist Daniel Schorr, then a correspondent for CBS. "We made comments as we went along." Schorr had no strong opinions at first about CBS's decision not to offer live coverage. "But after a while, as the controversy grew, we had to wonder whether CBS had made a mistake," he said. "But it was decided it was too late to make a change."

What made it relatively easy for NBC to drop the live shows, and for CBS to keep away, was that the hearings at first glance had not matched the high ratings and considerable excitement stirred by the Kefauver crime inquiries. According to the Hooper Service, then the major audience rating agency for television, the McCarthy hearings in the New York area in the first couple of days drew about as many viewers as the popular variety show hosted by broadcasting veteran Arthur Godfrey, which roughly resembled the sort of "vaudeville" that Senator Maybank had mentioned. In 1951 the Kefauver hearings had won a larger share of the existing audience. But this comparison was fundamentally flawed. In 1951 the crime hearings had almost no competition from other television programs, whereas the McCarthy inquiry was up against CBS's imposing lineup of soap operas. Too, the cast of characters that Kefauver summoned before the cameras was much more vivid and dramatic than the drab, cautious politicians and bureaucrats who peopled the stage of the Army-McCarthy hearings. Even so, given the vast expansion of homes with television, industry analysts estimated that the reach of the Army-McCarthy hearings was far greater than the audience for Kefauver. They had exposed what Jack Gould of the *New York Times* called a fundamental weakness in television journalism—economics. If the committee should decide to hold evening sessions, when the networks collected far more money from sponsors than during the day, "all the networks would have an extremely difficult task" reconciling the public interest with commercial realities, Gould wrote.

This was true enough. But another, more basic problem had to do with the nature of television journalism—the rigid adherence to depicting exactly what was going on at the particular event without offering adequate explanation or interpretation. ABC and DuMont took pride in meeting their obligation to "public service" by devoting five or six hours a day to the hearings—gavel-to-gavel coverage. But was the public interest really being served by this limited approach, which neglected to provide viewers with context and perspective? This was the weakness that had beset the Kefauver hearings. And it was already evident in the first days of the Army-McCarthy proceedings, as exemplified by the failure of the networks to give due emphasis to Secretary Stevens's disclosure and the report by the Federation of American Scientists, both strongly suggesting that the Red hunt at Fort Monmouth was comparable to a snipe hunt.

Despite these problems, the broadcasters could not help but be encouraged by one unexpected development: the emergence of a star performer, a requirement for successful television. Surprisingly this was not Joe McCarthy, as might have been predicted, but rather Joe Welch, the Army's "sly counselor," as *Newsweek* called him. By the end of the first few days it was clear that Welch had quietly but undeniably taken command of the hearings. He had seized the initiative from McCarthy and was now determined to press his advantage.

9

The Purloined Letter

The millions watching the hearings on television had to put up with, as Joe Welch later recalled, "immense stretches of aridity." Yet most viewers stuck with the show because, Welch reasoned, they believed "that at any moment a rocket would take off from this dismal desert." McCarthy's side had fired the first missile on April 26, the third day of the hearings, when they presented the photo of Schine and Stevens. Welch had shot that down. Now, on the ninth day of the hearings, May 4, McCarthy sent up another rocket. But this one blew up in his face.

McCarthy made his bold move late in the afternoon, a few hours after Republicans had given up efforts to cut short the testimony. The four GOP senators on the committee backed off the idea, even though they had the necessary votes, in the face of protests from the three Democratic members and from Welch. The attorney, a professed political naif, sounded like a veteran campaigner when he warned that "a committee vote that was too close in numbers would not leave the American people happy." Drawing on his farming background in Iowa, Welch added that "the American people will demand and should have the long, hard furrow plowed."

The Republicans had the majority, but they also faced a dilemma: they wished to limit the political damage to their party from the continued bickering on TV, but they feared the public reaction to a cutoff, which would appear to be just what it was—a partisan effort to save themselves embarrassment.

So it was that after spending sixty-five minutes discussing the need to speed up the hearings, the committee gave up on the idea. Like Old Man River, the hearings rolled on. But not before another flare-up between McCarthy and Welch. The tension between the two had become a subtext to the proceedings, rivaling in intensity the basic conflict between the Army and McCarthy. The latest disagreement came when Welch backed off a statement he had made the day before. At the time he had seemed to accept the Republican proposal to end the public hearings after Secretary Stevens had concluded his testimony and Senator McCarthy had then been given his chance. But now Welch said that after talking to Jenkins and some committee members he had changed his mind, and that he would want to hear at least from Roy Cohn and Francis Carr in addition to Stevens and McCarthy. Not surprisingly, McCarthy did not take this elliptic explanation with good grace. Making a nasty pun, the senator accused the Army counsel of having "welched" on an agreement he made. He added, "I will only consult with Mr. Welch when he is under oath. I will not consult with a man who makes an agreement and breaks it. As far as I am concerned, it is bad faith."

Stuck with this decision, McCarthy determined at least to liven up the proceedings. Up to now he had been badly flummoxed by Welch. The senator was used to the outrage of indignant liberals—that he could tolerate easily enough. What he was not used to was the lofty scorn and subtle ridicule to which Welch had subjected him and his staff. McCarthy's frustration mounted as the hearings continued, leading him, as Welch plainly intended, to become increasingly desperate and self-destructive.

On the morning of May 4, with Secretary Stevens in the witness chair for the ninth consecutive day, McCarthy reached into his briefcase, pulled out a document, and showed it to the committee's executive director, Frank Carr. "Shall I hit them with this one?" McCarthy asked Carr.

"No, put it back," advised Carr, who retained enough presence of mind to see the trouble that would come from this document.

At first McCarthy seemed to accept this guidance and returned the papers to his briefcase. But fifteen minutes later he could no longer restrain himself. Once again he produced the document with which he now confronted Secretary Stevens, claiming it was "a carbon copy" of a letter supposedly written by J. Edgar Hoover to the Army three years earlier. In the letter, as McCarthy described it, Hoover warned of a ring of subversives at Fort Monmouth and listed thirty-four suspects. Here was tangible proof of what McCarthy had been claiming all along: that Army leaders had recklessly ignored a grave threat to the nation's security at Fort Monmouth until a courageous senator and his committee had forced them to act. It seemed at first to be McCarthy's finest moment in the hearings so far. But it took only a few seconds before Joe Welch broke in to ruin the effect.

"The mere fact that we have an impressive-looking purported copy of such a letter doesn't impress an old-time lawyer," Welch remarked. "I would like to have J. Edgar Hoover say that he wrote the letter and mailed it." Once again, as with his charge that the Schine-Stevens photo had been altered, Welch was not just guessing. He had spent the three weeks following his appointment, before the start of the hearings, combing the Pentagon's files on McCarthy and communism. He was certain there was no Hoover letter there.

Even before Welch's caveat, Ray Jenkins had rushed to judgment, just as he had with the by now notorious Schine-Stevens photo. He ruled that he was accepting the letter as authentic and that it could be used by McCarthy to cross-examine Stevens, "on the assumption that no party of interest and no counsel would refer to a spurious, manufactured document."

McCarthy then asked Stevens to read the letter, but the secretary refused without Hoover's permission. Welch also refused even to look at the letter because he feared that would breach the laws governing confidential FBI matters. In response to nagging from Jenkins about finding the original letter, which should have been in the Army's files, as McCarthy told the story, Welch promised: "We'll find that letter if we have to keep fourteen colonels up for fourteen nights, and we'll get it if it's there. After we've got it, then you'll have the question of what to do with it." It was a pledge he had no trouble making since he was convinced that no such letter existed.

Indeed on the following day, May 5, the tenth day of the hearings, Stevens took the stand to say that the Army had been unable to find any copy of the purported letter from Hoover that McCarthy had introduced with such fanfare the day before. That made sense, as the committee soon discovered, since Hoover had not sent that letter to the Army. According to Robert Collier, a committee aide who had been dispatched to interview Hoover, instead of the three-page letter that McCarthy introduced, the FBI director had sent a fifteen-page memorandum with the same date, January 26, 1951, to Maj. Gen. A. R. Bolling, the Army's chief intelligence officer. This memo, Collier testified, contained "unevaluated" allegations about thirty-four persons at Fort Monmouth.

The letter McCarthy had presented to the committee contained seven paragraphs that were identical with seven paragraphs from Hoover's memo. But the McCarthy version differed in that it contained notations after each name, saying that the FBI information was either "derogatory" or not derogatory. The FBI, Hoover emphasized to Collier, had never provided such evaluations. And he recommended the committee ask Attorney General Brownell to rule on whether national security strictures would allow either the letter or the memo to be made public.

When Welch got his chance to question Collier, he made sure to underline McCarthy's latest humiliation. "As I understand your testimony," Welch remarked to the witness, "this document is a carbon copy of precisely nothing, is that right?"

Collier did not disagree.

As Collier's testimony continued, the proceedings neared farce. But it was a farce with elements of tragedy, in that it dramatized the self-destructive inanity of the security obsession that had overwhelmed the nation and the Eisenhower presidency. Collier, a member of the committee staff and a former FBI agent to boot, had been asked to compare what McCarthy had presented to the committee with what the FBI had originally produced and sent to the Army three years earlier. But he was unable to do this to anyone's satisfaction; like everyone else connected with the hearing, he felt constrained from reading either document because of the dire legal consequences that might follow.

Thus Welch asked Collier, "Am I correct in thinking that you did not read the fifteen-page document in the files of the FBI?"

"You are correct," Collier responded. "I purposely avoided it because it contains security information."

What about the shorter document that McCarthy had submitted? Welch asked.

"It has been a little hard, I will admit, to carry it around all night and not read it," Collier acknowledged. "However I will say truthfully that insofar as possible I have avoided reading the entire document. I merely read it with the idea of identifying it."

So here was the trusted agent of the Senate committee assigned to the crucial mission of authenticating, or not, a controversial document bearing on national security, fighting off the demon of temptation. If he had surrendered to it, it would have helped him fulfill his responsibility to the committee. Collier's inhibitions particularly exasperated McCarthy, who wanted Collier to absolve him of any guilt for violating security regulations by confirming his contention that there was no such information in the letter he himself had submitted. But Collier refused. "I do not feel entitled to read the document for the purpose of ascertaining the facts you suggest," he said politely.

"Mr. Chairman," McCarthy exploded, "I wonder how ridiculous we can get here. I am trying to have this young man just look at the letter he had carried around in his pocket all night and tell us there is no security information in this document."

But Collier would not budge, and Mundt backed him.

How "ridiculous" indeed. What made this strange colloquy even more ridiculous, though McCarthy would have been the last to acknowledge this, was the nature of the documents they were debating without reading—a fifteen-page FBI report and a condensed version of it, both of which had absolutely no probative value except as evidence of Director Hoover's cunning.

The FBI report was a typical example of J. Edgar Hoover's recklessness in the heyday of his power and influence, amounting to the crudest kind of hearsay. The FBI itself made a point of saying it did not even attempt to verify the information. Instead Hoover passed this material on to other agencies in the government for two reasons. By doing so he protected himself in case any of the information that had been whispered to the FBI by unidentified sources (who had motives all their own) proved incendiary, Hoover could always claim he had sounded the alarm. Even if nothing came of it, simply by providing such information, which might bear on national security, Hoover, in the climate of the 1950s, was able to intimidate the agencies he dealt with.

The fifteen-page Hoover memo was one factor, along with items in the right-wing press and information from fervent Red-hunting groups, that had led to a full-scale Army investigation at Fort Monmouth. But Murrey Marder, national security correspondent of the *Washington Post*, had reported in November 1953 that the Army's probe turned up no evidence to suggest espionage. Instead the allegations the Army looked at, many of them presumably drawn from the FBI's list, were based mostly on supposed statements made by individuals accused of membership in reputedly controversial organizations. But these groups had never been listed as subversive, and many respected Americans belonged to them.

Thus one of the accused, a leader of the American Veterans Committee, was blamed not for favoring the admission of Communists to the AVC but for "not taking a positive stand" against such action. Among the members of the AVC, Marder noted, was Dwight Eisenhower, who had recently accepted an honorary membership.

Another employee was reported to have confessed to a co-worker that he "fell for the Communist party propaganda line" while in service during World War II, an unlikely admission to have been made by someone who was actually a Communist. What the suspected employee had said, by his own account, was that he had seen Army orientation films on the defense of Stalingrad and concluded they were intended to bolster relations with the Soviets, who were then U.S. allies in the struggle against Hitler.

Indeed, that phase of Soviet-American relations was blotted out of the memory of most anti-Comunists. It should have

been no big surprise that the Russians had come into possession of some classified U.S. military documents, however
dated. During the war the Soviets had official representatives
at Fort Monmouth, among other U.S. military installations,
where they were frequently given access to classified documents. At the same time the United States was sending ship-
loads of classified military equipment to the Kremlin for use
against German forces.*

A few days after the *Post* story debunking the Fort Monmouth spy scare, Secretary Stevens in effect confirmed its gist,
saying the Army had been "unable to find anything relating to
espionage" among the scientists, engineers, and technicians it
had suspended. But all this was forgotten or overlooked by the
committee and its staff. They continued to treat McCarthy's
document and its origins as if they were tantamount to the
Rosetta stone. The committee did indeed seek a ruling from
Attorney General Brownell as to whether either of the documents at the heart of the controversy could be discussed publicly.

Meanwhile, in the wake of the disclosure that the document McCarthy had introduced was not what he represented
it to be, the committee sought to pursue the next issue: Where
had the document come from? And for this purpose the committee naturally turned to Senator McCarthy. After trying to

---

*The author was stationed at Fort Monmouth for nine months in
1952–1953 at a time when the alleged spy ring was supposedly operating
and Maj. Gen. Kirke Lawton was in command. The security apparatus appeared to be taking no risks. As a private E-2, the author trained to repair
radar sets and spent three weeks studying a model called the SCR-584.
It was an old set but still in use at the time. The atmosphere was highly
secretive. All the manuals and schematics were stamped RESTRICTED. SE-
CURITY INFORMATION. A master sergeant who had served in World War
II remarked that he could not understand why such a fuss was being made
about this set. "We must have lend-leased the Russkies thousands of them
during the war," he said.

give the impression in questioning Collier that the fifteen-page FBI memorandum and the letter he had confronted Stevens with amounted to the same thing, the senator was himself called to testify.

McCarthy gathered up his papers and moved to the witness table, beckoning for Cohn and Carr to join him. To give McCarthy and his aides room, Welch, who had been seated close by the witness table, suggested that he and his associate, James St. Clair, would move to the seats McCarthy had occupied.

McCarthy turned that down in another demonstration of petulance and ill will for Welch. "No, I don't want Mr. Welch examining my notes over there," he said.

At Mundt's suggestion, Welch took a seat near other Army officers seated at the subcommittee table. McCarthy could not resist another exhibit of pettiness. "In other words, take a cold chair," he told Welch.

McCarthy had barely taken his seat when, in response to a gentle query from Jenkins about the origins of the letter, he answered the question on everyone's mind—or rather, announced that he would not answer it. "First let me make it very clear that I will not under any circumstances reveal the source of any information which I get as chairman of the committee," he told Jenkins. "One of the reasons why I have been successful, I believe, to some extent in exposing Communists is because the people who give me information from within the government know that their confidence will not be violated." All McCarthy would say was that he got the controversial letter from an officer in Army Intelligence.

Jenkins's response to this stonewalling was to back off by announcing he did not intend to ask McCarthy the name of the person who gave him the document.

Welch showed no such forbearance. When he took over the questioning, he reminded McCarthy that the oath he had taken when he was sworn in as a witness included "a promise, a solemn promise to tell the truth, the whole truth, and nothing but the truth."

McCarthy responded with scorn. "Mr. Welch, you are not the first individual who tried to get me to betray the confidence and give out the names of my informants. You will be no more successful than those who have tried in the past."

But Welch concentrated on the oath. "When you took it, did you have some mental reservation," he asked McCarthy, "some Fifth or Sixth Amendment notion that you could measure what you would tell?"

"The answer is there is no reservation about telling the whole truth," McCarthy insisted.

Well then, Welch challenged the senator, "tell us who delivered the document to you."

But McCarthy again refused.

Welch pressed on, asking a series of questions about to whom else McCarthy had shown the documents, eliciting such answers as "I don't recall," "I wouldn't know," and "It might." All these rejoinders made him sound, as Roy Cohn later observed, "like the many dozens of witnesses he himself had criticized for being unresponsive at subcommittee hearings."

The issue came into focus the very next day, May 6, the eleventh day of the hearings, when Attorney General Brownell responded to the committee's request for a ruling on the FBI memo and the purported letter. Brownell held that the fifteen-page memo contained confidential sources of information while the three-page letter was an unauthorized use of confidential information. Therefore neither document should be made public.

McCarthy disagreed vehemently. He demanded that Brownell be summoned to an executive session of the committee to defend his ruling. When Mundt turned down that idea, McCarthy made plain he would defy Brownell's gag order. Railing against what he called "blackout orders" issued by President Truman in 1948 and continued by Eisenhower, which restricted congressional access to security information, McCarthy declared, "I don't think that any Congressional committee is bound by the opinion of anyone in the executive as to whether or not they are entitled to certain information."

In the midst of this brouhaha Senator Dirksen saw yet another opportunity to advance his favorite cause, curtailing the hearings and limiting the damage to his party. Dirksen had been pushing the idea of a speedup in one variation or another since the beginning of May. But it had been turned down because of Republican fears of seeming to smother the hearings before they had gotten at the truth, whatever that turned up to be. On Saturday, May 8, Dirksen revealed he would revive the idea of expediting the proceedings by limiting the public testimony to Stevens and McCarthy, much the same proposal Welch had rejected a few days before. The only difference was that under Dirksen's latest version of the cutback, other witnesses would be heard but only in closed session. McCarthy called the idea "a good thing." And Senator Dworshak also applauded the proposal.

But Democrats led by John McClellan stood firm in opposition, and McClellan also made clear who would get the blame for a cutoff. "The Republicans have the votes and can do anything they want to," he said. "But they will bear the responsibility for their actions."

Now the Republicans would have to decide whether they were willing to face that music, in other words whether they had the courage to back up their cowardly instincts. It was a tempting idea. All the complaints heard about the foolishness and wastefulness of the hearings made it seem like a no-lose proposition. Certainly for McCarthy, Dirksen's proposal offered a chance to limit further damage to his reputation.

But for Karl Mundt the stakes were higher. He was enough of a realist to guess that the public mood of disgust with the hearings might escalate immediately if they were brought to a halt with a partisan vote. In their hearts the Republicans feared a backlash.

So once again on May 11, as the committee faced the thirteenth day of hearings, Chairman Mundt decided that the most prudent course was to leave the decision up to Secretary Stevens. The secretary had been a tower of equivocation and irresolution all through the Army's wrangle with McCarthy and through his long days as the star witness of the hearings. But on this point he stood firm. He would not agree to limit the public hearings. "I don't want to be an obstructionist," he said. "But I think we must get the facts in this case before the committee, similarly to what I have done."

Later, Drew Pearson would write in his diary that Stevens had stuck to his guns despite being pressured by the president to allow the hearings to go silently into the night. But that was not the case. According to the diary of Eisenhower's press secretary, Jim Hagerty, Ike wanted the hearings to continue. The president knew the Army had been hurt already and reasoned that Dirksen's so-called "compromise" would ratify the outcome as a defeat. The closed sessions, he told Hagerty, would help McCarthy, "who would use his old trick of coming out and telling reporters anything he wanted. He would have a forum and the Army would not."

But while the extension of the hearings seemed to work to Eisenhower's advantage—or so he believed—it also created a problem. The president had tried to stay as far away from the hearings as he could. But by backing Stevens's desire to have them continue he had put himself and his administration out on a limb. It was a gamble. As a result of the testimony of the next witness before the hearings, Eisenhower would find himself drawn in more deeply than before. This witness, for the fourteenth day of the hearings, was a government lawyer, John Adams, counselor to the Army.

As the Army's legislative liaison, Adams had filled the unenviable role of go-between in dealing with McCarthy and his staff. It was not an assignment he was particularly well suited for, nor was he ever comfortable in it. Then forty-two years old, Adams had been a journeyman most of his working life, a reliable and useful hand, lacking flair or distinction but without serious drawbacks. Born in Ashland, Kentucky, he had moved with his family to South Dakota where he grew up and attended the state university law school and then obtained his first job in the state attorney general's office. During World War II, infantry lieutenant Adams fought in North Africa, Italy, and France, and left the service with a major's oak leaves and the Bronze Star.

Entering Republican politics, he came to Washington and moved ahead slowly but steadily from a staff job on Capitol Hill through the middle levels of the Pentagon bureaucracy, until Robert Stevens took over the Department of the Army and made Adams his counsel. He was in some ways similar to Stevens, perhaps too much so for the good of both men. Like Stevens, he was low-key, almost diffident in manner, a demeanor that concealed a fierce emotional intensity.

Although he had worked in the capital for nearly a decade, Adams had been a stranger to any sort of notoriety until circumstances forced him into assembling the chronology of the Army's tangled relationship with McCarthy. It was an action that thrust McCarthy on the defensive, ultimately imperiling his political life, but at the same time it opened a can of worms for the Army, creating a crisis for Adams unlike any he had ever faced.

There was probably no good way anyone could have handled the Army's dealings with McCarthy. Adams's superiors in the Eisenhower administration surely must have realized this, nevertheless they were not inclined to view Adams with favor or even much tolerance. After Stevens's February debacle at the notorious chicken lunch in the Capitol, Fred Seaton, an influential Eisenhower confidant and aide to Defense Secretary Charles Wilson, uncharitably told Adams, "Don't get into these things and wait until there is a mess and expect us to get you out."

As the hearings approached, with Attorney General Brownell and White House Chief of Staff Sherman Adams and Seaton sharing the impression that John Adams lacked the experience and backbone to represent the Army, he suffered the ultimate put-down. As the greatest opportunity of his professional life arrived, he was denied the chance to prove himself and instead supplanted by Joseph Welch as the Army's legal representative in the hearings.

Now that his moment in the sun had arrived, as a witness, Adams to his own great regret was to bear out the misgivings held about him. He started off smoothly enough. The burden of Adams's testimony dealt with his efforts to fend off pressures from McCarthy and Cohn to gain favorable treatment for Private Schine. His recounting was so extensive that at one point Ray Jenkins asked, without meaning to be facetious: "Did you and the secretary have any time to attend to your other business outside of looking after the future of Schine?"

"I have never been in a situation like this before," Adams responded. One matter that caused him particular concern was McCarthy's determination, expressed in what Adams referred to as an "ultimatum" to subpoena members of the Army Loyalty and Security Appeals Board to testify before the committee. This, as Adams explained, "was a matter of vital importance to the Army."

These quasi-judicial panels were responsible for deciding highly sensitive issues stemming from challenges to the loyalties of military personnel. Adams along with the Army brass felt they would be unable to function if they were subject to being summoned before the McCarthy Committee and ordered to account for their decisions.

Just before McCarthy made his demand to interrogate the Security Board members, Adams had told him and Cohn that it would be impossible to station Private Schine in New York, as Cohn and McCarthy had insisted. "The two matters," Adams said dryly, referring to Schine's assignment and the subpoenas, "seemed to me related."

So far so good. As a firsthand participant in the events so much debated before the committee, Adams had done a persuasive job of bolstering the Army's case against McCarthy. He seemed to get stronger as he went along, gaining confidence. That may have led to his downfall. Driven by his newfound self-assurance and his own intense resentment at what he and the Army had been subjected to, Adams made a disastrous mistake for a lawyer. He told the committee more than it needed to know, and what he said would come back to haunt not just the Army but the president.

The issue was McCarthy's threat to subpoena the Security Board members. Concern about this possibility, Adams revealed, had led to a meeting in the attorney general's office with Brownell and other high administration officials to discuss their strategy for blocking McCarthy. For the occasion, an all-star cast had been assembled. Besides Brownell himself, those in attendance included Sherman Adams (no relation to the Army counsel), the president's chief of staff, whose reputed power was such that it had led to the oft-repeated Washington witticism, "What would happen if Sherman Adams died and Ike became president?" Also on hand were William P. Rogers, the deputy attorney general, and, more surprisingly and somewhat inexplicably, Henry Cabot Lodge, Jr., U.S. ambassador to the United Nations.

This was a startling disclosure because it brought the White House directly into a controversy from which Eisenhower had been striving to remain clear. More broadly, Adams's testimony about the attendees at the meeting contradicted the Army's claim that it had acted on its own in dealing with McCarthy. Indeed, it was Sherman Adams, Ike's right-hand man, who after listening to John Adams recount the pressures brought on him because of Schine, suggested to Adams that he compile a chronology. This led to the detailed charges against McCarthy that the Army would make public two months later.

Adams dropped this bombshell on Wednesday, May 12, the fifteenth day of the hearings. So cluttered were the minds of the senators by the details of the machinations of both sides that it took until Friday, May 14, before anyone got around to pursuing the issue. It was a Democrat, Senator Symington, whose curiosity was whetted by the presence of Ambassador Lodge at the January 21 meeting.

"Why was Lodge there?" Symington asked.

"I don't know," Adams replied. "I didn't arrange for his presence."

When Symington would not drop the subject, Welch broke in with a point of order. "This was a high-level discussion of the Executive Department," he explained, and therefore Adams had been instructed not to discuss what was said there.

Symington was not pleased with that news. "Does that mean that we are going to get the information about low-level discussions but not about high-level discussions?"

Symington and his fellow Democrat Senator Jackson would not let the matter rest and demanded that the Army present a written explanation of the gag order on Adams after the luncheon recess.

But following the recess Joe Welch had no better answer than he had presented in the morning sessions. In his best self-deprecating manner, Welch told the senators: "I am only a bearer of messages, not a formulator of policies." He now found himself in a situation, Welch confessed, that was "a little beyond my depth." This being Friday, Welch promised he would devote the weekend to consult with people who knew more about the gag order than he did.

The weekend came and passed, and on Monday, May 17, Adams showed up with a letter from the president to the secretary of defense, explaining that because of the need for executive-branch officials to be completely candid in offering advice, "it is not in the public interest that any of their conversations concerning such advice be disclosed." The ban on disclosure, Eisenhower contended in his letter, was intended to preserve the separation of powers and to prevent "the arbitrary exercise of power by any branch of government."

McCarthy, outraged, denounced the White House action as a cover-up. He charged that he and his staff had been the victims of a smear by the attorney general, who he demanded be called upon to explain himself. "I don't think the president is responsible for this," McCarthy declared. "I don't think his judgment is that bad."

Democrats also objected. McClellan called the president's action "a grave mistake" and predicted that unless it was modified it would mean the end of the hearings. Dirksen argued that the ruling would hinder McCarthy in making his case against the Army. And he managed to push through a motion to recess the hearings for a week. Some thought the proceedings would never resume unless the president yielded

But Ike, who during all the controversies raging around McCarthy had managed to avoid finding any principle worth fighting for, now chose to stand up for executive privilege. Meanwhile, smelling McCarthy's blood in the water, he also called for the hearings to resume. "Let the chips fall where they may," the president said, a statement made easier since he was not required to swing the axe.

The reality was that the committee had no choice but to bow to Eisenhower's wishes. They were too far along to quit now on what most people would see as a technicality. The president had preserved executive privilege. More important, in practical terms he had kept his advisers from being called to account by McCarthy, Jenkins, and Cohn. McCarthy had suffered yet another defeat. And the Wisconsin senator's temper, as the next stage in the hearings would demonstrate, was growing ever shorter.

10

Time Out for Tears

The resumption of the hearings after their abrupt weeklong recess found McCarthy letting out his frustration at one target after another. A particular grievance was the strategy meeting in Attorney General Brownell's office, which John Adams had revealed, and about which Eisenhower had denied McCarthy or anyone else further information. Endowing this gathering with sinister portent, McCarthy hammered away at the idea that it was here that the administration had hatched a plot to "smear" him.

Secretary Stevens was another focus for the senator's anger, understandably so. Stevens's continued zigging and zagging on the witness stand bolstered McCarthy's charges of bad faith against the Army. The senator pointed out that Stevens had denied knowing who was responsible for "putting out" the Army's charges against McCarthy. But testifying as the hearings resumed on May 24, the nineteenth day of proceedings, Stevens accepted responsibility for that action himself.

Challenged by McCarthy, Stevens offered a semantical explanation for the apparent contradiction. In his initial statement, Stevens claimed, the expression "putting out" was intended only to apply to the public release of the charges, which he claimed the Army had not done, as opposed to preparing the thirty-four-page document. Unimpressed by this distinction, McCarthy responded by contending that Stevens either had a "bad memory" or had committed perjury.

McCarthy's sarcasm was so heavy that Stevens complained to Mundt. "I resent that remark," Stevens said indignantly. "I tell the truth."

Mundt agreed that McCarthy's questioning was "improper," a comment to which McCarthy did not take kindly. "We'll see whether it's improper or not," he snapped. "I don't enjoy seeing the Secretary come up here and contradict himself under oath."

As the week wore on, McCarthy's mood did not improve, even when Stevens finally left the witness stand and on Thursday, May 27, the twenty-second day, McCarthy finally got his chance to present his case against the Army. The testimony of the lead witness for McCarthy's side, Roy Cohn, led to another outburst of McCarthy's irritation, this time triggered by Senator McClellan. Following up on a point he had raised earlier, McClellan suggested that under Brownell's order banning disclosure of national security matters, both McCarthy and whoever gave him the purported Hoover letter might be guilty of a crime.

"If anyone wants to indict me," McCarthy replied, "they can go right ahead. I would like to make it clear that I think that the oath which every person in this government takes to protect and defend this country towers far above any presidential secrecy directive." In fact, he said, he wanted to notify the nation's two million federal employees "that I feel it is their duty to give us any information which they have."

If McCarthy was trying to provoke Eisenhower, he succeeded brilliantly. The very next day the White House issued a statement declaring that the responsibilities of the executive branch "cannot be usurped by an individual who may seek to set himself above the laws of our land." Although this statement was attributed to the attorney general, it was clear on whose authority it was based. Eisenhower's own press secretary, Jim Hagerty, read the statement to reporters at the White House.

In private, Ike vented his full fury to Hagerty. "This is nothing less than wholesale subversion of the public service," he fumed. "McCarthy is making the same plea of loyalty to him that Hitler made to the German people. I think it is the most disloyal act we have ever had by anyone in the government of the United States."

Republicans on the committee had other concerns. The longer the hearings went on, the more fed up and worried they and other GOP leaders became. So they made yet another attempt to limit the damage they were suffering, this one more successful than their earlier efforts. On May 26, two days after the resumption of hearings, by a 4-to-3 vote, the Republicans pushed through a resolution dropping the charges against Assistant Secretary of Defense Struve Hensel and McCarthy Committee staff director Francis Carr.

It was presented as an even swap which would placate both sides. The charges against Hensel had been brought by McCarthy, who accused him of "masterminding" the Army's case against him. Carr had been charged by the Army with involvement in the pressure campaign to obtain preferential treatment for David Schine.

The Democrats angrily protested the move and called it a "whitewash." Hensel claimed to be unhappy because he was denied the chance publicly to clear his name. By their action the Republican majority had denied him that opportunity as well as sparing Carr the ordeal of cross-examination by hostile Democrats and Joseph Welch. This maneuver stirred such public criticism that a few days later McCarthy announced that Carr wanted to testify after all. Even so, Republicans had managed to shrink the scope of the hearings a bit and thus hasten the day when they would be spared further agony.

The strength of GOP feelings on that issue was reflected by the remarks of Vice President Nixon, a man clearly much closer to the attitudes of partisan Republicans than the president. While Ike supported the hearings, Nixon, in a speech on May 27, spoke of the proceedings with scorn. "I have been asked many times what I think of the television performance now originating in the city of Washington," he told a GOP fund-raising dinner at New York's Waldorf-Astoria. "My answer is that I prefer professionals to amateurs at any time." He himself had not seen a single day of the hearings, Nixon boasted. But this did not discourage him from evaluating their worth. "The quicker the hearings can be concluded and public attention devoted to more important subjects, the better it will be for the country," he said.

If Nixon dismissed the hearings out of hand, the president seemed to see a deeper meaning to the issues they raised. On May 31, a few days after Nixon spoke at the Waldorf, Ike came to New York too, to speak at Columbia University where he had been president before ascending to the White House. On Morningside Heights he expressed the belief that knowledge and understanding would "drive from the temple of freedom all who seek to establish over us thought control, whether they be agents of a foreign state or demagogues thirsty for power." When reporters asked his aides if Eisenhower was referring to Senator McCarthy, the answer came back, "Who else?"

Next day McCarthy endured another pounding, one that was to have a far-reaching impact on his political destiny. It came from the senator who was fast assuming the role of the Anti-McCarthy, and whose rhetoric took on a special significance because he was a rock-solid member of the Senate Republican caucus, Ralph Flanders of Vermont.

Flanders had been an early adversary of McCarthy, going back to McCarthy's first months in the Senate. But the Vermonter had been cautious in challenging his Wisconsin colleague and had seemed determined to calibrate his indignation. This caution reflected the seventy-four-year-old Flanders's own strong conservative roots and his inherent New England restraint. Considering that McCarthy was the self-appointed scourge not only of communism but of any politician with leftist leanings, it would have been hard to find anyone in the Senate less likely than Flanders to emerge as his chief tormentor. Before he took on McCarthy, Flanders had established himself as an unyielding foe of big-government liberalism and a champion of free enterprise. His own early life resembled that of a Horatio Alger hero.

Born and raised on a Vermont farm, Flanders's formal education ended with a high school diploma. But that was good enough to help him get his first job as an apprentice in a machine-tool plant. A fast learner and a hard worker, young Flanders studied mechanical drawing at night school and earned a degree in mechanical engineering from a correspondence school. Soon he was contributing articles to machine-shop journals, and before long he was named associate editor of a respected trade journal in New York City. Five years later he moved back to Vermont, recruited by a Springfield manufacturer. In the best Horatio Alger tradition, he married the boss's daughter and became manager and later president of the company.

As he wrote more articles, Flanders expanded his scope to include a broad range of economic policy issues, particularly the alleged flaws of the economic reforms of the New Deal, then regnant in the land. His writing and his business success made him a national figure and stirred the interest of the Republican party, which in those depression years was desperate for fresh blood. After one unsuccessful try for the U.S. Senate in 1940, Flanders rode to victory in 1946 on the same wave of public discontent with Democratic rule that brought McCarthy to the Senate.

Flanders was flatly opposed to Democratic spending and taxing measures. His legislative record, such as his support for the Taft-Hartley Law, anathema to organized labor, was based on what he defined as a true conservative philosophy: belief in "production of more, not redistribution of limited, wealth," coupled with devotion to self-discipline and competition instead of "enjoyment of life" and "togetherness."

Still, the longer Flanders stayed in the Senate, the more his conservatism moderated. He supported Eisenhower over conservative hero Bob Taft in the contest for the 1952 Republican nomination and began to call himself a "liberal" Republican while acknowledging he had trouble defining the word. But he had no difficulty picking a fight with McCarthy early in both their Senate careers. Their first tiff was over a relatively mundane issue, the price of sugar, which during the days of wartime scarcity had been controlled by the government. McCarthy, from sugar-beet producer Wisconsin, naturally wanted a quick decontrol of prices while Flanders from Vermont, consumer of sugar except for what little it derived from its maple trees, fought for gradual decontrol. Harsh words flew back and forth on the Senate floor, and McCarthy's eventual limited victory was clouded by the resentments that remained.

With time Flanders found more substantive grounds for disagreement with McCarthy, namely his reckless pursuit of alleged Communist-inspired subversion. As far back as 1951 the Vermonter even toyed with the idea of introducing a resolution excoriating McCarthyism, but this initiative never left the drafting board. Flanders privately made excuses for the Wisconsin senator by lauding the impact he was having on the residue of Roosevelt's "soft as taffy" stance on communism. Wishful thinking—that Eisenhower's election would solve the problem—also helped Flanders ease his conscience. "I believe McCarthy can be washed out as thoroughly as a Kansas flood washes out the stockyards," he wrote a friend in anticipation of Abilene-bred Ike capturing the presidency. But by the time Eisenhower had been in the White House for a year, Flanders had come to realize how little the president was prepared to do to stem the tide of McCarthyism.

As McCarthyism waxed, Flanders's reluctance to take him on waned. He was pushed over the edge in March 1954 during a trip to his hometown of Springfield, Vermont. There on March 5, 1954, at a Friday night talk to a public affairs group at the First Congregational Church, he encountered a wave of outrage at McCarthy. "They tackled him, and he went home and wrote the speech on yellow foolscap," recalled Elizabeth French, his secretary. "He handed it to me for typing Monday morning."

In that address delivered on March 9—which as it happened was the day Ed Murrow targeted McCarthy on national television—Flanders charged that McCarthy was so obsessed with the threat of domestic communism that he was guilty of overlooking greater dangers to U.S. security from abroad. But he softened his criticism by praising McCarthy for cleaning out the "cobwebs and spiders" left in the cellar by the Truman administration.

But this time, on June 1, when Flanders took the Senate floor to denounce McCarthy, he had no balancing commendation. Instead his language was harsh enough that it might have come right out of McCarthy's own book of attack rhetoric. McCarthy's extremism, Flanders charged, was aiding the Communists. "Were the junior senator from Wisconsin in the pay of the communists he could not have done a better job for them," Flanders said.

He all but called McCarthy an anti-Semite and likened him to Hitler. Referring to the "foreboding" about McCarthy among Jewish Americans, Flanders recalled McCarthy's "strange tenderness" for the Nazis involved in the Malmedy massacre. Beyond that, Flanders added, "his anti-communism so completely parallels that of Adolf Hitler as to strike fear into the heart of any defenseless minority."

Flanders's remarks received widespread attention, making page one of the *New York Times*, among other papers. Also in the *Times* story was a brief paragraph in Flanders's speech that crossed a line, alluding to the suspect but previously unmentionable nature of the friendship between David Schine and Roy Cohn. The hearings, Flanders said, had not yet dug into "the real heart of the mystery," the relationship between Cohn, Schine, and McCarthy. Without using their names, referring to them only as "the staff assistant" and "the private," Flanders remarked on Cohn's "almost passionate anxiety" to keep Schine on board. He also asked pointedly whether Schine had some "hold on the Senator." Could it be that McCarthy, whom Flanders referred to as "Dennis the Menace," after the obstreperous comic-strip character, "so effective in making trouble for his elders, has at last gotten into trouble himself? Does the committee plan to investigate the real issues at stake?"

McCarthy responded by challenging Flanders to testify under oath before the committee about whatever information he had on the so-called "real issues." But Flanders ducked the confrontation, insisting that all his information came from what he read in the newspapers.

It was probably just as well for McCarthy that Flanders did not take him up on his dare. The Wisconsin senator was having enough trouble dealing with Joe Welch. On Tuesday, June 1, the twenty-fourth day of the hearings, Welch questioned the authenticity of eleven memoranda that had served as the basis of McCarthy's counterattack to the Army's initial public charges against him made in March. The occasion was the appearance at the witness table of Mary Driscoll, McCarthy's personal secretary, whom McCarthy referred to as "this young woman." In fact she was a grandmother who had run his office for six years. Even before the interrogation began, she seemed terrified. Her chin trembled, and her voice was so low that her testimony was almost inaudible. It was clear from Welch's line of questioning that he suspected that the memoranda, instead of being written contemporaneously with the events they described, had been patched together weeks later in an attempt to make McCarthy's countercharges more convincing. Strengthening Welch's suspicions that the memos were fake was his awareness that the Army memos they responded to had also been faked.

In her testimony Driscoll demonstrated that whatever she lacked in memory she made up in loyalty to her boss. A series of questions from Welch about which typewriter in her office had been used to type which document drew a series of non-informative responses from Driscoll and provoked a protest from McCarthy. Welch's line of questioning "was the height of something or other," McCarthy complained.

Welch explained he was just trying to find out whether the documents were "the real McCoy." He added, "I have nothing but admiration for Mrs. Driscoll. But I have the deepest suspicions about the genuineness of these memoranda."

Driscoll had not been around politicians as long as she had without figuring out a way to fend off smarty-pants lawyers. Like a fox, she played dumb. "You are confusing me, Mr. Welch," she protested at one point. And in response to another question, "I can't remember."

Lacking the evidence to back up what McCarthy called his "innuendos," Welch finally abandoned the hunt. But not before he had cast a shadow over McCarthy's case.

Precious few bright spots were appearing for McCarthy. One occurred while Welch was cross-examining Cohn on why Schine had worked for the committee without pay. "Was it because he would be subject to less discipline?" the counsel asked. At which point McCarthy interrupted to ask Welch if he was representing the Army without pay, which he knew to be the case. Welch winced, and then grinned.

"You got me there," he replied. "Score a touché for the Senator."

Flailing about in an effort to regain the initiative, McCarthy tried to exploit an opportunity created when the legal logjam that had suppressed the transcripts of Secretary Stevens's monitored phone conversations was broken and the first transcripts released. In the conversation McCarthy seized upon, the party on the other end of the line, on February, 20, 1954, was Democratic senator Symington. Symington and Stevens were old friends from their days at Yale and from the business and military world. It seemed only natural to Republican Stevens that he call his longtime pal, the Democratic senator, and ask for advice on how to handle McCarthy.

"If you are going to play with McCarthy you have to forget about those Marquis of Queensbury rules," Symington ventured. Beyond that, Symington suggested that if Stevens wanted strategic advice he should seek out Symington's fellow Missourian, Clark Clifford, the legendary Washington lawyer and lobbyist who was widely credited with having masterminded Harry Truman's upset victory over Dewey in 1948.

Stevens did no such thing. But to the increasingly desperate McCarthy, the disclosure of the conversation seemed a heaven-sent opportunity. On June 4, the twenty-seventh day of the hearings, McCarthy accused Symington of having set up the whole confrontation between the Army and McCarthy by getting Clifford, "one of the top aides of President Truman," to mislead "a fine, naive and not too brilliant Republican

Secretary of the Army." McCarthy now demanded that Symington take himself off the committee and testify under oath on his conversations with Stevens. He called for Clifford to be subpoenaed to testify too.

But Symington stood his ground, as he had against McCarthy from the beginning. At first glance Symington seemed a most unlikely fellow to get into a political brawl with Joe McCarthy or anyone else. He was a patrician figure—wealthy, socially prominent, a top-notch athlete (prowess he had displayed on the Yale tennis team), and a man-about-town in the New York of the 1930s. His wife, born Evelyn Wadsworth, was the daughter of a leading Republican politician and granddaughter of John Hay, President Lincoln's private secretary and Theodore Roosevelt's secretary of state. Evelyn Symington was herself a captivating beauty and a professional chanteuse, much in demand at nightclubs.

When Symington's business interests took him to Missouri, he became friends with the state's senior senator, Harry Truman, whom he served as chief troubleshooter and eventually, after Truman succeeded to the presidency, secretary of the air force. In that post Symington became deeply absorbed with protecting and promoting the institutional health of the air force in particular and the military establishment generally. His family history of wartime service and sacrifice also led him in that direction. Symington's grandfather had ridden with General George Pickett on his famous charge at Gettysburg. He himself had enlisted in the World War I Army at age seventeen, just as his second son, James, enlisted in the Marine Corps during the Korean War. Five of his cousins had been killed in action in World War II and Korea. Such tragedy might have made pacifists out of some men. But Symington became a committed hawk and a frequent critic of his friend and sponsor, Truman, over the conduct of the war in Korea, where Symington felt the United States should be more aggressive.

Despite his split with Truman, he ran for the U.S. Senate in 1952 and easily defeated his Republican foe while Eisenhower was swamping Democrat Adlai Stevenson in the state. Not surprisingly, Senator Symington's continued championship of the armed forces contributed to his resentment of McCarthy's probe of the Army. Adding a personal element to the tension between the two men was the genteel Symington's aversion to McCarthy's coarseness.

Symington brought several handicaps to his increasingly public feud with McCarthy. He had no formal legal training and was not a skilled debater, and his sometimes wooden manner hindered him in the give-and-take of a committee hearing. He fretted that under pressure he might lose control of his emotions. Thus when McCarthy baited him by sneeringly referring to him as "sanctimonious Stu," Symington tried to ignore the insult rather than respond in kind.

Still, Symington did not lack for self-confidence. He had been a great success in everything he tried, as a corporate maker and shaker and as a high appointed official. Six times the votes of Republicans and Democrats had unanimously confirmed him for high federal office; and he had won his Senate seat on his first venture into electoral politics. So, unlike many of his Senate colleagues in both parties, he was not afraid of McCarthy and would not back away from meeting the threat the Wisconsin senator posed to the values Symington cared about.

In this particular dispute McCarthy had a strong case. Democrat Symington's willingness to advise a Republican cabinet officer, even one he was chummy with, smacked of ethical insensitivity, particularly since he knew that he might have to sit in judgment on the resolution of the problems Stevens was asking him about. Under the circumstances, McCarthy's demand that Symington testify about his controversial role was not unreasonable. But at this stage of the hearings, reason and fairness did not influence Symington as much as his anger at McCarthy. At long last he abandoned the restraint inherent in his refinement and dismissed McCarthy's "diatribe" as "just another diversion."

He then proceeded to offer an explanation of his conversation with Stevens in chaste terms. When Stevens brought the Army's troubles to him, Symington suggested he get "a good lawyer." That was a description that certainly fit Clark Clifford, and that was about all that needed to be said. "I will always go under oath for anything I say, because I always speak the truth," he said loftily. Dissatisfied, McCarthy again cried foul, protesting Symington's conduct and demanding that he testify. But Symington brushed him off.

Meanwhile Welch had continued his efforts to add to McCarthy's increasing anxiety and frustration by gnawing away at the testimony of his chief lieutenant, Roy Cohn. Not that Cohn was an easy mark. Despite his air of cocksure arrogance, he was no fool. He had learned from his first dismal experience under Welch's cross-examination, when the Boston lawyer managed to turn attention from the photograph the secretary of the Army had taken with Private G. David Schine, to how that photo had been altered. By the time he was thrust into the spotlight again, Cohn had concluded that, as he later put it, the hearings "were less a search for truth than a gigantic personality play."

McCarthy understood this too, Cohn believed, but McCarthy lacked the ability, or the will, to analyze his own conduct objectively. Not so Cohn. He had studiously reviewed the transcript of his self-described "debacle" as a witness and determined to make amends. Instead of rambling, he would speak to the point. Rather than being smart-alecky and aggressive, he would be reticent and deferential. He even went to the length of rehearsing his testimony, meeting the night before he was scheduled to testify with McCarthy and other

McCarthy aides in McCarthy's home. Cohn did indeed do a good job of preparing himself. But his best efforts would come to naught because of the temperament of the man he served.

Cohn did nothing to embarrass himself during the direct examination by Ray Jenkins. And he stood up fairly well under Welch's intensive cross-examination—though needling would be a more accurate term. On June 2, Cohn's fourth day of testimony, Welch returned to the supposed root cause of the battle, Private Schine.

If Schine had been given the commission he and Cohn sought from the Army, would the "collision" between McCarthy and the Army still have taken place?

Cohn was polite but firm. "I'll put it this way, sir," he said. "The collision between the Senator and the Army was not caused by the Schine matter."

Welch pursued another tack, the relationship between the witness and his friend, the private. "Were you his boss?" he asked.

"I don't think anybody has a boss, except for the chairman of the committee," Cohn replied.

That seemed unremarkable enough. But with Welch as the inquisitor, there was no safe answer for Cohn. "Well, do you all just romp around there?" Welch asked, drawing the laughter he surely expected.

But he failed in his main purpose, to goad Cohn into an outburst. "Well, sir, that might be amusing," the witness said. "But the boys down there, as I've explained, don't romp around."

Satisfied that he had done as much or as little with Cohn as he could, Welch was ready for the next witness. But Cohn was not yet ready to leave the witness stand. "I would still like to answer the pending question, if I may," he told Welch.

Welch picked up the gauntlet. "Are you still troubled about that question of 'romping around'? Does that bother you?"

Once more the audience laughed, provoking a halfhearted scolding from Chairman Mundt—in which, as one rhetorician to another, the erstwhile head of the National Forensic League expressed his admiration for Welch's skill with words and audiences. "Mr. Welch," Mundt said, "has the happy faculty of asking rib-tickling questions."

Encouraged, Welch returned to his confrontation with Cohn. "I want a speech on 'romping around,' which you say you are prepared to make."

Cohn parried that thrust with a touch of sanctimony. "Well, Mr. Welch, apparently this is all very funny to you, sir, but it's not to me. The people downstairs work much harder than they have had to earn the pay that they get," Cohn said. "They do their work and they do it well and the result is that Communists have been eliminated from defense plants and government agencies and money has been saved to the taxpayers of the country."

While the evidence for Cohn's claim would certainly be hard to come by, particularly the assertion about the benefits for taxpayers, it was one of his better moments in the hearings. Cohn presented himself as a sincere and dedicated public servant rather than an unscrupulous and reckless muckraker. In fact he did so well that Welch, reflecting on the afternoon's exchange and on the impact it would have on millions of viewers, sought the next day to mitigate whatever harm he might have done to his own carefully wrought image.

"Mr. Cohn," Welch told the witness on June 3, as he began a fifth grueling day of testimony, "my mail and my telegrams reflect, sir, that you are held in gratifying high esteem in this country. There apparently are a good many people who think I was unfair to you yesterday. Would you kindly set them at rest, if you could, by saying I was fair?" This was certainly an extraordinary request. The tormentor, Welch, seeking absolution from his target. Not surprisingly, Cohn did not leap at the opportunity. "I am sure you are doing your job as you see it, sir," was all he would allow.

But Welch was not satisfied. "Well, would you mind picking up my word? Would you say it was fair?"

With Welch all but begging, Cohn could afford a bit of magnanimity. "I'm sure, sir, you did not mean to be unfair." And with that, having gained a measure of forgiveness from his victim, Welch returned to the attack.

The next day, June 4, Welch jabbed at Cohn about an issue he knew he was sensitive about: his avoidance of the draft by getting successive appointments to West Point, followed by his failing to meet the entrance requirements for the academy. "Mr. Cohn, there had I think been some articles published about you and your draft status, of which you are probably aware, are you not?"

"I would say articles have been published about me on just about everything else," Cohn replied. But Welch mysteriously dropped the matter there, saying he would delay further questioning until Cohn had his whole file before him "so you can reel it off to us."

The matter was thus left hanging, which was enough to make Cohn uneasy. The exchange about his draft status took place on a Friday. Cohn brooded about it over the weekend and then on Monday, June 7, went to see Welch with a proposition. By Cohn's later account, each man had an issue he wished to avoid. For Cohn it was his draft status. For Welch the counterpart was the case of Fred Fisher, the young lawyer in his firm originally slated to serve on the committee but then sent back to Boston when he acknowledged having once belonged to the National Lawyers Guild, because of its reputation for devotion to left-wing causes. This was a concern that would not go away for Welch, because McCarthy had several times threatened to raise the issue on national TV. So he had reason to go along with Cohn's proposition. Both men shook hands on a promise not to raise either issue. That night Cohn went to McCarthy's home and got his approval of the deal.

But two days later, on June 9, the thirtieth day of the hearings with Cohn on the stand, McCarthy broke his word to his own loyal aide. It was a moment that brought Joseph Welch to the verge of tears and beyond. But along with the sorrow and shock he expressed over McCarthy's thrust, Welch certainly was entitled to feel enormous satisfaction because his grand strategy had succeeded.

It began quietly enough near the end of another prolonged grilling of Cohn, when Welch recalled that Cohn had testified earlier that he knew of a "disturbing" situation at Fort Monmouth involving subversives and security risks as far back as the spring of 1953. "I am sure that was to you a disturbing and alarming situation," Welch said, and then pointed out that Cohn had first met Secretary Stevens in September of that same year. And yet, Welch said, Cohn did not "tug at his lapel and say, 'Mr. Secretary, I know something about Monmouth that won't let me sleep nights.' You didn't do that, did you?"

Cohn did not recall exactly what he had said or when to Stevens about the threat to security at Monmouth. Welch pushed on: "Mr. Cohn, tell me once more: Every time you learn of a Communist or a spy anywhere, is it your policy to get them out as fast as possible?"

"Surely we want them out as fast as possible, sir."

"And whenever you learn of one from now on, Mr. Cohn, I beg of you, will you tell somebody about them quick?"

Cohn explained that in his work at the committee, the pace of his efforts was governed by those with experience enough to know when and how to respond to the danger of subversion.

Welch would not let it rest. "May I add my small voice, sir, and say whenever you know about a subversive or a Communist or a spy, please hurry. Will you remember those words?"

Still on the defensive, Cohn assured Welch that it was the practice of himself and his colleagues on the McCarthy Committee to "proceed as expeditiously as is humanly possible to get out Communists and traitors."

But by now McCarthy had lost patience entirely and demanded the floor. Many found it easy to blame McCarthy for what came next. But it was not hard to understand what impelled him. For thirty days he had endured Welch's well-bred, taunting voice, his cultured sarcasm, his grating fondness for self-deprecation. And all the while the senator saw his own reputation—more than that, the empire he had built on paranoia—slowly crumbling away. And not on the merits. No one had attacked the premises of the ideology he had shaped. Instead he had been made to seem personally obnoxious and, almost as bad, irrelevant. It was more than he could bear. And now the dam burst and history began ticking away McCarthy's final moments as the country's most intimidating politician.

"Have you a point of order?" Mundt asked him.

"Not exactly," McCarthy replied. "But in view of Mr. Welch's request that the information be given once we know of anyone who might be performing any work for the Communist Party, I think we should tell him that he has in his law firm a young man named Fisher whom he recommended to do work on this committee who has been for a number of years a member of an organization which was named years and years ago as the legal bulwark of the Communist Party. I have hesitated bringing that up," McCarthy added, smiling and literally licking his chops, "but I have been rather bored with your phony requests to Mr. Cohn here that he personally get every Communist out of government before sundown."

Welch had listened to McCarthy in silence. And when he spoke it was more in sorrow than in anger. But what eloquent sorrow. When he started his response McCarthy had turned to talk to an aide. Welch asked for his attention.

"I am listening with one ear," McCarthy said.

"This time I want you to listen with both," Welch replied. "Until this moment, Senator, I think I never really gauged your cruelty or your recklessness," Welch said. Then he went on to explain that he had indeed intended to name Fisher to assist him on the committee work until Fisher disclosed his membership, abandoned years before, in the Lawyers Guild, whereupon he decided it was best all around for Fisher to return to Boston.

"Little did I dream you could be so reckless and cruel as to do an injury to that lad," said Welch, fudging the truth more than a bit since he had long considered that McCarthy might launch just such an attack, and indeed both he and James St. Clair had warned Fisher to be prepared for McCarthy to smear his name. "It is true he is still with Hale and Dorr," Welch continued. "It is true that he will continue to be with Hale and Dorr. It is, I regret to say, equally true that I fear he shall always bear a scar needlessly inflicted by you. If it were in my power to forgive you for your reckless cruelty, I would do so. I like to think I am a gentleman, but your forgiveness will have to come from someone other than me."

Welch had said his piece, long considered in case of just this exigency, and there the matter would have ended. Except for McCarthy, who could not let bad enough alone. Striving desperately to justify himself, he accused Welch of base hypocrisy in his questioning of Cohn and tried once more to bring up Fisher's ties to the Lawyers Guild cloudy past.

"Senator, may we not drop this?" Welch asked, almost plaintively. "We know he belonged to the Lawyers Guild, and Mr. Cohn nods his head at me." Now Welch turned to Cohn: "I did you, I think, no personal injury," he said.

"No, sir," Cohn agreed.

"Let us not assassinate this lad further, Senator," he told McCarthy. "You have done enough." Then he added the words that drove a dagger into McCarthy's political life and became an indelible fragment of the history of that stormy era: "Have you no sense of decency, sir, at long last? Have you left no sense of decency?"

Still McCarthy would not give up. "I know this hurts you, Mr. Welch," he said.

"Senator, I think it hurts you too, sir," Welch added presciently.

Again McCarthy sought to return to Fisher's background. As he did, he turned to Roy Cohn, sitting next to him, who was sadly shaking his head. "I know Mr. Cohn would rather not have me go into this," he said. But go into it he did, citing the language of HUAC describing the Lawyers Guild as "the foremost legal bulwark of the Communist Party" and demanding to know more about Welch's decision to have Fisher serve as his assistant.

But Welch cut him off. "I will not discuss this further with you," he told McCarthy coldly. "You have sat within six feet of me and could have asked me about Fred Fisher. You have brought it out. If there is a God in heaven it will do neither you nor your cause any good. I will not ask Mr. Cohn any more questions. You, Mr. Chairman, may, if you will, call the next witness."

Before Mundt could do that the audience burst into applause, which Mundt did not attempt to discourage. Welch stroked his chin, his face a somber mask, his eyes welling up. McCarthy stared straight ahead.

Mundt put off summoning the next witness and called a recess instead.

The impact of Welch's rebuke was heightened by the dexterity of the TV camera crews. Three separate cameras were aimed at each of the principals in this climactic exchange—McCarthy, Cohn, and Welch, catching them not only as they spoke but as they reacted to the words of the others. As for

McCarthy, he seemed in a state of shock. While the audience and senators marched past him into the corridors, he looked around for someone to talk to. "What did I do?" he asked plaintively, addressing no one in particular, palms spread outward.

For all his pain at McCarthy's slur on Fred Fisher, Welch had reason to feel jubilant. The blow he had struck at McCarthy was the political equivalent of a knockout punch. He had set the stage day in and day out since April, relentlessly goading McCarthy into this ultimate outburst. He had to know that whatever agreement he had reached with Cohn—to ignore Cohn's draft record in exchange for leaving Fisher out of the fight—would be meaningless if McCarthy could be driven to the breaking point. And Welch did all he could to push him there. His sarcastic grilling of Roy Cohn about his supposed failure to alert Secretary Stevens soon enough to the Communist threat at Fort Monmouth could have had no other purpose. Then, when McCarthy broke, Welch exploited the moment. He was also fully aware of what he had accomplished, according to Robert Griffith's *Politics of Fear*, an incisive study of McCarthy's rise and decline. A lawyer who walked out of the hearing room with Welch, past the reporters and the exploding flashbulbs, told Griffith: "Welch looked at me and without changing expression, the tears still streaming down his face, asked, 'Well, how did it go?'"

Welch's heart-tugging excoriation of McCarthy was the emotional climax of the hearings. But the proceedings dragged on for another week before coming to their official end. On June 10, the day following the confrontation over Fred Fisher, Republicans had finally succeeded in arranging for the end of the hearings by limiting the number of witnesses who followed Cohn to Senator McCarthy and Francis Carr. That meant the proceedings would finish the following week. The Democrats wanted David Schine as a witness, but the Republicans, who had had more than enough of the hearings by this time, turned that idea down by a 4-to-3 vote.

In those closing days, the damage Welch had inflicted upon McCarthy was signaled by the increasing willingness of the Democrats to challenge the Wisconsin senator, something they had done only rarely in the past. The first such incident was a confrontation between Roy Cohn and Robert Kennedy, whose resentment of Cohn had not abated during the bitter hassle of the hearings. The storm broke on June 11 while McCarthy was testifying and was being questioned by Senator Jackson.

Jackson made no attempt to hide his skepticism about the psychological warfare plan that David Schine had created to combat communism. The plan had been cited by McCarthy as substantiating Schine's qualifications for his involvement in the controversial investigation of the USIA that both he and Cohn had conducted. But as Jackson relentlessly pointed out, this blueprint amounted to nothing more than a potpourri of notions, some commonplace, some dubious, from tapping the support of church leaders to using Hollywood pinups in the worldwide struggle for hearts and minds.

Watching Jackson quiz McCarthy, with the help of Robert Kennedy in his role as aide to the Democrats, Cohn became convinced that Kennedy saw this as an opportunity to "gibe at us" and was using Jackson's questions "to fire a barrage of ridicule" at Cohn, Schine, and McCarthy. "What kind of program is he going to carry out with the use of pinups?" Jackson wanted to know.

"Pictures, cartoons can have an important place in any information program," McCarthy answered.

"I am directing the question to pinups," Jackson persisted.

McCarthy was at a loss to explain. "I don't know what he is referring to as a pinup."

"Really, Senator," Jackson continued, "do you think this qualified a man to investigate a multimillion-dollar information agency?"

McCarthy tried to fight back. But the old fire and confidence were gone. "Looking this over, I couldn't subscribe to every item here without going into more detail," McCarthy said.

"Bobby and Jackson would not give up," Cohn later recalled. "They picked at point after point in Dave's plan, finding something hilarious in each." And each time Cohn's anger mounted. At the end of the session he came face to face with Kennedy and complained bitterly about his tactics. He carried a file labeled "Jackson's record," toting it, one reporter wrote, "like a weapon." According to Kennedy, Cohn told him to warn Jackson, "We are going to get to him on Monday."

"Don't you make any warnings to us about Democratic senators," Kennedy snapped.

"I'll make any warnings to you I want," Cohn replied.

Then he started to swing at Kennedy, but others separated them. The next day's headline in the *New York Daily News* said, "COHN, KENNEDY NEAR BLOWS IN HATE CLASH."

Later Kennedy felt abashed at losing his temper. But in truth his defiance of Cohn and McCarthy signified more than his lack of self-discipline; rather it reflected the shift in power that had taken place.

The final challenge to McCarthy came a few days later on June 14 when Senator Symington once again confronted the Wisconsin senator. The clash was triggered by Symington's interrogation of Frank Carr, the committee's executive director. In a sense Symington was following the pattern established by Welch a few days earlier in his questioning of Roy Cohn—of turning the tables on McCarthy by challenging his vigilance and his staff's efficiency in pursuing their crusade against the

Communist threat. Just as Welch taunted Cohn about being slow in sounding the alarm about Fort Monmouth, Symington chided Carr about his laxness in maintaining security procedures. In a series of questions about the committee's internal security procedures, Symington suggested that a substantial number of staffers who worked for the committee or elsewhere in the Senate, and who lacked appropriate clearance, might be able to lay their hands on committee documents.

Pressing the point, Symington said to Carr: "It would be unfortunate if we had a subversive on our staff and he hadn't had clearance, and then he examined an agency and in that agency he got information which made it possible for him to betray the country."

Trapped, Carr did the best he could. "It would be unfortunate and most unusual," he told Symington.

"Klaus Fuchs was unusual, wasn't he?" Jackson snapped.

Carr could no nothing but agree. "He certainly was," he said.

The reference to Fuchs, the British scientist whose theft of nuclear secrets probably did more than any other piece of espionage to aid the Soviet quest for an atomic bomb, seemed far-fetched on the surface. But Symington had another, subtler point he was trying to make. From his days in the Truman administration, Symington, like McCarthy, had many informants in the bureaucracy. One of them had let him know that the controversial Don Surine and another McCarthy aide had been denied clearance by the Department of Defense. McCarthy's response had been to transfer both men to his personal staff.

Symington did not go into all this, but the hint of what he knew about the clearance problems of McCarthy's aides so flustered McCarthy that he confused Symington with McClellan and raised a point of personal privilege.

"Senator McClellan was talking about the possibilities of subversives on our staff," McCarthy said. "If he knows of any subversive then he should take the stand and tell about him." His annoyance mixed with amusement, McClellan told McCarthy, "Get your names straight." McCarthy corrected that error, but Mundt turned down the claim to privilege, pointing out that Symington had not mentioned any member of the staff as being subversive.

But after Symington concluded his questioning of Carr, McCarthy found new justification to protest. "Senator Symington has been here by innuendo trying to smear the staff of young men who have been working to dig out Communists." If Symington had such information, McCarthy contended, he should take the stand and testify about it under oath. "Do you have any information to indicate that there is anyone on my staff who is subversive as you have indicated in your questioning?" he challenged Symington.

Symington evaded the question but gave McCarthy an answer he would not soon forget. "In all the years that I have been in this government, I think the files of what you call *my* staff, *my* director, *my* chief of staff have been the sloppiest and the most dangerously handled files that I have ever heard of."

At this moment a bell summoned the senators to a roll-call vote, Mundt called a recess, and Symington with his colleagues began to stride out of the room. McCarthy was beside himself. "Mr. Chairman, even though the Chair is leaving, I want to make this record, and, Mr. Reporter, will you take this down?" McCarthy demanded. "May I say that this is the most dishonest, the most unfounded smear upon some of the outstanding young men I have ever seen work to uncover Communists. And before this is over, the American people will have a better picture of it."

But the American people had already gotten a clear picture, and it was certainly a very different impression from what McCarthy had in mind. The point had been made a few days earlier during one of the several McCarthy-Symington skirmishes that had marked the closing sessions of the hearings.

"You're not fooling anyone, Mr. Symington," McCarthy said as he and his Democratic adversary continued to bait each other. "You're not fooling anyone at all."

Symington hit back swiftly. "Let me tell you something, Senator," he said. "The American people have had a look at you for six weeks. And you're not fooling anyone either." It would serve as an epigraph for the hearings and an epitaph for McCarthy's career.

11

To the Bitter End

A s bad as Karl Mundt had thought that chairing the Army-McCarthy hearings would be, the experience turned out to be even worse than he feared. As he later recalled, he considered "this distasteful job," as he had originally described it, the most miserable assignment of his long career on Capitol Hill. Not only was he obliged to endure the complaints and bickering of his Senate colleagues, he also had to bear the wrath of the public. On one day alone five thousand telegrams landed on his desk. Their senders all had one thing in common: they were angry at Chairman Mundt. About half thought he had been too harsh on McCarthy, the others thought he had been too easy.

Now, with the worst behind him and the end of the hearings in sight, it seemed to Mundt that a celebration might be in order—a chance to wash out the bad tastes of the past ten weeks and restore a measure of amity. Mundt wanted to do this with flair. He would invite not only his colleagues but witnesses and staffers on both sides as well as the members of the press. Straining for humor, the invitations were sent out as mock subpoenas, commanding one and all "to appear before a SUBSTANCE SEEKING SENATE COMMITTEE, to aid in an investigation of Vagaries, Vintages and Viands" on June 21, in the Senate caucus room. "Fail Not to Leave Behind all Peeves, Prejudices, Points of Order and Pistols under pain of exclusion and/or rejection," the invitation admonished in a final burst of archness.

Unfortunately many of those on Mundt's guest list were more interested in retribution than reconciliation. So absorbed was Mundt with his own difficulties and his anticipated relief that he grossly underestimated the intensity of the ill will the hearings conducted under his stewardship had generated. No sooner had they received their invitations than the Army's representatives sent their regrets, and so did the Democratic members of the committee.

Far from being willing to abandon their "peeves and prejudices," the three committee Democrats had caucused June 18, the day after the hearings finally ended, and demanded a wholesale "housecleaning" of the committee staff whose work McCarthy had defended so vehemently during the hearings. No new investigations should go forward without this cleanup, the Democrats insisted. For good measure they also called on the Justice Department to consider perjury indictments against some witnesses. The Democrats did not name their preferred targets, but no one doubted that they had Cohn and McCarthy in mind.

What made the Democratic response all the more ominous to Mundt and his Republican brethren was that many of the same points were made in a closing statement by Michigan senator Charles Potter, one of four Republicans on the committee. Until this occasion Potter, like Senator Dworshak, had been almost invisible during the hearings. Like his fellow war hero, Eisenhower, Potter had always had trouble finding a voice and a focus in politics. But at the last minute, at the end of the hearings, a veteran Michigan political reporter named Tommy McIntyre, who was dedicated to the destruction of

McCarthy and who had become Potter's press secretary, prepared and issued a press release over Potter's signature which at least in part aligned him with McCarthy's Democratic critics. Potter's statement too called for the firing of Cohn and his cohorts and perjury action by Justice, thus confronting Mundt and his fellow Republicans with the threat of a new committee majority—the three Democrats plus the suddenly energized Potter.

This by itself would probably have been enough to doom Mundt's strained effort at goodwill, but there was more. No sooner had the Democrats made known their demands than McCarthy fired back at them, calling their proposals "dishonest" and "dangerous to the country."

And McCarthy had another arrow in his quiver. He announced that he was planning to make "very serious charges of wrongdoing" against a Democrat not on the subcommittee. The alleged wrongdoing, McCarthy said, had nothing to do with communism but rather dealt with an improper attempt to use influence on a government agency.

McCarthy's statement was of a piece with many other ambiguous threats he had made since rising to prominence. But this one had a somber footnote. His warning made the Washington papers on the morning of Saturday, June 19. That same morning Senator Lester Hunt, a Wyoming Democrat and a longtime critic of McCarthy's Senate conduct, drove to his office from his home in northwest Washington and shot himself through the head with a .22 caliber rifle. He died a few hours later in a Washington hospital.

Friends attributed Hunt's suicide to concerns about his health; he was being treated for a kidney ailment at Bethesda Naval Hospital. And ill health was the reason that Hunt had given a week earlier for his abrupt decision not to seek reelection to a second Senate term, a withdrawal that seemed to dim Democratic chances of regaining control of the closely divided Senate in the forthcoming midterm elections. But the truth, which Hunt did not mention, was far darker. He was being hounded by Republican Senate leaders who threatened to broadcast throughout his home state the fact that his son, Lester Hunt, Jr., had been arrested a year earlier for soliciting an undercover Washington police officer, part of a sting operation designed to trap gay men.

Because this was a first offense and a misdemeanor, the police agreed not to prosecute young Hunt, who was then president of the student body at the Episcopal Theological School in Cambridge, Massachusetts, and a civil liberties activist. But then word of the matter reached Senator Herman Welker of Idaho, a ferociously partisan Republican and so close to McCarthy that he was sometimes referred to as "Little Joe from Idaho." With or without McCarthy's knowledge, Welker let Hunt know that his son would be prosecuted unless he himself did not seek reelection.

At first Hunt refused to drop out of the race, so Welker and New Hampshire senator Styles Bridges bullied the Washington police into prosecuting Hunt, and also leaked the story to the *Washington Times-Herald*. As the months wore on, Hunt was caught in mounting cross-pressures. Apart from the *Times-Herald* story, young Hunt's arrest had drawn little attention. But now Republicans were threatening to use his son's misadventure against him by spreading the news in his reelection campaign in Wyoming. Meanwhile Democrats, desperate to take charge of the Senate in the next term, and convinced Hunt was their best if not only chance to hold the Wyoming seat, were urging him to run. In addition to these political conflicts, he was tormented by guilt over his son's behavior, blaming himself for not spending enough time with the young man.

Eventually he caved in and agreed not to run again. But friends claimed that some Republicans were not satisfied; they wanted him to resign immediately so that the Republican governor of Wyoming could appoint a member of his own party to fill the vacancy, thus consolidating the narrow one-vote advantage the Republicans held in the Senate. Given the turmoil in Hunt's mind and the despair in his heart, it would not have taken much to push him over the edge and get him to pull the trigger on his .22.

If McCarthy had targeted him for attack, it would have not been surprising given the pattern of their relationship. The two men were close to being on the worst of terms. Their first open clash came in 1949, Hunt's first year in the Senate, when he was a member of the Armed Services subcommittee looking into the war crimes trials of the Nazis involved in the Malmedy massacres, an issue that McCarthy was trying to make a cause célèbre. McCarthy, who did not belong to the subcommittee but had finagled an invitation to sit in, characteristically all but took over the proceedings. At one point his grilling of the Army officer who had been the chief prosecutor at the trials became so heavy-handed that Hunt interrupted and reminded McCarthy, "This hearing is not a prosecution of the witness before us. We will get his full statement and then decide on its propriety."

"I entirely disagree," said Senator McCarthy. "It's a mistake for me to sit in on this if that is the purpose of the committee." Later after Hunt and the subcommittee chairman, Raymond Baldwin of Connecticut, had rejected McCarthy's demand that the Army prosecutors take lie-detector tests, McCarthy stormed out of the meeting and claimed the decision proved that the committee did not really wish to get at the truth.

More broadly, Hunt had long been disturbed about McCarthy's reckless approach to investigating and the harm he had done to innocent individuals. With chilling prescience he wrote to a friend, "There have been many suicides due to the smearing received either in committee hearings or from remarks made in the United States Congress." Hunt was so troubled by this that he introduced a joint congressional resolution in 1951 to abolish or at least limit the absolute immunity granted members of Congress for their official statements. Hunt's proposal would have made lawmakers open to damage suits for libel or slander. "If situations confront the Congress in which it can no longer control its members by the rules of society, justice and fair play, then Congress has, I feel, a moral obligation to take drastic steps to remedy those situations," Hunt wrote in a *New York Times* magazine article promoting his idea.

Although the link between McCarthy and Hunt's death is only circumstantial, it cannot be dismissed out of hand. McCarthy, as the saying goes, had means, motive, and opportunity. His pal, "Little Joe" Welker, would certainly have told him of the stress besetting his old adversary, Hunt. And it would have been a fair bet that a vague threat of the sort McCarthy issued would have been seen by Hunt as aimed at him. The reference to interfering with a government agency could mean Hunt's efforts to prevent charges being filed against his son. McCarthy, of course, could not have expected that Hunt would take his own life. But it is plausible that McCarthy's implied threat of exposure would have been sufficient to persuade Hunt to surrender to the demands of Republicans and resign on the spot. And that would have strengthened the GOP's Senate hand just when McCarthy was in need of all the help he could get.

Although no one will ever know what was in Lester Hunt's mind that final Saturday morning of his life, the suspicions of a causal link to McCarthy were evident enough that Karl Mundt felt obliged to issue a denial of sorts. He wanted it understood, Mundt said, that Hunt was "positively" not the senator referred to by McCarthy as under investigation by the committee staff. Mundt claimed the reference was to "an old case." But Mundt did not say who the unfortunate senator was that McCarthy had in mind. And nothing more was heard from McCarthy about the wrongdoer he was supposedly on the verge of exposing. Mundt's unpersuasive denial really amounted to a confession, or at least an acknowledgment, that McCarthy had earned such a reputation for himself that in a case like Hunt's the senator from Wisconsin would immediately come to mind as a potential victimizer.

Before Hunt's suicide, Drew Pearson reported on the pressuring of Hunt by Welker and Bridges in his syndicated column published in several Wyoming newspapers and in Bridges's home state of New Hampshire. The *Washington Post* did not run the column, probably because the paper shied away from references to homosexuality. But another syndicated columnist, Marquis Childs, known for being more restrained than Pearson, did get the gist of the story into the *Post* ten days after Hunt's death. Childs avoided explaining the reasons for the arrest of Lester Hunt, Jr., referring to the incident as a police action. But otherwise he pulled no punches. "In the recent suicide of Senator Lester Hunt, Democrat of Wyoming, his friends believe that the threat of a smear contributed to a shocking tragedy," Childs wrote. Childs targeted Welker for warning Hunt that the facts of his son's arrest "would find their way into every mailbox in Wyoming."

But Childs did not spare McCarthy: "The conviction is spreading that Sen. Joseph McCarthy, as chairman of the Senate committee on Government Operations and its investigating subcommittee, is using funds voted by the Senate to investigate other Senators. Nothing like that has ever happened before. It came in Senator McCarthy's hint that he was considering charges to be made against another Senator." Childs conceded there were other reasons why Hunt might have taken his life, including ill health. "If this were an isolated incident it might pass without comment," he wrote. "But today it threatens to become a pattern."

Hunt's tragedy did serve one purpose as far as Karl Mundt was concerned. It gave him an excuse to cancel his ill-conceived party. "It is not known if a later date will be set," Mundt said. It was the last anyone would hear of that celebration.

On this morbid note the hearings concluded. To those directly involved, it seemed at times as if they would go on forever. They did consume 36 days spread over almost two months, a length of time exceeded in modern congressional history only by the World War II inquiry into the Japanese attack on Pearl Harbor, which went on almost twice as long, and the investigation of President Truman's dismissal of Douglas MacArthur during the Korean War, which endured for 41 days. The Army-McCarthy committee heard from 22 witnesses, consumed 188 hours of television time, and spread its work out on 7,424 pages of transcript.

Although Chairman Mundt's clumsy plans for a celebration fell flat, a good many people around the country pronounced themselves relieved, if not delighted, that the hearings had ended. Adlai Stevenson called the proceedings a "melancholy spectacle" and declared that they had done "irreparable injury to the prestige of our country around the world"—though he, like others who made similar assertions, offered no evidence of this purported harm. Editorial comment tended to follow predictable lines. The newspapers that had been McCarthy's strongest defenders throughout his career stood foursquare behind him now. "We think these hearings were beneficial if for no other reason than that they alerted or realerted millions of Americans to the communist conspiracy," said the right-wing *New York Daily News*. Cried the equally conservative *Los Angeles Herald Examiner*, "Let's get behind Senator McCarthy and show him the public is united in his efforts to rid the country of the communist evil."

For McCarthy's critics, the hearings provided that much more reason to condemn him. The public would decide the case, said the *New York Times.* "In the larger sense," the *Times* declared, "the issue was not between McCarthy and the Army or the Senate but rather between McCarthy and the U.S. Constitution." Another severe McCarthy critic, the *Washington Post*, dismissed the idea of firing Roy Cohn as an answer to the problem posed by the hearings. It declared the "real problem to be Senator McCarthy, his influence and his control. And his is peculiarly a problem for the whole Senate rather than Senator McCarthy's committee."

This was a problem that the Senate—or more precisely its Republican members—appeared in no great hurry to solve, until they were forced to by the one man in their number who was unwilling to let McCarthy go unpunished, Ralph Flanders of Vermont. Seeking to take advantage of the blows McCarthy had been suffering on television, Flanders did not even wait for the hearings to end before he acted. On June 11, within forty-eight hours of McCarthy's dramatic confrontation with Joe Welch, Flanders introduced a motion to strip McCarthy of his key Senate prerogatives—his chairmanship of the Permanent Subcommittee on Investigations and its parent, the Senate Government Operations Committee. The supposed predicate for this action, or so Flanders said, was McCarthy's failure to respond to charges about his alleged mishandling of his financial activities which had been investigated in 1952 by a committee headed by Iowa Democrat Guy Gillette. But it was evident to everyone in Washington that what had given new life to this old controversy was the Army-McCarthy hearings.

When the charges by Gillette's committee were first made in 1952, McCarthy had dismissed them as "a smear." But Flanders had a ready retort now. "It is no defense," he said, "to call the charges 'a smear.'"

Still the Senate panjandrums in both parties who had let McCarthy run rampant for four years were unwilling to move against him. Republican Majority Leader William Knowland immediately rebuffed Flanders, claiming the sanction he proposed against McCarthy was not justified. And anyhow, Knowland contended, debate over Flanders's proposal would tie up the Senate for weeks, damaging chances of passing Eisenhower's legislative program. Hardly anyone raised his voice to disagree. Flanders seemed up against a brick wall. Few senators, even if they were not allied with McCarthy, were willing to back such an unprecedented move against one of their colleagues.

But help was on the way in the form of advice and organizing muscle from an organization called the National Committee for an Effective Congress (NCEC), a liberal lobbying group which had made opposition to McCarthy its prime interest. To Flanders's credit, as imbued as he was with the determination to overturn McCarthy, he was willing to listen to advice from those who shared his sentiments but had a more pragmatic sense of tactics. Guided by Maurice Rosenblatt, NCEC's founder, and other McCarthy foes in the Senate and elsewhere, Flanders scrapped his foredoomed proposal to take away McCarthy's chairmanship. In its place he substituted another less extraordinary but nonetheless severe remedy: censure. As radical as censure was, unlike Flanders's initial gambit it was not unprecedented. In more than a century and a half the Senate had censured five of its members, the most recent being Hiram Bingham III, Republican of Connecticut. He had been punished in 1929 for hiring a staff member to work on tariff legislation who was also working for Connecticut's manufacturers association. Bingham stayed in the Senate until 1932 when he was defeated for reelection in the Democratic landslide that year.

In asking for support of his new resolution, Flanders sought a balanced, above-the-battle tone. He even offered praise for McCarthy, saluting him for "alerting his fellow citizens to one part of the communist danger—that of internal subversion." But, as Flanders phrased it, McCarthy had also presented "the opportunity to appraise our national political morality." This was a pretty bland and amorphous incentive to persuade senators to deal with an issue most of them would much rather have avoided. Support was so difficult to come by that Flanders agreed to wait ten days before bringing his resolution to the floor, heeding Democrats who promised they would use the time to rally more votes for the measure. But when the appointed time arrived, it did not seem the Democrats had delivered the backing they promised. As James Reston, Washington bureau chief of the *New York Times*, reported, the first night of the debate was devoted to criticizing Flanders rather than to censuring McCarthy. "There was very little evidence" that Flanders had the votes to carry his proposal, Reston reported.

Disappointed Democratic critics of McCarthy complained that Flanders should have waited until the final report of the Army-McCarthy hearings had been made public, and that his case against McCarthy lacked specifics. When that report finally did appear, at the end of August, it was a heavily compromised document that added little to the debate. It was overshadowed by Flanders's drive for censure, which by then commanded the attention of the Senate and the nation.

When Flanders made his case on July 30, Senate Majority Leader Knowland opposed it, and leading Democrats such as Minority Leader Lyndon Johnson and John McClellan, the ranking Democrat on the panel that had conducted the Army-McCarthy hearings, were anchored firmly on the sidelines. Yet perhaps because the televised hearings had stirred such interest in McCarthy and his tactics, the public seemed to believe that Flanders had initiated something important. The largest crowds of the session jammed the Senate galleries the afternoon that Flanders was expected to launch the debate. When his speech was delayed until evening, the galleries thinned out. But they were packed again when he finally spoke that evening.

In calm tones Flanders read his remarks for twenty minutes, calling McCarthy a "Fifth Amendment Senator" because of his failure to answer questions raised by the Gillette Committee that had investigated his activities two years earlier. By giving that committee the back of his hand, Flanders charged, McCarthy had "spread contempt over the Senate as a whole."

McCarthy sat through most of Flanders's oration, though he sought to give the impression that he was more absorbed with papers on his desk than with his accuser's rhetoric. His chief defender that night was Everett Dirksen, who charged that much of Flanders's support came from liberals and the Communist party, eager to make trouble for the GOP.

Meanwhile Flanders's allies pressed their case. On July 31, the night after the debate began, Arkansas senator J. William Fulbright responded to claims that the case against McCarthy lacked specifics. Fulbright, one of the Democrats outside the leadership recruited by Rosenblatt and his NCEC forces, offered a six-point bill of particulars against the Wisconsin senator. Among Fulbright's charges were McCarthy's urging federal employees to violate the law by giving him information on alleged security threats, his mistreatment of General Zwicker, and his "unwarranted attack" on George Marshall.

But it was hard to tell whether any of this ammunition had altered the heavy odds against censure. Fulbright's complaints, after all, were nothing new. That Sunday, with the Senate taking the day off, Senator Knowland, as opposed to Flanders's effort as ever, announced that the censure debate would not be allowed "to drag on." Knowland hinted that Flanders's proposal might be turned over to a committee for study. To Oklahoma Democrat Mike Monroney, that sounded a lot like a plan to bury censure, and he told Knowland so.

For his part, Knowland reminded Monroney that the Democratic party had never censured McCarthy, though it had controlled the Senate when McCarthy was "very powerful." Said Knowland, "Now that perhaps he has been a little crippled, it can do what it was not willing to do then."

Monroney's reply recalled the spectacle of the Army-McCarthy hearings. "If he is crippled, he has crippled himself before the country by his own exposure of McCarthyism on the television sets of the nation," he said.

But Knowland was firm in insisting that consideration of censure be turned over to a committee. "I would not censure a criminal, even had I seen a criminal act committed," he claimed, "without at least giving the person his day in court."

One measure of the political influence McCarthy was believed to wield by his colleagues, including some Democrats, was the stance of Robert Kennedy's older brother, Massachusetts senator John F. Kennedy. His aide, Theodore Sorensen, who was to help draft the future president's memorable 1961 inaugural address, drafted remarks for Kennedy to deliver, declaring his support for censure. But Kennedy's argument was based on the narrowest of grounds—McCarthy's backing for Roy Cohn. Otherwise Kennedy sounded defensive to the point of being apologetic as he emphasized how steadfast he had been in supporting McCarthy's legislative proposals and investigations. To cover himself further, Kennedy joined with Hubert Humphrey in supporting an ill-conceived measure which outlawed the Communist party in the United States and swept through the House and Senate with barely any dissent.

But Kennedy never had to deliver that speech because the battle over censure took a surprising turn, pivoting on Knowland's proposal for a study committee but triggered by McCarthy's own habitual recklessness. At first Knowland's idea for a committee study generated little enthusiasm and created some odd political allies among its opponents. Idaho's Welker, one of McCarthy's ardent supporters, agreed with liberal Democrats Monroney and Fulbright that a censure vote should be taken quickly, though Welker made clear that he and the two Democrats would be on opposite sides of the roll call.

Said Welker, "I am not going to censure a Senator who is carrying the ball alone in a crusade to save America, if he may have said something in an ill-tempered vein." As for Flanders's complaint that McCarthy had shown "contempt" for the Senate, Welker retorted, somewhat irrelevantly, "No one can tell me that Irishman would not give the shirt off his back to anyone who needed it except a dirty, lying, stinking Communist."

Indiana Republican Homer Capehart probably spoke for most of his colleagues when he argued that instead of judging McCarthy, "What we ought to do is forget him." For the first two days of the three-day debate, this appeared to be a likely course for the Senate to follow. Much of the argument was carried either by die-hard McCarthy haters among the Democrats or equally obsessed McCarthy supporters among the Republicans. Knowland's proposal for a study committee charted the path of least resistance that most senators, like Capehart, seemed to want to follow.

At this point McCarthy stepped in with the kind of tactic he had tried so often during the televised hearings, one that had helped put him in his present state of jeopardy. He took the floor to enter into the *Congressional Record* a letter written by Harry Woodring, Franklin Roosevelt's failed secretary of war. Woodring, who had opposed aid to Britain and France, had been dismissed by Roosevelt in 1940 when the president realized that Woodring was not up to handling the military crisis that would soon plunge the country into World War II. Democrat Woodring's letter, dated June 23, 1954, and addressed to a New York businessman of no particular reputation, accused McCarthy's old target, George C. Marshall, of selling out Nationalist China under orders from the Truman administration. Woodring added: "I can tell you that he would sell out his grandmother for personal advantage."

In this manner did McCarthy render one of the greatest public services of his ill-starred Senate career. His exercise in vituperation, renewing his slander of an American whom many considered a national hero, reminded the Senate of the image the junior senator from Wisconsin had presented in the nation's living rooms, courtesy of television, for thirty-six tedious and frustrating days that spring. And it helped drive home to them the reality that this impression would persist unless his colleagues made clear to the country their disapproval of his behavior. Slowly but steadily the realization built among McCarthy's peers that this was a responsibility they could not ignore.

It was Irving Ives, liberal Republican of New York, who transformed Knowland's easy-way-out approach of smothering censure by study committee into a telling weapon against McCarthy. Ives persuaded the Senate to amend Knowland's proposal in a way that put teeth into it—the censure study committee was instructed to report back to the Senate before final adjournment. In that fashion Ives dispelled the hope of McCarthy sympathizers that the drive for censure would wither away from inattention over time. Adding more muscle to this requirement was another amendment which gave the committee subpoena power. When the roll was called, Knowland's motion, with its two crucial amendments, carried 75 to 12.

Three days later Vice President Nixon appointed a committee of three Republicans and three Democrats drawn from the recommendations of the leadership from both sides. By now the recognition that the Senate would at long last have to deal with McCarthy had spread to the Senate leadership of both parties, as reflected by the three Democrats and three Republicans that Lyndon Johnson and William Knowland chose for the committee. They were among the senators least likely to allow McCarthy an excuse to create a distraction. None of them had taken a strong public stand on McCarthy, either for or against. All were conservative, highly respected members of the "club," an inner sanctum in that most exclusive of American clubs. On the Republican side were Arthur Watkins of Utah, a lawyer, former prosecutor, and state district judge; Frank Carlson of Kansas, former governor of his state and a longtime friend of Eisenhower's; and Francis Case of South Dakota, a Marine veteran of World War II. The Democrats came from similar well-settled backgrounds: Edwin Johnson of Colorado, former two-term governor of his state; John Stennis of Mississippi, a former prosecutor and state court jurist; and a new face in the Senate, freshly appointed to fill a vacancy, Sam Ervin, Jr., a respected judge from North Carolina, a man then little known who would achieve his own celebrity two decades in the future.

Not one of these six was from the East, the region most roiled over McCarthyism. Instead most came from the Far West, the Mountain States, and the South. The respect in which they were all held by their colleagues would serve to provide a buffer against criticism, so much so that if McCarthy were reckless enough to attack any of them personally, he would risk bringing down on himself the wrath of most of the Senate.

The collective character of the committee was epitomized by its chairman, Arthur Watkins of Utah, a man almost unknown outside his state and beyond the parameters of the Senate's inner circles. Watkins's life had not been spent making a big noise about himself or anyone else. The son of Mormon pioneers, in his first years out of college he worked as a Mormon missionary in the slums of New York City. After he was released from Mormon service he stayed in New York to take a law degree from Columbia University, then moved to Utah to practice law and to win election as a state judge, a post he kept for twelve years. His first big success came in 1947 when, prodded by GOP leaders and against his better judgment, he took on a New Deal Democratic incumbent and upset him by fewer than five thousand votes. In his first term he built a reputation as a party loyalist and an isolationist skeptic of the country's post–World War II ventures. In 1952 he was reelected after turning down an offer from McCarthy to campaign for him in Utah. One of the last things he wanted in life or politics was to chair the committee on censuring McCarthy. But party leaders told him they needed his judicial experience to lend gravitas to the committee. Given the Mormon tradition of service in which he was reared, Watkins saw no other choice but to accept.

The choice of Watkins and his equally stolid fellow panel members reflected the Senate's pervasive disapproval of the Army-McCarthy hearings, whose supposed excesses were generally blamed on television. One of the new panel's first decisions was to ban television coverage of its hearings. Not only TV but even news photographers were barred. In a sharp departure from the leadership of most Senate inquiries, Watkins made plain he wanted as little coverage of his committee as possible. "Let's get off the front pages and back among the obituaries," he declared. The hearings would be conducted according to "rules of evidence in courts of the U.S., state and federal." This stricture cut down on the kinds of freewheeling tactics that McCarthy and even Joseph Welch had practiced during the Army-McCarthy hearings. The committee gave McCarthy or his counsel the right to cross-examine witnesses. It also agreed to pay the $10,000 salary of the lawyer McCarthy had retained, an up-and-coming star of the Washington legal firmament named Edward Bennett Williams.

A drinking buddy of McCarthy's, Williams had graduated from Georgetown Law School in 1945 and then gone to work for one of the capital's leading law firms, Hogan and Hartson. But he was interested in larger challenges, bigger headlines, and fatter fees than he was getting from the auto injury cases he was trying as a young associate, so Williams set up his own firm, determined, he said, to specialize in civil liberties. True to his goal, at least initially, he defended the likes of Robert Rossen and Sidney Buchman, two Hollywood writers cited for contempt of Congress for refusing to answer the questions of HUAC about alleged Communist activities.

If some might see a contradiction between such efforts and his representation of McCarthy, that did not disturb Williams. Both men were similar in temperament, though Williams was far more disciplined than his client. Both were devout Catholics and also devoted to their Irish origins. And Williams was at least as much of an anti-Communist as McCarthy claimed to be. Beyond that both men, as Murray Kempton put it, were "anti-Harvard, anti-sissy, and anti-genteel." They resented the elitists who staffed the upper echelons of the federal government, particularly the State Department. Williams had been McCarthy's lawyer in legal battles with Senators Benton and Tydings and in a tax dispute with the IRS. Now the opportunity to defend him against censure amounted to, by a long shot, the most important legal challenge the thirty-four-year-old Williams had yet faced, and he had no intention of passing up such a chance. Moreover he could rationalize the decision by casting McCarthy not as the great threat to constitutional protections that his critics perceived but rather as a victim of persecution by his enemies in the Senate.

So imbued was Williams with this new cause that he sought to persuade McCarthy's ally, *National Review* publisher William F. Buckley, to assist him in the defense. A great deal hung on clearing the name of McCarthy, a great American, Buckley later recalled Williams telling him. But Buckley demurred and suggested that Williams instead sign on L. Brent Bozell, a lawyer and another McCarthy admirer. Williams took the suggestion with what turned out to be disastrous consequences.

The relationship between Williams and his new client was in trouble from the start. Williams had taken on McCarthy's defense only after being promised by the senator that he would not butt into his lawyer's handling of the case—a pledge Roy Cohn could have told Williams that McCarthy was probably innately incapable of keeping.

On the very first day of the hearings, August 31, the conflict between McCarthy's ego and William's lawyerly sense of his own responsibility became evident. The issue that prompted the trouble was McCarthy's effort to challenge the impartiality of one of the three committee Democrats, and one of its most respected members, Ed Johnson of Colorado. McCarthy's complaint against Johnson was based on a clip from a March 1954 story in the *Denver Post* which quoted the senator as saying, "In my opinion, there is not a man among the Democratic leaders of Congress who does not loathe Joe McCarthy." When Williams objected to Johnson early on, Chairman Watkins had briskly explained that the status of Senator Johnson, who had been named to the committee by the full Senate, was not subject to committee review. Johnson himself had already explained that he did not personally loathe McCarthy: "In response to a telephone call from Denver, I agreed that some of my Democratic colleagues did not like Senator McCarthy."

Dissatisfied with the Watkins ruling, McCarthy began to argue his case when Watkins cut him off, reminding him that his lawyer had already spoken on this issue. "We are not going to permit both of you to argue the same matter," the chairman said. McCarthy, as was his wont, persisted anyway, demanding to know whether Johnson had been accurately quoted. He got as far as saying "Mr. Chairman, I should be entitled to know whether or not . . ." when Watkins banged down his gavel and snapped, "The Senator is out of order."

McCarthy went on and finished his sentence ". . . whether it is true or false."

Down came the gavel again. Said Watkins: "We are not going to be interrupted by these diversions and sidelines. We are going straight down the line." Afterward, out of range of Watkins's gavel, McCarthy, sounding as if he were mimicking Jimmy Durante, told reporters, "This is the most unheard of thing I have ever heard of." His counsel tried to calm him. "Now don't get excited," Williams told him. The futility of such a plea had been demonstrated time and again to a national television audience that spring.

Similarly Watkins gave short shrift to an argument that lawyer Williams contended was "the heart of our defense," the claim that McCarthy should not have to answer for conduct in earlier Congresses. "Our counsel and others have also looked at the precedents," Watkins said. "We do not agree with you. That is obvious or we would not have the charges before us at this time."

If the Army-McCarthy hearings reminded some viewers of a television variety show, the McCarthy censure proceedings, with their emphasis on legalisms, resembled nothing so much as an appellate court. Chairman Watkins's determination to bore the public near to death if necessary in order to avoid the wild-and-wooly goings-on at the duel between McCarthy and the Army was reflected, and reinforced, by his choice of committee counsel. He was E. Wallace Chadwick, a man as unlike the windy, overbearing Ray Jenkins as Watkins himself was unlike Joe McCarthy. A former Republican congressman from Pennsylvania, Chadwick in his single term in Congress had managed to impress members on both sides with his competence and professionalism. Neither as flamboyant as Jenkins nor as witty as Joseph Welch, his greatest strength in this situation, besides his skill at the law and a bulldog's determination, was lack of an ego.

He made his presence felt on the first day of the hearings when in his uninflected voice and dreary manner he began reading the bulk of the charges and evidence against McCarthy into the record. Williams suggested as a time-saving alternative that the committee just place all the material into the record with a single stroke. But the committee turned that idea down. Its members were far more interested in getting the case against McCarthy into the public record than in sparing some of the details.

And so the proceedings rolled on, lacking much in the way of drama or emotion but, like the mills of the gods, grinding exceedingly small. On September 13, after nine consecutive days of hearings, the committee recessed to write its report. Although the senators judging him tried to avoid offering any hint of what their verdict would be, McCarthy had a pretty good idea that he would not hear good news. After the last session, Williams asked that counsel Chadwick and his assistant be barred from aiding in the writing of the committee report because of their "role as advocates," and that "real counsel, independent to this committee" be retained instead. McCarthy himself complained that Chadwick could "hardly write a fair report" since he had "very, very vigorously prosecuted me." But the committee rejected his motion. The committee, said Watkins, had "absolute confidence" in its counsel's fairness.

The committee moved to judgment with deliberate speed. On September 27 it released its report, in which the six members voted unanimously to censure McCarthy on two counts. One was for "contemptuous, contumacious and denunciatory" behavior toward the Senate Elections Subcommittee, under Senator Gillette, which had investigated him in 1951–1952. This was the inquiry that had followed in the wake of the earlier probe of McCarthy's involvement in Millard Tydings's defeat in 1950. Six times the subcommittee had asked McCarthy to testify, the Watkins report pointed out; but each time

McCarthy had refused and instead had called the subcommittee "completely dishonest" and charged that using public funds to investigate him was tantamount to stealing from the taxpayers.

The second count was for his "reprehensible" behavior toward General Zwicker during the probe into subversion at Fort Monmouth. "Senator McCarthy knew that General Zwicker was a loyal and outstanding officer who had devoted his life to the service of his country and was strongly opposed to Communists and their activities," the report said. He also knew that Zwicker was only carrying out the orders of his superiors in granting an honorable discharge of Maj. Irving Peress, the dentist whose left-wing views had made him a principal target for McCarthy's probe of the Army. "Under these circumstances," the Watkins Committee held, "the conduct of Senator McCarthy was inexcusable."

Although it criticized McCarthy on other grounds, the committee shrewdly turned away from incorporating these alleged misdeeds into the censure recommendation. This strategy was intended to make it easier to defend against the assault the committee was sure to face from McCarthy's partisans. For example, in weighing the allegation that McCarthy had abused Ralph Flanders—of whom he had said, "I think they should get a man with a net and take him to a good, quiet place"—the committee called McCarthy's remarks "highly improper." But it pointed out this was an attack on an individual senator who had made "provocative speeches." It was not an attack on a senator for an official action he had taken as a member of a committee, and therefore was not grounds for censure.

Such distinctions did not impress McCarthy. He sought to depict the action against him as an offense against the institution to which he belonged, even if he had generally disregarded its prestige and traditions. "If the Senate upholds this report and all its implications, it will have gone a long way toward abdication of its constitutional right to investigate wrongdoing in the executive departments," he declared.

The Senate faced a tortuous choice. For many of its members, conscience and a sense of obligation toward the legislative body whose prerogatives McCarthy now professed to be defending inclined them in favor of censure. But for many— including those leaning toward censure—political considerations raised a red flag. McCarthy may have lost ground with the majority of Americans, but he still had a hard cadre of supporters, and these partisans felt bound even closer by the threat of censure.

After the dramatic face-off with Welch, the pollster George Gallup wrote to a friend that McCarthy had probably hit bottom. "The people who have not been won over to date probably cannot be won by any known tactics. Even if it were known that McCarthy had killed five innocent children, they would probably still go along with him."

The decision for the Senate would be hard enough, and Majority Leader Knowland saw no reason to add to the difficulties by debating the issue just before the midterm elections. On September 24, three days before the Watkins Committee issued its report, Knowland declared that the Senate would reconvene on November 8 after the November 2 elections, so it could act "in an atmosphere free from pre-election tensions."

But if Knowland had gotten the November 2 monkey off the Senate's back, there were plenty of other tensions when they returned. The Republicans were in an even bleaker mood than before, having lost control of both houses of Congress to the Democrats. It was a setback to which some believed the fracas between the Republican senator from Wisconsin and the Republican administration had contributed. As for the Democrats, they returned with greater confidence as a result of their victory at the polls, but no less cautious than before about the McCarthy controversy. Under the leadership of

Lyndon Johnson they were mostly content to let the Republicans carry on the censure fight among themselves until the moment for voting arrived, a strategy that promised potential gains at minimum risk.

No Democrat was more cautious than Massachusetts senator Kennedy. His office was being flooded with letters from his state's strong cohort of McCarthy supporters, and the pro-McCarthy *Boston Post* was challenging his Americanism. He had been in constant pain since summer from a severe onset of Addison's disease, an affliction he never publicly acknowledged. When he underwent surgery late in October, his condition was listed by the hospital as critical. His illness was attributed to his wartime service, a diagnosis the press accepted. Nevertheless he soon felt well enough that he could have notified Sorensen and taken a public position on censure. He avoided taking any stand, and absented himself from the eventual Senate roll call on McCarthy's fate. Later, as his credentials for the presidency were challenged by liberals in his party, he claimed that he would have voted for censure.

On both sides most senators sensed that having gone this far down the road to censure, the Senate was unlikely to stop short. But no one expected McCarthy to go down without a fight, and he did not disappoint. No sooner had the Senate returned to business on November 8 than McCarthy was on his feet in protest. "Highly improper," McCarthy complained about Knowland's motion, at Watkins's request, to make a few typographical changes in the report of the select committee, a routine procedure. When Watkins explained that in addition to the typos he also wished to delete one other "obvious error," McCarthy could not resist the opening. "I have found so many obvious errors that I should like to know which one the Senator is deleting," he snapped.

A few minutes later the Senate adjourned for the day, having accomplished nothing of substance. But McCarthy had set the tone for the debate to follow. On his way out of the men's room he slapped a reporter on the back and declared, "I'm back in shape."

Next day he could not even wait for the Senate to begin debate before throwing the first punch. It was at this point that Brent Bozell, the assistant whom Williams had hired on William Buckley's suggestion, made his presence felt. He handed to McCarthy and released to the press a speech that Buckley described as elegant but that also sealed McCarthy's doom. The address Bozell wrote and McCarthy delivered charged that the Communist party had "extended its tentacles to that most respected of American bodies, the U.S. Senate; that it has made a committee of the Senate its unwitting handmaiden." That predictably infuriated a number of senators, among them South Dakota's Francis Case, a member of the committee, who said McCarthy's rhetoric offered proof of the count in the censure indictment that he had been "contemptuous" of a Senate committee.

That speech opened the way for the Democrats at last to enter the debate on the floor, from which they had carefully abstained. Lyndon Johnson, soon to be majority leader of the Senate, assigned Mississippi's John Stennis, a member of the committee, to let the Senate know where the Democrats stood. Stennis denounced McCarthy for pouring "slush and slime" on the Senate in his "handmaiden to communism" speech, adding that if the Senate did not censure McCarthy, "something big and fine will have gone from this chamber, something wrong will have entered and been accepted."

McCarthy seemed satisfied to accept his fate. He now wanted to become a victim and to use his martyrdom to expand and strengthen his own personal political base outside the Republican party. Boosting such hopes, on Sunday, November 15, his supporters outside the Senate launched a ten-day nationwide drive to collect ten million signatures urging the Senate to reject the censure charges against McCarthy as inspired by Communist propaganda.

That Tuesday, as the debate roiled the Senate, McCarthy had himself admitted to Bethesda Naval Hospital for treatment of an elbow contusion. The next day the Senate voted to recess for ten days, until November 29, to give McCarthy time to recover.

McCarthy's foes were openly skeptical of his hospitalization. Liberal senator Wayne Morse, an independent from Oregon, recalled that after being thrown from a horse *he* had nevertheless shown up in the Senate in a wheelchair with his jaw wired (a medical procedure which some of those who had felt the lash of Morse's tongue hailed as a great improvement). McCarthy's supporters grasped at the delay as a last straw, hoping it would give the anti-censure petition drive enough time for a maximum effort. The petitions might not have much impact on the Senate roll call; but as McCarthy's backers wanted to believe, they would help keep his great anti-Communist crusade rolling in the post-censure era.

Meanwhile some Democrats were not shy about pointing to the elements of a conspiracy. The delay, they worried, would permit McCarthy's supporters to filibuster against censure and thus perhaps prevent action before the current Congress ended. That would mean the entire record of censure would be wiped out and McCarthy's foes would have to start over from scratch. But even die-hard opponents of censure, like Majority Leader Knowland, realized that such a scheme would likely be viewed by the public as a high-handed frustration of majority rule and would engender a damaging backlash.

During the recess some of McCarthy's Senate supporters worked in the back rooms, trying to write a compromise resolution. The proposal advanced chiefly by Illinois's Everett Dirksen and New Hampshire's Styles Bridges was that in return for an apology from McCarthy the Senate would slap

Joe's wrist but stop short of censure. But McCarthy himself, visited in his hospital room first by Arizona Republican senator Barry Goldwater and lawyer Williams and then by Dirksen, sneered at the idea. "I don't crawl. I learned to fight in an alley," he told Dirksen. "That's all I know."

On its return from recess November 29, as its first order of business the Senate voted to limit debate to three days, thus nullifying the Democrats' nightmare scenario. The proposal to prevent a filibuster was made by, of all people, Senator Joseph McCarthy. He now recognized the outcome as inevitable, and like a man declining a blindfold before facing a firing squad wanted to give the impression that he was not afraid to confront his fate.

He had never meant to offend anyone, McCarthy told the Senate, his right arm still in a sling. "I admit," he added, "that at times I have been extremely blunt in expressing my opinions. I do not claim to be a master of words." But he hastened to make clear that this was no apology. "In the facts and opinions that I held," he said, "I am unchanged."

Before the final vote the Senate did drop the censure count against McCarthy for his abuse of General Zwicker. In its place went a condemnation section against McCarthy for his "Communist handmaiden" sneer at the Watkins Committee.

On December 2 the Senate voted 67 to 22 to "condemn" rather than "censure" McCarthy, a hairsplitting semantic change designed to placate McCarthy's backers. Some of McCarthy's supporters professed satisfaction at the word change, but Senator Watkins pointed out that the last censure resolution adopted by the Senate had used the word "condemn" rather than "censure," adding that "condemn" was the word historically used in censure resolutions. Asked if he himself was comforted by the switch, McCarthy allowed his natural Irish wit to show in a rare moment of self-amusement. "Well," he said, "it wasn't exactly a vote of confidence."

Whatever the semantics, the forty-four Democrats present unanimously backed the resolution; the Republicans were evenly divided, twenty-two voting for, twenty-two against. For McCarthy the indignities continued even after the vote. The next day Eisenhower phoned Arthur Watkins, the man most responsible next to McCarthy himself for censure, specifically to tell him he had done "a splendid job."

For the defense lawyer, Edward Bennett Williams, it was a rare defeat but one he could easily live with. As he knew from the start, win or lose the censure fight would make him famous. He won rave notices in the press. Typical was Richard Rovere's comment in the *New Yorker* that Williams "is one of the most capable trial lawyers in Washington and an extremely personable young man." In the future the censure case would help Williams gain some infamous clients, among them Estes Kefauver's old punching bag, Frank Costello, and the future target of Robert Kennedy, Jimmy Hoffa.

As for his former client, McCarthy would have benefited from more of Williams's advice—if only he would have listened to it. Anger and depression do not foster good judgment, and McCarthy was no exception to that rule. He now did the worst possible thing: he struck back at the president. In a statement McCarthy recalled that he had campaigned vigorously "from coast to coast" for Eisenhower's election. Many of his critics had suggested that he apologize to the Senate for his conduct there, McCarthy noted. "I feel that, instead, I should apologize to the American people for what was an unintentional deception upon them." For his pains he was denounced by every Republican leader of note, including Everett Dirksen and the future leader of the conservative movement, Barry Goldwater.

McCarthy lingered in the Senate for two and half more years. Not only was he shunned by his political allies, he was ignored by the press. Some observers speculated that journalists and their editors had conspired to create a news "blackout" on anything he said or did. But such a conspiracy, which sounds like something McCarthy himself might have thought of, seems on its face unlikely. It would have been hard to enforce among the conspirators, and more to the point it was unnecessary. What McCarthy said and did no longer counted for news. The televised fight with the Army had robbed him of his influence and weakened and narrowed his support. A computer check of the historical index of the *New York Times*, the nation's "paper of record," offers evidence of his fall into obscurity. In 1954, when McCarthy was at the height of his fame and in the depths of his troubles, his name showed up more than 1,900 times. But the next year, 1955, following his censure, the use of McCarthy's name fell below 400. In 1956 it dropped to fewer than 250, and in the months of 1957 before his death on May 2 his name appeared only 75 times. "I think it was very sad," said Ruth Watt, chief clerk of McCarthy's subcommittee. "If he sent out a press release, you never saw it unless it was on the back page."

The demise of his political career was matched by his physical collapse. McCarthy had always been a heavy drinker, and by 1954 some friends guessed he was putting away a quart of whiskey a day. Reports of his public drunkenness became commonplace. "By the end of 1955 and 1956 he was in pretty bad shape," recalled Ruth Watt. He was in and out of Bethesda Naval Hospital where he was treated for cirrhosis as well as hepatitis and delirium tremens. He died on June 2, 1957, with his wife, Jean, by his side. The official cause of death was acute hepatitis. Joseph Raymond McCarthy was buried on a bluff overlooking the Fox River in Appleton's St. Mary's cemetery.

In the immediate aftermath of the Army-McCarthy hearings that proved to be McCarthy's undoing, many people had trouble seeing a point or purpose to the proceedings. "The bitter battle ends with no clear cut winners—only losers," said the *Buffalo News*. But with the passage of time, the condemnation of McCarthy, and the unraveling of his career, it became evident that while there may have been a number of losers, the biggest one by far was McCarthy himself. And just as clear was that there was one big winner. And that was television.

12

Unfinished Business

In his own postmortem on the Army-McCarthy hearings, delivered more than a decade after the event, Roy Cohn sought to minimize the impact of the televised confrontation in toppling McCarthy. The hearings were "a setback" to McCarthy, Cohn conceded, but he suggested that "there were other perhaps more fundamental reasons for his decline." For one thing, Cohn argued, McCarthy had been stage center for more than three years, and the public had become bored with his act. More particularly, Americans had lost interest in the threat of subversion.

But Cohn's argument overlooks the major cause of this changed public attitude: the increased revulsion of many Americans for McCarthy as a result of what they saw of him during the hearings. Much of this had more to do with personality and appearance than with ideology and substance. Even the artifices McCarthy employed worked against him. The cream-colored makeup he wore "gave a startling aspect to his jowls," Michael Straight of the *New Republic* observed. And when he leaned across the table to speak, "a roll of flesh beneath his black eyebrows came down over his upper eyelids, making slits of his eyes, and giving his face an almost Satanic look."

Beyond that, what also came across, as Straight and others pointed out, was McCarthy's disregard of the rules and codes to which most Americans felt obliged at least to pay lip service. With his slander of Samuel Reber's brother at the start of the hearings, and his assault on Frederick Fisher near the end, he demonstrated his contempt for widely accepted values that help make society civilized. So when Joseph Welch asked him, at the culminating moment of the hearings drama, "Have you no sense of decency?," it was a question that resonated with millions of Americans.

"McCarthy demonstrated with appalling clarity precisely what kind of man he is," James Reston wrote in the *Times* ten days before McCarthy's dramatic confrontation with Welch. Among the public there was great disagreement over the substance of the charges and countercharges between him and the Army, Reston noted. "But on one thing there seems little division: the Senator from Wisconsin is a bad-mannered man." And this was an impression impossible to avoid from the televised confrontation.

Those who doubt the significance of the hearings in McCarthy's downfall point out that the broadcasts were limited to two networks, one of them, DuMont, struggling to keep its head above water. Also, the proceedings failed to provide the sensational appeal of the Kefauver hearings with its panoply of mobsters. Moreover ABC and DuMont, in televising the hearings, were competing against a lineup of well-established daytime programs on CBS and NBC. Despite this the telecast scored some important successes. WNAC-TV, the Boston ABC outlet, captured 35 to 40 percent of the Boston television audience with the hearings. These were the highest consistent ratings of any station since television's advent in Boston, many of whose Irish-Catholic citizens viewed McCarthy as a champion of the causes closest to their hearts. In early May in New York City, ABC and DuMont coverage attracted close to 60 percent of the TV audience and raised the number of sets in use from 50 to 75 percent over the average. "Most noticeable in bars and restaurants in the midtown area was the silent attention which the hearings received," observed the *New York Herald Tribune* about the reaction in New York. And generally around the country, "a substantial portion of the public is watching intently and the audience seems to be growing," *Television Digest* commented after the first weeks. "It seemed that little else was talked about," *Newsweek* reported following week one. "From coast to coast—in homes, bars, clubs, offices, even in GI day rooms—men and women clustered around television sets to watch the developing battle between Sen. Joseph McCarthy and the Army officials. And while they looked, they argued among themselves. Who was lying? Who was telling the truth?"

In dismissing the impact of the hearings, the historian Michael Gauger asserts that "the critical point" is that the hearings fell "far short of expected ratings," though he does not explain who did the expecting. In reality, the reasons for the decisive impact of the hearings on McCarthy personally (though not on the attitudes he represented) are far broader and more nuanced than the issue of how the TV audience compared with prior expectations. It is true that the hearings failed to produce what has become the great cliché of any public controversy, "a smoking gun" that made the sinfulness of one side or another undeniable. But the hearings were about something else, something more emotionally powerful, as McCarthy himself well understood.

"People aren't going to remember the things we say on the issues here," he told Roy Cohn when they chatted during a recess. "They are only going to remember the impressions." And of course impressions were what television was all about. In this case their cumulative impact altered history's course.

Comparisons with the public's reaction to the Kefauver crime probe are somewhat beside the point because of the immense expansion of the television audience in the years after 1950, when Kefauver put on his show. About 26 million television set–owning families made up the potential audience for Army-McCarthy, more than a fivefold increase from the Kefauver era, and the number of stations had quadrupled to more than 400. About 45 million Americans, nearly half the adult population, watched at least part of the 188 hours of live broadcasts, not to mention the millions who viewed the recaps on CBS and NBC and listened to the radio accounts carried by four national networks. About 65 million read reports of the hearings in their newspapers, much of which would probably not have been published or read except for the drama provided by the television coverage.

The Army-McCarthy hearings were the greatest news event yet generated by the television culture that was just beginning to shape American life. Newspapers gave it as much space as they did mainly because it was on television. And it was the camera that provided the impact. All the memorable highlights, such as the doctored photo of Stevens and Schine, and the showdown between Welch and McCarthy, gained force from the fact that people could see them, either as they happened or a few hours later.

The influence of the hearings also needs to be judged in the context of the times. The polls help tell the story. In January 1954 Gallup gave McCarthy a 50 percent favorable rating in his polls, his zenith. By March, with his feud with the Army receiving regular coverage, McCarthy's favorability was down to 46 percent. A month later, as the hearings got under way, it plummeted to 38 percent. In May, with the hearings in full swing, McCarthy lost three more points, dropping to 35 percent, and by the time the hearings ended in June he was at 34 percent. The hearings alone did not lower McCarthy's ratings.

But they were the biggest single factor that kept him from recovering lost ground in the seesaw effect that is common to public reaction to political personalities and controversies. Probably more significant than the public reaction as gauged by Gallup was the response of McCarthy's peers in the Senate. That was registered in no uncertain terms six months after the hearings in the overwhelming vote for censure. By 1954 McCarthy had been the nation's most controversial politician for nearly four full years. He had been under constant scrutiny and attack from the time of the Tydings Committee hearings, whose report detailed McCarthy's malicious and dishonest behavior in helping turn Tydings out of office. That report had prompted Democratic senator William Benton of Connecticut to seek McCarthy's expulsion, setting the stage for the Senate Elections Subcommittee probe of McCarthy's financial activities. McCarthy's defiance of the committee was one of the prime charges against him in the censure resolution of 1954. But no harm had come to McCarthy from his behavior three years earlier. Indeed, as late as February 1954, two months before the hearings began, the full Senate approved funds for McCarthy's committee to carry on its work by a margin of 84 to 1. It was the televised hearings, coming on top of Edward R. Murrow's attack, that made a critical difference. Both the weeks of hearings on ABC and DuMont, tedious as they often seemed, and the one-hour Murrow documentary not only exposed McCarthy's flaws to a wider audience than ever before, they also showed his vulnerability. He could be attacked, first by Murrow and then by Welch and Symington, and his critics could escape unscathed. In the political calculus of the Senate, where risk is always balanced carefully against reward, that lesson finished McCarthy. Many of his colleagues had disliked him for years. Now they felt emboldened to act on their impulses.

The most telling analysis of the hearings' importance came from Maurice Rosenblatt, who as head of the lobbying group

NCEC had made the destruction of McCarthy his avocation as well as his vocation. "The hearings," Rosenblatt wrote in a memorandum to his staff and supporters on June 23, less than a week after the proceedings adjourned, "served to unmask the personality and disclose what the press has long concealed as to the nature of the man and his methods." Among national Republican leaders, who previously had "only paid attention to the Democratic votes McCarthy allegedly attracted," he was "finally being recognized as a political liability." The White House and Eisenhower's attorney general, Herbert Brownell, who had always been cautiously disapproving of the Wisconsin senator, "are more firmly committed against McCarthy than ever before," Rosenblatt wrote. As for the Democrats, "milling around without leadership or purpose," they had now indicated they would back any "sound move" against McCarthy as long as it was advanced by a Republican.

What it came down to for senators in both parties is that the hearings had transformed the debate about McCarthy in their own minds. It was no longer a question of whether they agreed with his purposes or supported his methods. He had become an embarrassment, one they could no longer afford to tolerate, because he was damaging their own standing with their constituents.

While it may have taken pundits and professors some time to appreciate the significance of TV's role in McCarthy's downfall, the lesson did not escape those who had most at stake, McCarthy's colleagues on Capitol Hill. Fearful of this new power on the political scene, the Congress, starting with the Watkins Committee hearings on censure, kept its distance from television, with a few spasmodic exceptions such as the Senate investigation into labor racketeering spearheaded by Roy Cohn's almost-sparring partner, Robert Kennedy.

In 1966 and again in 1971 Senator William Fulbright's televised hearings on Vietnam policy created something of a stir. But not until twenty years after Welch and McCarthy had their confrontation did televised hearings achieve comparable drama and impact. That came with public television's broadcast of the Senate Watergate hearings, memorably chaired by North Carolina senator Sam Ervin. In background and appearance, Ervin could hardly have been more different from the Army's counsel, Joe Welch. But he used some of the same weapons—humor and the impression of righteousness—to undermine Richard Nixon, much as Welch had prodded McCarthy to the brink of self-destruction.

Long before the Ervin Committee drilled Watergate into the public consciousness, however, television had gone about taking charge of American politics. One big milestone came in January 1955, only six months after the Army-McCarthy hearings concluded, when Dwight Eisenhower held the first televised presidential press conference in the East Room of the White House. Five years after that, John Kennedy, combining coolness with charisma, outpointed a saturnine and sweaty Richard Nixon over television, in a debate most Americans who listened on the radio thought the young senator from Massachusetts had lost.

Yet as it rose to dominate national politics not just on Capitol Hill but in every campaign battleground in every section of the country, television showed little awareness of its limitations, as pointed up by its coverage of the Army-McCarthy hearings—perhaps because there had been no mention of such shortcomings at the time. Television was too busy accepting kudos and patting itself on the back to wonder how it might have done a better job. "In my memory, TV never performed a service which received more unsolicited evidence of appreciation of viewers," proudly declared Ted Bergmann, managing director at DuMont, which along with ABC carried the load for the industry. "The promotional value for the TV broadcasting industry is inestimable," declared *Billboard*. Even critics of the hearing praised television. In an editorial lamenting the hearings as a blow to American prestige, *Collier's* magazine added: "This is not a rap at television. The wrangle over Private Schine, with all its ramifications, was of wide public interest, and the TV people had the same duty to cover it as the press and radio. And technically the television production was good."

Where TV fell short was not in its technical production but with the journalistic end result. In simplest terms, TV's coverage of the Army-McCarthy hearings followed the same narrow trail blazed by the Kefauver crime hearings. Once again television's failure to look beneath the surface, its emphasis on entertainment—in this case personality—at the expense of substance, and its reluctance to question political authority was exposed.

The most important story of the hearings, buried under the unending points of order and partisan posturing, was how the United States Army and the administration of Dwight Eisenhower had allowed themselves to be bamboozled and intimidated by a demagogue distinguished more by his ambition than his political skill. This was the issue, more important than who provided McCarthy with the faux Hoover letter or who cropped the photo of Stevens and Schine, that television should have explored if it was genuinely to serve the public interest.

Coverage by the print press also missed the forest for the trees. But it was TV that aired the hearings, made them a national event, and therefore had a greater responsibility and opportunity to cut through the pomposity and persiflage and give its viewers a fuller grasp of the forces that had shaped the confrontation. The absence of such an understanding made it possible for *Collier's*, echoing other critics, to jeer at the proceedings as a "a sprawling, brawling travesty," and for politicians as far removed on the ideological spectrum as

Adlai Stevenson and Richard Nixon to dismiss them as foolish nuisances.

The domination of the hearings by personality rather than substance certainly contributed to their drama, but it also prevented a more enduring impact. While the hearings proved to be a disaster for the nation's leading demagogue, except for his demise they offered little for civil libertarians to celebrate. McCarthy's adversaries on the committee focused on his reckless tactics and his bully-boy manner. But no one seriously challenged the underlying rationale for the McCarthy era: the belief that Americans simply because of their association, however peripheral, with relatively innocuous but unpopular organizations posed a threat to the security of the Republic.

In this regard, no one in television or elsewhere in the media questioned the role of Joseph Welch. Although he emerged as the hero of the anti-McCarthy forces, he lacked the nerve to tackle the premise of McCarthyism head-on. But by his cunning, which earned him a place in history, he in effect endorsed the idea of guilt by association. When Fred Fisher first told him of his link to the relatively innocuous National Lawyers Guild, Welch might have told the young man that he had done nothing to threaten national security, and then dismissed the matter. Instead, acting on the advice of Jim Hagerty, he sent Fisher packing and then leaked the story to the *New York Times* to inoculate himself against damage from further disclosures.

The best account of the atmosphere in which that decision was made is provided by Fisher himself. On the way to the meeting with Jim Hagerty, Fisher recalled Assistant Defense Secretary Streuve Hensel complaining "that he had crawled on his knees to Senator McCarthy long enough and now would stand up and walk." Fred Seaton, Hensel's Pentagon colleague declared "that never since the Civil War had the country been in greater danger." Yet before the evening was over, that sense of resolve had melted away in favor of what was thought to be the safe way out.

Shaping the decision was the sense of McCarthy's omniscience. This turned out to be as misplaced as the overestimation of his political potency that had influenced Eisenhower's dealings with him in the 1952 campaign. One conviction shared by those involved in the discussions about Fisher was that McCarthy would certainly find out about the young lawyer's connections to the nefarious Lawyers Guild, probably the very next morning.

Such thinking, fostered by paranoia, defied common sense. The Harvard chapter of the Guild, by Fisher's own account (against which we have no contravening evidence), seems to have been spectacularly inoffensive. Whatever Fisher had done as a member of that organization was sufficiently unremarkable that it had escaped the attention of the presumably intensive Hale and Dorr vetting process to which Fisher had been subjected before he was hired by the law firm. And there was nothing to indicate from McCarthy's later conduct and remarks that he knew anything more about Fisher's background than was provided by the *New York Times*, through the courtesy of Joseph Welch. In the end, in a practical sense it did not matter whether McCarthy was all-knowing or not, because those who feared him behaved as if he was.

A few years after the hearings ended, Welch would recall his experience with the Sacco-Vanzetti case and claim he was still troubled by knowing that "there were men in Massachusetts who said in substance, and loudly, 'I no longer care about their guilt or innocence. Their death is politically desirable.'" Yet when it was time for him to make a decision about Fred Fisher, he seemed himself less concerned about Fisher's guilt or innocence because he felt it was "politically desirable" to dismiss him from the case.

No wonder that Fisher, though he behaved with grace and civility, was puzzled by what had happened to him. "Just what if anything I am accused of I am unable to understand," he said after McCarthy's assault on his reputation. "Without any prior notice or chance to explain or defend myself, I find an attempt made to brand me as subversive and unpatriotic, simply because as a law student I, like many others, joined a legal organization whose purposes I believed to be entirely proper." Welch ducked the issue, and television never addressed it.

The hearings did force the end of McCarthy's career and free Eisenhower from the burden of dealing with him. But neither the committee nor Joseph Welch confronted the issue of *McCarthyism*, as distinguished from McCarthy the personality, a failure that was overlooked by the television coverage. This was the business the hearings left unfinished, in fact did not even touch upon. As a result, the broader questions raised by the McCarthy era—how Americans could reconcile their heritage of freedom with the dangers of the nuclear age—were never seriously aired. The politics of fear and paranoia, while they ebbed and flowed, never really went away. They persist to this day in the midst of the so-called war on terror.

The Army-McCarthy hearings not only launched television on the road to primacy in political coverage, they also paved the way for television to shift the balance of political communication. And by doing so television changed the criteria by which politicians win elections and persuade the public of the merits of their policies. The telling impact of personality and character as conveyed by the television cameras during the Army-McCarthy hearings was not lost on candidates and their strategists. And so the national political debate, which had always tended to be short on substance and rationality, grew even more superficial, more reliant on impressions and emotions, and more subject to manipulation by candidates and their operatives.

At times television journalism has demonstrated an ability to escape the reach of candidate contrivance and serve as a catalyst in reforming the social order. This was first illustrated during the tumult of the civil rights revolution in the early 1960s. Journalism in general earned enhanced prestige from the fortitude of individuals, print reporters, and television correspondents alike, who penetrated the walls of bigotry and brutality that had long shielded racism in the Old Confederacy to chronicle the assault of Southern blacks on the barriers of segregation. "If the news media had not carried into American homes the scenes of black children, Freedom Riders and other protesters being hosed, beaten, bitten by dogs and stuck with cattle prods, the conscience of the nation might never have been massively stirred," wrote Harris Wofford, President Kennedy's liaison to the civil rights movement. Wofford justly paid tribute to all branches of journalism. But as with the Army-McCarthy hearings, it was the greater impact of televised images that influenced the nation's newspapers to splash across their front pages the scenes to which Wofford referred.

Television's next big accomplishment was to help force a shift in U.S. policy on Vietnam. The opportunity came with the Tet offensive launched by the Communists, coinciding with the Vietnamese New Year in January 1968. Even before the Tet attack, television news had made the Vietnam War its own, giving Americans at home an unprecedented, often wrenching linkage with their sons in combat. It was this compelling intimacy that led the *New Yorker* to label the fighting in Indochina "the living room war." Despite subsequent popular opinion to the contrary, the coverage was generally favorable. From 1962 to 1967, according to an analysis by the historian Lawrence Lichty and former CBS Saigon bureau chief, reporters "generally reflected the optimistic news related by the military, the optimistic news they hoped for, and the optimistic news the American people thought possible, if not inevitable." There were a few exceptions, notably the *New York Times'* David Halberstam and Morley Safer of CBS. But as the journalist Edward J. Epstein concluded in a 1973 study for *TV Guide*, television tended to present "a picture of slow but sure progress in the war"—in other words, supporting with the rest of the press the official U.S. policy line that "there was light at the end of the tunnel." A *Newsweek* poll showed that for the first few years of the war TV coverage had actually increased popular support for the war. But abruptly, the surprising attack by a supposedly defeated foe that penetrated the grounds of the U.S. embassy in Saigon stunned the nation and changed the outlook of television along with the rest of the press. Both NBC and CBS aired half-hour specials entitled "Vietcong Terror" and "Saigon Under Fire." The print media followed along. But television led the charge, its coverage climaxed by the on-camera execution in a battle-torn Saigon street of a Viet Cong prisoner by South Vietnamese Gen. Nguyen Ngoc Loan.

Dismayed by Tet, the esteemed CBS anchor Walter Cronkite, who had come to fill Edward R. Murrow's niche as the nation's most prestigious television journalist, flew to the battlefield to see for himself. "To say that we are mired in a stalemate seems the only realistic yet unsatisfactory conclusion," was his grim assessment upon his return.

"The shock waves rolled through the government," George Christian, Lyndon Johnson's press secretary, later recalled. Johnson himself was devastated. "If I've lost Walter Cronkite, I've lost the country," he told an aide. The upheaval over Vietnam forced Johnson, a man seemingly designed by the Creator to wield the powers of the White House, to stun the political world by announcing he would not seek reelection.

Despite such contributions to public edification, television continued to struggle against itself. The same qualities that gave it sway in political discourse—its ability to project immediacy and to stir the emotions—also undermined its potential to fulfill David Sarnoff's vision of a torch of enlightenment. "The inherent limitations of our media make it a powerful means of communication, but also a crude one, which tends to strike at the emotions rather than the intellect," Roger Mudd, then one of the stars of CBS news, declared soon after television's coverage of the Tet offensive. "For television journalists, this means a dangerous and increasing concentration on action, which is usually violent and bloody rather than on thought," the broadcaster said in an address at his alma mater, Washington & Lee University. "The industry somehow still is unable or unwilling now to move beyond its preoccupation with razzle-dazzle."

Just as disturbing as Mudd's criticism was his network's response to it. Summoned to corporate headquarters in New York, Mudd was scolded by CBS president Richard Salant in front of fifteen or twenty other network executives, and then punished by no longer being allowed to fill in as anchor when Walter Cronkite was absent from the CBS Evening News. This dimmed prospects that CBS or any of the networks would benefit from criticism and from their own experience.

Thus more than two decades after Mudd's comments, when the 9/11 attacks confronted the nation with its most serious international crisis since Vietnam, television news once again exhibited its customary obsession with spectacle, along with its unquestioning support for the administration in power. Television became the most potent instrument available to President George Bush to promote the idea of what the self-styled "war president" declared to be "the Global War on Terrorism."

As awful as the events of 9/11 were, TV found a way to hype them, spearheading a binge of what the late Susan Sontag called "self-righteous drivel and outright deceptions" which involved all other media and nearly every political leader of note. The coverage was highlighted by the endless repetition of the images of the missile-airliner crashing into the second of the Twin Towers, and of the towers collapsing. After a while, as *New York* magazine's Michael Tomasky wrote, "as the footage of the towers' collapse seen for the thousandth time ceased to shock, so too did the thousandth tale of the heroics of the firehouse or of the nobility of Mayor Giuliani begin to pall. So much ground zero reportage came to sound less like journalism and more like an extended therapy session."

That appears to have been what the networks had in mind. For they presented 9/11 as a national trauma, which emotionally devastated not just eyewitnesses or other citizens of the New York metropolitan area but Americans who saw the tragedy only on television. This dubious nationalization of 9/11 certainly worked to Bush's advantage, paving the way for him to present himself as a "war president" and thus entitled to national support. Television correspondents eagerly embraced the war metaphor from the beginning. "If there is a war, it's a war against terrorism that started, rather ongoing right now, it started here at about quarter to nine this morning," declared Pat Dawson of ABC even as the flames consumed the Twin Towers.

But the spirit in which most of TV enlisted in the War on Terror was expressed in its most extreme by CBS anchorman Dan Rather in an interview with David Letterman a week after 9/11: "George Bush is the President. He makes the decisions, and you know, as just one American, wherever he wants me to line up, just tell me where."

Six years later Rather tried to explain, to a less sympathetic television host, Bill Moyers. "I didn't mean it in a journalistic sense," he said. "I know it may have come across that way. I meant it in a sense as an individual citizen. 'Mr. President, if you need me, if you need me to go to hell and back for my country, I will do it.'"

But what his television audience needed from Rather, never mind his president, was clear and objective reporting, not outbursts of misguided patriotism. As Moyers asked the CBS anchor pointedly, "Once we say, 'We'll line up with the President,' can we ever really say to the country, 'The President's out of line'?"

"Of course you can," Rather insisted. But in the months ahead, as Bush expanded the global war on terror and sent American troops to invade Afghanistan and Iraq, such challenging coverage was conspicuous by its absence from television commentary—and from other media as well.

The world of television news followed the administration drumroll, kept in line by a combination of complacency and intimidation. "I don't think there was enough skepticism, because I think most of us kind of believed that Saddam Hussein was building biological, chemical, and perhaps even nuclear weapons," Walter Isaacson, the former boss at *Time* who was then chairman of CNN, acknowledged long after the fact. Isaacson added, "There was a patriotic fervor, and the administration used it so that if you challenged anything you were made to feel there was something wrong with that."

Meanwhile the Bush White House had set about preaching the urgency of attacking Iraq, a decision that had already been privately made by administration higher-ups. Television gave time and prominence to the likes of James Woolsey and Richard Perle, both advisers to Defense Secretary Donald Rumsfeld, and to William Kristol, the leading intellectual light of the neo-conservative warhawks. It was not just the Bush-friendly Fox News that welcomed their war cries; they also showed up with great frequency on NBC, ABC, and CNN, where they filled the airwaves with belligerent rhetoric. They charged that Iraq had somehow inspired the 9/11 attacks, a claim for which they never mustered credible evidence, warned that Iraq was stockpiling weapons of mass destruction, and promised that invading U.S. forces would be welcomed by the Iraqis as heroes.

Presenting any of these heralds of war could be defended as part of legitimate news coverage. But the networks offered their viewers no one of comparable weight in opposition. Liberal commentator Phil Donahue was told by his bosses at MSNBC that he could have guests who supported the president on by themselves; but if he presented a Bush critic, he would also have to invite two Bush backers as counterweights. All of television, broadcast as well as cable, maintained a firm hawkish stance beginning immediately after 9/11.

"Just as television news programs are careful to filter Taliban propaganda and omit the most wrenching images of bombing victims, they do not dwell on criticism of the United States' effort," Alessandra Stanley, the *New York Times'* leading TV analyst, wrote in November 2001. "Mostly, the small pools of dissent are absent from American television. Most viewers, still aching over the attacks of Sept. 11, are in no mood to listen to views they dismiss as either loopy or treasonous," Stanley added, betraying her own bias with a dismissive vocabulary.

Instead of dissent, television relayed a steady fusillade of alarms and warnings which helped sustain the anxiety and distress that were handmaidens to the administration's policies. Of the twenty-three "terror alerts" announced by the government from 2001 to 2004, all led the evening news on broadcast and cable. But only about 10 percent of the reductions in alert status received comparable billing, national security analyst John Mueller points out. For example, each of the three networks used hundreds of words to announce the alert of May 23, 2002. "The level of worry is as high as it's been since September 11," one reported. An attack was said to be "very imminent" by another, while the third claimed "something big is going to happen in the next two to three days." But news that the alert had been canceled received fewer than fifty words from CBS and NBC while ABC did not mention it at all.

Given this sort of coverage, no wonder that Americans viewed their choices in the struggle for the White House in 2004 through a prism shaped by the war on terror. This despite the fact that the nation had gone three years without a serious episode of terrorism on American soil. Most of what terrorism had cost Americans in blood and treasure had resulted from the Bush administration's extension of its war on terror to Iraq.

The print media, including some of the nation's most prestigious newspapers, were also culpable in this distorted coverage. But television bears the heaviest burden. Despite the rise of internet sources, in 2004 about 70 percent of Americans got most of their political news from television, much as they did in 2000 and 1992. A study of nearly eight hundred residents of Tompkins County in central New York shortly after the 9/11 attacks showed that among liberals who relied for news mainly on television, their support for tougher policy actions increased while backing for civil liberties declined, bringing them closer to the viewpoint of conservatives. "TV pushed the two groups together in their thinking about post-9/11 policies such as the Patriot Act, and hardened their views on civil liberties," according to Dietram Scheufele, the University of Wisconsin communications professor who conducted the study.

By contrast, among liberals who watched little television but read newspapers regularly, only about 20 percent favored more government police powers, about half the percentage of those who were heavy television viewers. Newspapers, Scheufele pointed out, are more selective, give readers more options, and allow them to seek out their own viewpoints. "TV coverage is very linear, doesn't offer any choice, and is more image driven. You saw the plane hitting the building time and time again." TV's postattack coverage, he added, was increasingly characterized by language that emphasized a nation "under siege." "Television news, by uncritically 'echoing' the strategic messages of the Bush administration, served an important governing function by marshaling public support for the president and his preferred domestic security measures." The administration did not need a propaganda ministry; TV did the job on its own.

By the time of the 2004 elections, a Pew Research Center survey showed that beliefs about national security were twice as important as economic or social values and played a major role in shaping partisan allegiances. Among voters, 51 percent approved of the decision to go to war in Iraq, a view that most Americans would reverse in the coming months. But on election day 85 percent of the war approvers voted for George W. Bush, a significant chunk of the electorate, while 55 percent of all voters agreed that the U.S. assault on Iraq was part of the war on terrorism, and four of five of these voters backed Bush over Kerry.

Television's role in reviving the strain of paranoia in American politics, half a century after the medium came of political age by helping bring down Joe McCarthy, in his time the leading practitioner of the politics of fear, may seem paradoxical. But the attributes of television that shaped the coverage of 9/11 and President Bush's war on terror were evident in the treatment of the Army-McCarthy hearings: emphasis on superficial impressions and emotional appeals, to the neglect of substance and rational thinking; and, even more important, an unwillingness to question conventional wisdom and established authority.

In 1954 television accepted the notion that domestic subversives jeopardized national security and had penetrated crucial echelons of the U.S. Army. Similarly it bought into the claim that 9/11 was only the first blow against the United States by a worldwide conspiracy energized by Islamic fascism, in which Saddam Hussein's regime was a principal cohort. "I don't think there is any excuse for, you know, my performance and the performance of the press in general in the roll-up to the war," Dan Rather conceded afterward. "There were exceptions. There were some people, who, I think, did a better job than others. But overall and in the main, there's no question that we didn't do a good job."

In their rush to conform, too many journalists ignored the broader meaning of the First Amendment. Journalists talk about the First Amendment a lot, usually as a protection against government interference. But the First Amendment is more than a shield; it is a responsibility. It not only protects the press, it imposes an obligation and a duty.

One of the clearest and strongest expressions of the full meaning of the First Amendment came not in a newspaper editorial but in a judicial opinion written by Federal District Judge Murray Gurfein in June 1971 when he rejected the Nixon administration's efforts to prevent publication of the Pentagon Papers. Nixon's lawyers claimed that release of the papers would undermine national security, but Gurfein disagreed. "The security of the nation is not at the ramparts alone," he wrote in a judgment, the spirit of which was ultimately upheld by the Supreme Court. "Security also lies in the value of our free institutions. A cantankerous press, an obstinate press, a ubiquitous press must be suffered by those in authority in order to preserve the even greater values of freedom of expression and the right of the people to know."

The phrases Gurfein used—"cantankerous," "obstinate," "suffered by those in authority"—are not words generally considered pathways to success in television or any other form of journalism. But they do express what the Founders meant when they wrote the First Amendment. "It is not merely the opinion of the editorial writer or of the columnist which is protected by the First Amendment," Gurfein explained. "It is the free flow of information so that the public will be informed about the government and its actions. There is no greater safety valve for discontent and cynicism about the affairs of government than freedom of expression in any form."

Judge Gurfein's wisdom is worth recalling anytime politicians warn that the nation's security is imperiled from without or within. The decision he handed down, while it applied directly to newspapers, is just as relevant for all media, certainly including television news. It helps remind journalists what their rights are in covering the news. Just as important, Gurfein's words remind viewers and readers what they have a right to expect from the journalists who serve them.

Notes

Full citations of the references in the Notes may be found in the Bibliography that follows.

Abbreviations used in the notes.
NYT for *New York Times*
WP for *Washington Post*

1. THE CURTAIN RISES

page
3   Room 318: The room number was changed to SR325 in 1958 because of the opening of the new Senate Office Building.
3   The setting in Room 318: "The Russell Senate Office Building Caucus Room," "Special Dateline," Straight, 126; Doherty, 196–198.
4   The Army struck back: *NYT*, March 12, 1954.
5   Oppenheimer's difficulties: *NYT*, April 18, 1954.
5   The French admitted: *NYT*, April 23, 1954.
5   Nixon's warning: *NYT*, April 18, 1954.
7   Cartoon of Ike: *WP*, March 4, 1954.
7   "A lot of moral support": Griffith, 206.
8   "Some high school debate": ibid.
8   Eisenhower backed down: Ewald, 41–46.
9   In the national interest: Oshinsky, 297.
9   McCarthy's wedding: *WP*, September 30, 1953.
9   McCarthy was alerted: Cohn, 94.
10 Kefauver probe: see Chapter 3.

10 Among those impressed: author's interview with Ann Littlejohn, December 18, 2005.
11 Littlejohn persuaded: *WP*, December 9, 2005.
12 Hearings audience: Fenton, 138.
12 Sort of a "hostage": *NYT*, March 13, 1954.
12 "Bonnie, Bonnie, and Clyde": NYT, August 3, 1986.
13 Debs's conviction: Murray, *Red Scare*, 25.
14 *Atlantic Monthly* estimate and the bomb plots: Allen, 40–43.
15 Hoover and the Palmer raids: Murray, *Red Scare*, 201–202.
16 Goulden's book: *The Best Years, 1945–50* (New York: Atheneum, 1976).
17 Hiss case: Trachtenberg, Wheatcroft, Linder, "Trials of Alger Hiss."
22 Rosenbergs: Linder, "Trial of the Rosenbergs."
25 Mundt's orders to photographers: *NYT*, April 29, 1954.

2. A TORCH IN THE TROUBLED WORLD

26 A flying start: *NYT*, April 8, 1927.
27 Sarnoff's view: Weinstein, 33.
27 "Crawled along": "Still a Toddler."
28 The FCC's approach: Weinstein, 2.
29 A propaganda system: Chomsky and Herman.
30 Bagdikian's view: Bagdikian, 3.
30 "voluntary propagandists": Baughman, *Republic*, 1.
31 Hutchins Commission report: *NYT*, March 27, 1947.
31 Forrest's view: *NYT*, April 7, 1947.
31 Coaxial cable: Frank, 7.
32 Opening of the Eightieth Congress: Ritchie, 185.
32 Television going the way of radio: Baughman, *Republic*, 61.
32 Results of poll of TV set owners: Baughman, *Same Time*, 218.
33 1924 convention: Murray, *103rd Ballot*, 97ff.
33 Boom in radio sales: Allen, 137.
34 A promise to help out: Frank, 13.
35 Bleak Democratic outlook: Shogan, "1948 Election."
35 India Edwards's talk: Karabell, 155.
36 Murrow's visual aids: Frank, 21.
36 "Doves of peace": Ross, 128.
36 Scene in Room 22: Frank, 24.
36 Murrow vs. Heiskell: ibid., 26.
37 Reuven Frank's hiring, and early TV news era: ibid., 30-35.
39 Everyday reality: Frank Littlejohn, speech draft for John Charles Daly to broadcasting group, November 10, 1986, in author's possession.
39 Impact of cold war: Frank, 37.

40 Spread of blacklisting, Doherty, 7, 8, 25; Everitt, 44.
41 Compiling the blacklist: Schwartz.
41 A more ominous threat: Doherty, 23.
41 Postwar crime scare: Moore, 25-27.

3. RACKET BUSTER

44 Kefauver's early background: Gorman, 7–32; Fontenay, 13–20.
44 He married well: Bartlett.
45 "Shame on you": Gorman, 7.
45 "I ain't Mr. Crump's pet coon": ibid., 49.
46 "A natural desire": Bartlett.
46 Central villain: Moore, 30.
46 Truman's response: ibid., 44.
46 McCarthy's interest in crime probe: ibid., 44.
47 Origins of the crime probe: ibid., 44–57.
49 Only the fifth time: Gorman, 87.
49 Reaction to Detroit hearings: *Broadcasting/Telecasting*, February 26, 1951.
49 Privacy issue in St. Louis: Moore, 170.
50 Resembled a "Dragnet" script: *Los Angles Times*, February 28, 1951.
50 "This vital service": *Broadcasting/Telecasting*, March 12, 1951.
50 *Time*'s cover: "It Pays to Organize."
51 Reacted rather than initiated: Gorman, 87.
51 Hearings in New York: *NYT*, March 8, 9, 12-17; "Crime Hunt in Foley Square"; "Biggest Show on Earth"; "Biggest Show Panics the Public"; Gorman, 86-95.
52 "rattle of a seagull": "Mighty Interesting Visit."
53 O'Dwyer's testimony: ibid.
54 Public response: Moore, 184; Gorman, 90.
55 Rave reviews: *Billboard*, March 24, 1951.
55 Some critics worried: *WP*, March 22, 1951.
55 Jack Gould's view: *NYT*, March 18, 1951.
55 Community reaction: *NYT*, March 16, 1951.
56 Showered with honors: Gorman, 102.
56 "A skunk at a lawn party": *NYT*, March 25, 1951.
57 Praise from Seldes: *Printers Ink*, April 20, 1951.
58 "A good look around": Doig.

4. THE ROAD TO ROOM 318

60 The first press conference: Griffith, 1.
60 A gregarious type: Ritchie, 76.

61 "His IQ was goddamn high": Bayley, 70.
62 "He'd always have something": ibid., 69.
62 Feuding with Arrowsmith: Oshinsky, 181.
62 Brawling with Pearson: Reeves, 38.
62 Early years: Oshinsky, 1–21.
64 First run for the U.S. Senate: Griffith, 5–6.
65 1946 campaign: ibid., 8–11.
66 Same pattern of carousing: Oshinsky, 29.
66 McCarthy's Senate style: Griffith, 11–13.
67 Malmedy massacre: Bayley, 9.
67 McCarthy's priorities: Griffith, 22–26.
67 Dinner at the Colony: ibid., 29.
68 GOP 1950 platform: *NYT*, February, 7, 1950.
68 Nixon pounds away: Griffith, 48.
68 Wheeling speech and subsequent coverage: Bayley, 17–21; Evans, 181–193.
69 What McCarthy did not know: Oshinsky, 109.
71 McCarthy's interpretation: ibid., 112–114.
72 McCarthy's journalistic lobby: Griffith, 62; Ritchie, 75–82.
73 Uncovered no Communists: Griffith, 100.
73 Anti-Tydings tabloid: Ritchie, 80.
74 Benton's reaction: Griffith, 153–160.
74 Gillette Committee's report: Griffith, 180.
75 Attacks on Acheson and Marshall: Oshinsky, 194–201.
76 Complaints of Theis and Steele: Ritchie, 82.
76 Impact of wire service stories: Bayley, 63.
77 Lippman's view: Oshinksy, 187.
77 *Denver Post* policy: "The Fetish of Objectivity."
78 McCarthy's Senate campaign: Bayley, 93.
78 Sounded like cheerleading: Oshinsky, 237.
78 Attack on Stevenson: Bayley, 104.
79 Underwhelming triumph: *Guide to U.S. Elections*, 358, 635.
80 Browbeating Harris: Bayley, 183; Oshinsky, 274–276.
81 "A frightening precedent": *NYT*, March 4, 1953.
82 Peress case: Griffith, 246–247; Oshinsky, 365–372; Adams, 117–120.
84 Ike's early years: Ambrose, *Soldier*, 37.
85 Military tradition: ibid., 53.
85 Alsop's reaction: Oshinsky, 392.
85 McCarthy's blast at Zwicker: ibid., 393.
86 Reston's view: *NYT*, March 4, 1954, cited in ibid.
86 A notable instinct: "A Conversation with Fred Friendly."
87 Stevenson's attack: *NYT*, March 7, 1954.

5. ST. ED AND THE DRAGON

88   Murrow's inaction: Oshinsky, 398.

88   Kintner and Agronsky: Bayley, 194.

89   Shoeshine boy quip and ACLU programs: Doherty, 170–171.

89   Defending Radulovich: Kendrick, 37–39.

91   Surine's threat: Wershba.

92   Murrow's reaction: ibid.

93   "Murrow could say 'twenty-six'": Persico, 14.

94   Murrow's early years: Persico, 15–31; Kendrick, 72–85.

95   Murrow at Washington State: Persico, 39ff.

96   With the National Student Federation in New York: Kendrick, 109ff.

97   Marriage to Janet: Persico, 81–82.

98   Soviets balked: ibid., 83–84.

99   Not everyone agreed: Smith, 9–10.

99   Murrow burnishes his image: Kendrick, 147.

100   "The wave of the future": Sevareid, 86.

100   "Everything is quiet in Vienna tonight": Persico, 137–138.

100   Murrow in London: Kendrick, 173ff.

101   His foot tapped continuously: Persico, 157.

101   Not a milk run: ibid., 157.

101   "The midgets have been real": Manchester, 601.

102   Murrow come to television: Kendrick, 335–343.

102   *Person to Person*: Persico, 343–345.

103   Murrow and Korean War: Kendrick, 324–328.

103   A shot against the Red Scare: Persico, 293.

103   "Choose your battles": ibid., 342.

104   Preparing the McCarthy report: Wershba.

105   McCarthy program: "A Report on Senator Joseph R. McCarthy."

107   Misgivings: Cogley, "The Murrow Show," *Commonweal*, March 26, 1954; Gilbert Seldes, "Murrow, McCarthy and the Empty Formula," *Saturday Review*, April 24, 1954.

109   Gould's column: *NYT*, March 11, 1954.

109   "Good Tuesday": *Variety*, March 17, 1954.

109   McCarthy shot back: *NYT*, March 12, 1954.

110   Flanders's blast: "Words from a Quiet Man," *Time*, March 22, 1954.

111   Murrow responds to McCarthy: *NYT*, March 13, 1954.

112   "When you shoot wildly": *NYT*, March 14, 1954.

112   McCarthy's equal time: *NYT*, April 7, 1954.

114 Gould's comment: *NYT*, April 9, 1954.
114 "But Murrow said it on television: "The Scorched Air: Murrow vs. Senator McCarthy."
114 "Deflated the balloon": *Billboard*, March 20, 1954.

6. AT WAR WITH THE ARMY

115 Mundt's background: "Karl Earl Mundt."
117 Army report: *NYT*, March 12, 1954.
118 Potter Demands Firing of Cohn: "The Self-Inflated Target."
118 McCarthy Fires Back: "The Case of Private Schine."
118 Eleven memos: *SSI*, Appendix, Exhibit 31.
120 A careful bead: "The Self-Inflated Target."
121 Cohn's early years: *NYT*, August 3, 1986; Wolfe.
124 That did not go over well: Johnson, 256.
125 Cohn hired his own assistant: "The Case of Private Schine."
126 European press jeered: *NYT*, March 12, 1954.
127 "Oh, my God! I've picked Schine!": "The Self-Inflated Target."
128 Dirksen background: *NYT*, April 7, 1960; "Everett McKinley Dirksen."
130 Dirksen asked rhetorically: *SSI*, 4–5.
130 McClellan's background: "John Little McClellan"; Straight, 237.
131 McClellan's view: *SSI*, 8.
132 "The worse it's going to be": *SSI*, 9.
132 "It's going to take time": ibid.
132 "Not the proper forum": *SSI*, 12.
133 "Dirksen's view": *SSI*, 13.
133 No precedent for transfer: *SSI*, 14.
133 Still another suggestion: *SSI*, 20.
134 Rogers declines post: *NYT*, March 23, 1954.
134 Effort to find a counsel: *NYT*, April 2, 7, 8, 1954.
135 Welch's appointment: *NYT*, April 3, 1954.
135 Vetting Fred Fisher: Fisher, 7; Oshinsky, 308.
136 Fisher's early years: Fisher, 80–107.
136 Background on Lawyer's Guild: *WP*, May 24, 1987; *NYT*, October 13, 1989.
137 Hagerty's initial inclination: Oshinsky, 409–411.
138 McCarthy's charge: *SSI* supplement to hearings, 4–5.
139 Too much for Eisenhower: *NYT*, March 25, 1954.
139 McCarthy names Hensel: *NYT*, April 21, 1954; Alsop.
140 Johnson passed the word: Caro, 552.
140 Network lineup: *NYT*, April 25, 1954.

7. THE SOLDIERING OF PRIVATE SCHINE

142 "Point of order": *SSI*, 33; Straight, 131.
143 Mundt's pledge and McClellan statement: *SSI*, 31–32.
144 Crisp in appearance: Straight, 132.
144 Welch asks about pressure: *SSI*, 48.
144 Put the issue in focus: *SSI*, 52.
144 Targeting Rebel's brother: *SSI*, 56.
145 Returned to the attack: *SSI*, 70.
146 "Let's have a ruling: *SSI*, 71.
146 "A very serious charge": *SSI*, 73.
146 Jackson steps in: *SSI*, 75.
146 Same Rebel speaks up: *NYT*, April 24, 1954.
148 Stevens's background: *Daily News Record*, February 1, 1983; *NYT*, February 1, 1983.
150 An earful from Ridgeway: Oshinsky, 378.
150 "I am going to kick the brains out": *SSI*, 2155–2156.
151 "Fighting Bob": *NYT*, February 21, 1954.
151 Chicken lunch: *NYT*, February 25, 1954; *WP*, February 25, 1954.
152 "The Army doesn't coddle Communists": *SSI*, 99.
152 Chat with Schine: *SSI*, 104–105.
153 Monitored phone conversations: *NYT*, April 24, 1954.
154 "My position is peculiar": *SSI*, 189.
155 "So damned mad": "The Terror of Tellico Plains."
155 Jenkins's early years: ibid.
156 "A boxer dog": *NYT*, April 11, 1954.
157 Restating a theme: *SSI*, 190.
158 "It is not a fact?": *SSI*, 191.
159 "You wanted it stopped, didn't you?": *SSI*, 196.
159 Visit to Schine's apartment: *SSI*, 202.
159 "Let me show you a picture": ibid.
160 Jenkins shrugged off the denial: *SSI*, 204.
161 Mundane but crucial facts: *SSI*, 192–193; *NYT*, April 27, 1954.
161 Statement by scientists: *NYT*, April 26, 1954.
161 "It was not fair": *SSI*, 211.

8. TURNING THE TIDE

163 Reston's view: *NYT*, April 23, 1954.
163 "A point of something": *SSI*, 256.
163 Not running a risk: Wanger, 36.

164 Welch's background: Fisher, 39ff; Straight, 185; "The Other Joe"; Johnson, 383.
166 "He gave me all a father could": Dolan, 168.
166 Sacco and Vanzetti case: Wanger, 15.
167 "A range of feelers": Smith, 605.
168 "What am I doing in this coffin?": Smith, 545.
168 Meeting with Dewey: Ewald, 298–299.
169 Dewey's private phone numbers: Fisher, 6.
169 Welch says he's not up to the job: Straight, 185.
169 Claimed to have been terrified: Welch.
169 "You were imposed upon": *SSI*, 256.
170 "Sick of being interrupted": *SSI*, 258.
171 A turning point: Wanger, 39.
171 "It increases the significance": *SSI*, 273.
172 Jenkins referred back: *SSI*, 276.
172 "The third person had no relevance": *SSI*, 279.
172 "Not the slightest difference": *SSI*, 283.
175 "Someone with clairvoyance": *SSI*, 295.
175 "Worst witness": Cohn, 182–183.
176 In another controversy: *WP*, May 1, 1954.
177 Juliana testimony: *SSI*, 523–551.
178 Pixie exchange: *SSI*, 543.
179 McCarthy's threat: *NYT*, May 1, 1954.
179 General Lawton's troublesome lectures: Ewald, 130–135.
180 Confession dragged out of him: *NYT*, May 1, excerpts from testimony.
182 Re Blatnik's reaction: *NYT*, May 1, 1954.
182 Dr. Mayo's comment: *NYT*, April 30, 1954.
182 Ike's indignation: *NYT*, April 29, 1954.
182 Privately more forthcoming: Ambrose, *Eisenhower the President*, 167.
183 Editorial reaction in U.S.: *NYT*, May 3, 1954.
183 "Domino theory": *NYT*, April 8, 1954.
183 Fall of Dienbienphu: *NYT*, May 8, 1954.
184 Editorial comments abroad: *NYT*, May 10, 1954.
184 Dirksen did not need Cassandra: *NYT*, May 3, 1954.
185 McCarthy's disappointment with Dworshak: *NYT*, May 1, excerpts from testimony.
185 Political reality: *NYT*, May 3, 1954.
185 "Bully in the Senate": *Washington Evening Star*, April 26, 1954.
186 "Harming the country": *NYT*, May 2, 1954.
186 Estimate of TV costs: *Broadcasting/Telecasting*, April 23, 1954.
186 "Too late to make a change": author's interview with Daniel Schorr, April 25, 2007.

187 Audience ratings for hearings: *NYT*, April 26, May 2, 1954.
187 Gould sees economic problems for TV: *NYT*, May 2, 1954.

9. THE PURLOINED LETTER

189 "A rocket would take off": Welch.
189 "The long hard furrow": *NYT*, May 5, 1954.
190 "He changed his mind": *SSI*, 656.
191 "Shall I hit them?": Cohn, 168.
191 As McCarthy described it: *SSI*, 703.
191 Welch's challenge to letter: *SSI*, 705.
191 Welch not guessing: Wanger, 40.
192 Jenkins rushed to judgment: *SSI*, 703.
192 Stevens refused: *SSI*, 706.
192 "Fourteen colonels": *SSI*, 712.
192 Collier's testimony: *SSI*, 720.
193 "A carbon copy of precisely nothing": *SSI*, 734.
193 "You are correct": *SSI*, 733.
194 "How ridiculous we can get": *SSI*, 738.
195 As Marder reported: *WP*, November 9, 1953.
195 Army unable to find espionage: *WP*, November 14, 1953.
197 "Take a cold chair": *SSI*, 758.
197 The question on everyone's mind: *SSI*, 759ff.
198 "A promise, a solemn promise": *SSI*, 767.
198 Brownell's ruling: *NYT*, May 7, 1954.
198 Railing against the "blackout": *WP*, May 8, 1954.
199 Dirksen tries to curtail testimony: *NYT*, May 9, 1954.
200 Stevens would not go along: *WP*, May 12, 1954.
200 Stevens won't quit: Oshinsky, 437–438; Ewald, 333–334.
201 A journeyman most of his life: Ewald, 96.
202 "Don't get into these things": Ewald, 297.
202 Adams testimony: *SSI*, 1009ff.
204 "Why was Lodge there?": *NYT*, May 15, 1954, excerpts from testimony.
204 "Only a bearer of messages": *WP*, May 15, 1954.
205 "Not in the public interest": *NYT*, May 18, 1954, excerpts from testimony.
205 "Let the chips fall": *NYT*, May 20, 1954.

10. TIME OUT FOR TEARS

207 McCarthy hammered away: *NYT*, May 25, 1954, excerpts from testimony.

208 Stevens complains: ibid.
208 "It is their duty": *WP*, May 28, 1954.
208 White House statement: *NYT*, May 29, 1954.
209 Ike vents to Hagerty: Oshinsky, 434.
209 Dropping the charges against Hensel: *NYT*, May 27, 1954.
210 Nixon's view of hearings: *NYT*, May 27, 1954.
210 Eisenhower at Columbia: *NYT*, June 1, 1954.
211 Flanders background: "Words from a Quiet Man"; "Ralph Edward Flanders."
213 Pushed over the edge: Crozier.
213 "McCarthy obsessed": *NYT*, March 10, 1954.
213 McCarthy aiding Communists: *Congressional Record*, 83rd Congress, 2nd Sess., U.S. Senate, 7389–7390.
215 Driscoll's testimony: *SSI*, 1816ff.
215 Strengthening Welch's suspicions: Oshinsky, 456.
216 "Touché": *NYT*, June 5, 1954.
216 McCarthy accuses Symington: *NYT*, June 5, 1954, excerpts from testimony.
217 Symington's background: Straight, 284ff; "(William) Stuart Symington, II."
218 In chaste terms: *NYT*, June 5, 1954.
219 Cohn no easy mark: Cohn, 184–188.
220 Needling Cohn: *NYT*, June 3, 1954, excerpts from testimony.
221 "Say I was fair": *NYT*, June 4, 1954, excerpts from testimony.
222 Cohn's draft status: Cohn, 201–202.
223 McCarthy approved the trade: Cohn, 203.
223 "Disturbing and alarming": *SSI*, 2424.
224 McCarthy loses patience: *SSI*, 2424–2425.
225 "I want you to listen with both": *SSI*, 2428.
226 "No sense of decency": *SSI*, 2429.
226 Dexterity of camera crews: Doherty, 208.
227 "What did I do?": Straight, 315.
227 "How did it go?": Griffith, 259fn.
227 Republicans arrange for end to hearings: *NYT*, June 11, 1954.
228 "What kind of program": *NYT*, June 12, 1954, excerpts from testimony.
228 Cohn was convinced: Cohn, 71.
229 Face to face: Schlesinger, 113.
230 "It would be unfortunate": *SSI*, 2704.
230 Symington's informants: Oshinsky, 469fn.
231 An answer McCarthy would not forget: *SSI*, 2706.
232 "You're not fooling anyone either": De Antonio.

11. TO THE BITTER END

233 Worse than he feared: *NYT*, August 17, 1974.
233 Mock subpoenas: Rash Papers, Container 1, Army-McCarthy Hearings.
234 Sent their regrets: *NYT*, June 20, 1954.
234 A wholesale "housecleaning": *NYT*, June 19, 1954.
234 Same points made: *NYT*, June 19, 1954.
234 Behind Potter's stand: Rovere, "Untold Story."
235 "A very serious charge": *NYT*, June 19, 1954; Rosenblatt Papers, Part II, Box 5, Folder 10.
235 A .22 caliber rifle: *NYT*, June 20, 1954.
236 Hunt's ordeal: Ewig.
237 McCarthy stormed out: Ewig, citing U.S. Congress, Senate, 81st Congress, Committee on Armed Services, *Hearings on Malmedy Massacre Investigations*, Washington, D.C., 1949, 637.
237 "There have been many suicides": Ewig.
238 A constitutional amendment: Hunt.
238 Mundt wanted it understood. *NYT*, June 10, 1954.
239 Drew Pearson reported: Ewig.
239 "A shocking tragedy": Childs.
240 Length of hearings: *NYT*, June 20, 1954.
240 "A melancholy spectacle": *NYT*, June 18, 1954.
241 Editorial comment: *NYT*, June 19, 1954; *WP*, June 19, 1954.
241 Flanders's motion: *NYT*, June 12, 1954.
241 Knowland's rebuff: *NYT*, June 13, 1954.
242 NCEC's role: Oshinsky, 474–475; Griffith, 284–291.
242 Flanders aims for censure: *NYT*, July 19, 1954.
243 "Very little evidence": *NYT*, July 31, 1954.
243 A heavily compromised document: *NYT*, August 24, September 1, 1954.
243 Largest crowds: *NYT*, July 31, 1954.
244 Fulbright's charges: *NYT*, August 1, 1954.
244 Not allowed "to drag on": *NYT*, August 2, 1954.
245 "If he is crippled": "Condemnation Proceedings."
245 JFK's stance: Reeves, 151.
246 "Carrying the ball alone": "Condemnation Proceedings."
246 McCarthy stepped in: ibid.
247 Members of the club: *NYT*, August 6, 1954.
248 Watkins's background: "Arthur Vivian Watkins"; "Man with a Hard Gavel."

249 As little coverage as possible: Oshinsky, 478.
249 "Rules of Evidence": *Facts on File*, August 12, 1954, 1.
249 A drinking buddy: *NYT*, August 14, 1954; "Edward Bennett Williams"; Buckley.
250 Most important challenge: Thomas, 68–70.
251 Conflict with McCarthy's ego: "New Kind of Hearing for Joe."
252 "The most unheard of thing": *NYT*, September 1, 1954.
252 "We do not agree": ibid.
253 Made his presence felt: "New Kind of Hearing for Joe."
253 "Absolute confidence": *Facts on File*, September 16, 17, 1954.
253 Two counts of censure: "The Censure of Joe McCarthy."
254 If the Senate upholds this report: *WP*, September 28, 1954.
255 Gallup wrote friends: Oshinsky, 465, citing George Gallup to Gerard Armbert, June 14, 1954, in John Foster Dulles Papers, Princeton University.
255 "Free from pre-election tensions": *Facts on File*, September 30, 1954.
256 On his feet in protest: "Joe and the Handmaidens."
257 Additional ammunition: *NYT*, November 12, 1954; "Joe and the Handmaidens."
257 An "elegant speech": Buckley.
257 "Slush and slime": *NYT*, November 13, 1954; "Joe and the Handmaidens."
258 Senate votes to recess: *NYT*, November 19, 1954.
259 McCarthy makes the motion for censure: "Splendid Job."
259 "Not a vote of confidence": *NYT*, December 3, 1943.
260 Ike praises Watkins: *NYT*, December 5, 1954.
260 McCarthy lashes out at Eisenhower: *NYT*, December 8, 1954.
260 Rave notices for Williams: Rovere, "Letter."
261 "A news 'blackout'": Oshinsky, 496.
261 "I think it was very sad": Watt, oral history.
261 Physical collapse: Oshinsky, 504.
262 No winners, only losers: *NYT*, November 19, 1954.

12. UNFINISHED BUSINESS

263 "More fundamental reasons": Cohn, 211.
263 "A startling aspect": Straight, 182.
264 "Appalling clarity": Reston.
264 Important successes: Gauger.
265 "The silent attention": *New York Herald Tribune*, April 23, 1954.
265 "Watching intently": "Telecasting Notes."
265 "Argued among themselves": "The Country: Looking and Deciding for Itself."

265 "They will remember the impressions": Cohn, 210.
266 Poll results: Fenton, 136–139; *WP*, March 14, May 23, 1954.
267 Tydings hearings: Oshinsky, 217.
267 Most telling analysis: Rosenblatt Papers, Part 1, Box 21, Folder 12.
269 Views of radio audience: Kolbert; *NYT*, October 6, 1996.
269 "In my memory": *Television Digest*, June 19, 1954.
269 "The promotional value": *Billboard*, May 1, 1954.
270 "Not a rap at television": "After the Brawl."
271 Best account: Fisher.
274 "Massively stirred": Wofford, 236.
274 Vietnam coverage: Donovan and Scherer, 85–91; Epstein.
275 "Shock waves": Turner, 232.
276 "Razzle dazzle": Mudd, 254–258.
276 Self-righteous drivel": *New Yorker*, September 24, 2001.
277 "It started here": Moyers.
277 Rather tried to explain: ibid.
278 Isaacson acknowledged: ibid.
279 Donahue was told: ibid.
279 "They do not dwell": *NYT*, November 9, 2001.
279 A steady fusillade. Mueller, 39–40.
280 About 70 percent: Pew Research Center Survey, March 20–24, 2008.
280 "TV coverage very linear": Scheufele et al.
281 Voter attitudes in 2004 election: Pew Research Center Survey, January 24, 2005.
282 Gurfein's opinion: *NYT*, June 20, 1971.

Bibliography

Abbreviation used for website biographies: BRC (reproduced in Biography Resource Center, Farmington Hills, Mich.: Gale Group. http://galenet .galegroup.com/servlet/BioRC.

ARCHIVAL SOURCES

Library of Congress, Manuscript Division.
Papers of Bryson Brennan Rash (cited in notes as Rash Papers) Papers of Maurice Rosenblatt (cited in notes as Rosenblatt Papers).
Senate Historical Office.
Ruth Young Watt, Chief Clerk, Permanent Subcommittee on Investigations, 1948–1979, Oral History Interview.

BOOKS

Adams, John G. *Without Precedent: The Story of the Death of McCarthyism.* New York: W. W. Norton, 1983.
Allen, Frederick Lewis. *Only Yesterday: An Informal History of the 1920s.* New York: Harper, 1964.
Ambrose, Stephen. *Eisenhower: Soldier, General of the Army, President-Elect, 1890-1952.* New York: Simon and Schuster, 1983.
———. *Eisenhower the President.* New York: Simon and Schuster, 1984.
Bagdikian, Ben H. *The New Media Monopoly.* Boston: Beacon Press, 2004.
Baughman, James L. *The Republic of Mass Culture: Journalism, Film Making, and Broadcasting in America Since 1941.* 3rd ed. Baltimore: Johns Hopkins Press, 2006.

———. *Same Time, Same Station: Creating American Television, 1948- 1961*. Baltimore: Johns Hopkins University Press, 2007.

Bayley, Edwin R. *Joe McCarthy and the Press*. Madison: University of Wisconsin Press, 1981.

Caro, Robert. *The Years of Lyndon Johnson: Master of the Senate*. New York: Random House, 2003.

Chomsky, Noam, and Edward S. Herman. *Manufacturing Consent*. New York: Pantheon Books, 1988.

Cohn, Roy. *McCarthy*. New York: New American Library, 1968.

Doherty, Thomas. *Cold War, Cool Medium: Television, McCarthyism and American Culture*. New York: Columbia University Press, 2003.

Dolan, John A. *Hale and Dorr: Backgrounds and Styles*. Boston: Hale and Dorr, 1993.

Donovan, Robert J., and Ray Scherer. *Unsilent Revolution: Television News and American Public Life, 1948-1991*. New York: Cambridge University Press, 1992.

Evans, M. Stanton. *Blacklisted by History: The Untold Story of Senator Joe McCarthy and His Fight Against America's Enemies*. New York: Crown, 2007.

Everitt, David. *A Shadow of Red: Communism and the Blacklist in Radio and Television*. Chicago: Ivan R. Dee, 2007.

Ewald, William B. Jr. *Who Killed Joe McCarthy?* New York: Simon and Schuster, 1984.

Fenton, John M. *In Your Opinion: The Managing Editor of the Gallup Poll Looks at Polls, Politics, and People from 1945 to 1960*. Boston: Little, Brown, 1960.

Fisher, Frederick G. III. *Patriot's Day: The Life and Times of Frederick G. Fisher, Jr.* Dublin, Ireland: privately published, 2000.

Fontenay, Charles L. *Estes Kefauver: A Biography*. Knoxville: University of Tennessee Press, 1980.

Frank, Reuven. *Out of Thin Air: The Brief Wonderful Life of Network News*. New York: Simon and Schuster, 1991.

Friendly, Fred W. *Due to Circumstances Beyond Our Control*. New York: Random House, 1967.

Gorman, Joseph Bruce. *Kefauver: A Political Biography*. New York: Oxford University Press, 1971.

Griffith, Robert. *The Politics of Fear: Joseph R. McCarthy and the Senate*. Lexington: University Press of Kentucky, 1970.

Guide to U.S. Elections. 2nd ed. Washington, D.C.: Cogressional Quarterly, 1985.

Johnson, Haynes. *The Age of Anxiety: McCarthyism to Terrorism*. Orlando, Fla.: Harcourt, 2005.

Karabell, Zachary. *The Last Campaign: How Harry Truman Won the 1948 Election*. New York: Knopf, 2000.

Kendrick, Alexander. *Prime Time: The Life of Edward R. Murrow*. Boston: Little Brown, 1969.

Manchester, William. *The Glory and the Dream: A Narrative History of America, 1932–1972*. Boston: Little, Brown, 1973.

Moore, William Howard. *The Kefauver Committee and the Politics of Crime, 1950–1952*. Columbia: University of Missouri Press, 1974.

Mudd, Roger. *The Place to Be: Washington, CBS and the Glory Days of Television News*. New York: Public Affairs, 2008.

Mueller, John. *Overblown: How Politicians and the Terrorism Industry Inflate National Security Threats, and Why We Believe Them*. New York: Free Press, 2006.

Murray, Robert K. *The 103rd Ballot*. New York: Harper & Row, 1976.

———. *Red Scare: A Study in National Hysteria, 1919–1920*. New York: McGraw-Hill, 1964.

Oshinsky, David M. *A Conspiracy So Immense: The World of Joe McCarthy*. New York: Free Press, 1983.

Persico, Joseph. *Edward R. Murrow: An American Original*. New York: McGraw-Hill, 1988.

Potter, Charles E. *Days of Shame*. New York: Coward-McCann, 1965.

Reeves, Thomas C. *The Life and Times of Joe McCarthy: A Biography*. New York: Stein and Day, 1982.

Ritchie, Don. *Reporting from Washington: The History of the Washington Press Corps*. New York: Oxford University Press, 2005.

Ross, Irwin. *The Loneliest Campaign: The Truman Victory of 1948*. New York: New American Library, 1968.

Schlesinger, Arthur M. Jr. *Robert Kennedy and His Times*. Boston: Houghton Mifflin, 1978.

Sevareid, Eric. *Not So Wild a Dream*. New York: Athenenum, 1976.

Smith, R. Franklin. *Edward R. Murrow: The War Years*. Kalamazoo, Mich.: New Issues Press, 1965.

Smith, Richard Norton. *Thomas E. Dewey and His Times*. New York: Simon and Schuster, 1982.

Straight, Michael. *Trial by Television: And Other Encounters*. New York: Devon Press, 1979.

Thomas, Evan. *The Man to See: Edward Bennett Williams: Ultimate Insider; Legendary Trial Lawyer*. New York: Simon and Schuster, 1991.

Turner, Kathleen J. *Lyndon Johnson's Dual War: Vietnam and the Press*. Chicago: University of Chicago Press, 1985.

Wofford, Harris. *Of Kennedys and Kings: Making Sense of the Sixties*. New York, Farrar, Straus, and Giroux, 1980.

PERIODICALS, JOURNALS, AND WEBSITES

"After the Brawl," *Collier's*, August 9, 1954.

Alsop, Joseph and Stewart, "McCarthy Acts Desperate," *Washington Post*, April 23, 1954.

"Arthur Vivian Watkins," *Dictionary of American Biography*, Supplement 9, 1971–1975. New York: Charles Scribner's Sons, 1994. BRC.

Bartlett, Charles, "The Crusading Kefauver," *The Nation*, March 3, 1952. http://www.thirdworld traveler.com/Herman% 20/Manufac_Consent_ Prop-

"Biggest Show on Earth," *Time*, March 26, 1951.

"Biggest Show Panics the Public," *Newsweek*, March 26, 1951.

Buckley, William F. Jr., "Edward Bennett Williams: RIP," *National Review*, September 16, 1988.

"The Case of Private Schine," *Time*, March 22, 1954.

"The Censure of Joe McCarthy," *Time*, October 4, 1954.

Childs, Marquis, "Smears and Tears Plague the Senate," *Washington Post*, June 30, 1954.

"Condemnation Proceedings," *Time*, August 16, 1954.

"A Conversation with Fred Friendly," *Nieman Reports*, No. 4, Vol. 53, Nieman Foundation, Harvard University.

"The Country: Looking and Deciding for Itself," *Newsweek*, May 3, 1954.

"Crime Hunt in Foley Square," *Time*, March 26, 1951.

Crozier, Barney, *Barre* (Vt.) *Times-Argus*, August 29, 1979, "Vermont Senator's Speech Heralded McCarthy's End," http://members.localnet.com.a

Doig, Ivan, "Kefauver vs. Crime; Television Boosts a Senator," *Journalism Quarterly*, Autumn 1962.

"Edward Bennett Williams," *Encyclopedia of World Biography*, Supplement, Vol. 22. Farmington Hills, Mich.: Gale Group, 2002. BRC.

Epstein, Edward J., "Changing Focus," *TV Guide*, October 13, 1973.

"Everett McKinley Dirksen," *Dictionary of American Biography*, Supplement 8, 1966–1970. New York: American Council of Learned Societies, 1988. BRC.

Ewig, Rick, "McCarthy Era Politics: The Ordeal of Senator Lester Hunt," *Annals of Wyoming*, Spring 1983.

"The Fetish of Objectivity," *Time*, May 3, 1953.

Gauger, Michael, "Flickering Images: Live Television Coverage and Viewership of the Army-McCarthy Hearings," *The Historian*, December 22, 2005.

Hunt, Lester C., "Dangers in Congressional Immunity," *New York Times Magazine*, June 24, 1951.

"It Pays to Organize," *Time*, March 12, 1951.

"Joe and the Handmaidens," *Time*, November 22, 1954.

"John Little McClellan," *Encyclopedia of World Biography*. 2nd ed. Farmington Hills, Mich.: Gale Research, 1998. BRC.

"Joseph McCarthy," *American Decades*. Farmington Hills, Mich.: Gale Research, 1998. BRC.

"Karl Earl Mundt," *Dictionary of American Biography*, Supplement 9, 1971–1975. New York: Charles Scribner's Sons, 1994. BRC.

Kolbert, Elizabeth, "Looks Aren't Everything," *New York Times Week in Review*, September 29, 1996.

Linder, Doug, "The Trials of Alger Hiss: A Commentary," http://www.law.umkc.edu/faculty/projects/trials/hiss/chronology.html.

———, "Trial of the Rosenbergs: An Account," http:///www/law.umkc.edu/faculty/projects/trials/rosenb/ROSENB.HTM.

"Man With a Hard Gavel," *Time*, September 13, 1954.

"Mighty Interesting Visit," *Time*, April 2, 1951.

Moyers, Bill, "Buying the War," http://www.pbs.org/moyers/journal/archive.

"New Kind of Hearing for Joe," *Time*, September 13, 1954.

"The Other Joe," *Time*, May 17, 1954.

"Ralph Edward Flanders," *Dictionary of American Biography*, Supplement 8, 1966–1970. New York: American Council of Learned Societies, 1988. BRC.

"A Report on Senator Joseph R. McCarthy," by Edward R. Murrow, transcript. The Beat Begins: America in the 1950s. http://www.honors.umd.edu/HONR269/archive/Murrow540309.html.

Reston, James B., "Unintended Achievements of Senator McCarthy," *New York Times*, May 30, 1954.

Rovere, Richard H., "Letter from Washington," *The New Yorker*, September 18, 1954.

———, "The Untold Story of McCarthy's Fall," *New York Review of Books*, October 28, 1965.

"The Russell Senate Office Building Caucus Room," http://aoc.gov/cc/cobs/rsob_caucus_rm.cfm.

Scheufele, Dietram A., Matthew C. Nisbet, and Ronald E. Ostman, "September 11 News Coverage, Public Opinion, and Support for Civil Liberties," *Mass Communication and Society*, Vol. 8, No. 3 (Summer 2005).

Schwartz, Richard A., "How the Film and Television Blacklists Worked," Florida International University. schwartz@fiu.edu.

"The Scorched Air: Murrow vs. Senator McCarthy," *Newsweek*, March 22, 1954.

"The Self-Inflated Target," *Time*, March 22, 1954.

Shogan, Robert, "The 1948 Election," *American Heritage*, June 1968.

"Splendid Job," *Time*, December 13, 1954.

"Still a Toddler, *Time*, February 25, 1946.
"Telecasting Notes," *Television Digest*, May 8, 1954.
"The Terror of Tellico Plains," *Time*, May 17, 1954.
Trachtenberg, Doug, "Hiss, Chambers Battle Before HUAC, Nixon 1948," *Roll Call*, June 17, 1999.
Welch, Joseph N., "The Lawyer's Afterthoughts," *Life*, July 26, 1954.
Wershba, Joseph, "Murrow vs. McCarthy: See It Now," *New York Times Magazine*, March 4, 1979.
Wheatcroft, Geoffrey, "Inside Story: Boo, Hiss," *The Guardian*, August 6, 1998.
"(William) Stuart Symington, II," *Scribner Encyclopedia of American Lives*, Vol. 2, 1986–1990. New York: Charles Scribner's Sons, 1999. BRC.
Wolfe, Tom, "Dangerous Obsession," *New York Times Book Review*, April 3, 1988.
"Words from a Quiet Man," *Time*, March 22, 1954.

GOVERNMENT DOCUMENTS

U.S. Senate, Committee on Government Operations, Special Subcommittee on Investigations. Special Senate Investigation on Charges and Counter-Charges Involving: Secretary of the Army Robert T. Stevens, John G. Adams, H. Struve Hensel, and Senator Joseph McCarthy, Roy M. Cohn, and Francis P. Carr (cited in notes as *SSI*).

SCHOLARLY PAPERS

Wanger, David Kushlan. "The Role of Joseph N. Welch in the Army-McCarthy Hearings of 1954." Unpublished Senior Honors Thesis, Department of History, Harvard University, 1984.
Weinstein, David Michael. "Live from the Nation's Capital: A History of Television in Washington, D.C., 1946–1958." Unpublished Ph.D. Dissertation submitted to the Faculty of the Graduate School of the University of Maryland, 1997.

MISCELLANEOUS

Fisher, Fred G. Jr. "Joseph N. Welch." Unpublished manuscript in author's possession.

DOCUMENTARY FILM

De Antonio, Emile, editorial director. "Point of Order!" New York: New Yorker Films Artwork, 1998.

Index

A NOTE ON THE AUTHOR

Robert Shogan is a former prizewinning national political correspondent for *Newsweek* and the *Los Angeles Times*. Born in New York City, he studied journalism at Syracuse University. After reporting for newspapers and magazines and writing books for more than forty years, he turned to teaching. He has been professional in residence at the Annenberg School of Communications of the University of Pennsylvania, and is now adjunct professor of government at the Johns Hopkins University. He lives in Chevy Chase, Maryland.